A Couple's Guide to Healing

IF THE MAN YOU
LOVE WAS ABUSED

MARIE H. BROWNE, R.N., PH.D., WITH MARLENE M. BROWNE, ESQ.

ADAMS MEDIA
AVON MASSACHUSETTS

Published by
Adams Media, an F+W Publications Company
57 Littlefield Street, Avon, MA 02322. U.S.A.
www.adamsmedia.com

ISBN 10: 1-59337-643-X
ISBN 13: 978-1-59337-643-7

Printed in the United States of America.

J I H G F E D C B A

Library of Congress Cataloging-in-Publication Data
is available from publisher.

This publication is designed to provide accurate and authoritative information with regard to the subject matter covered. It is sold with the understanding that the publisher is not engaged in rendering legal, accounting, or other professional advice. If legal advice or other expert assistance is required, the services of a competent professional person should be sought.

—From a *Declaration of Principles* jointly adopted by a
Committee of the American Bar Association and
a Committee of Publishers and Associations

Many of the designations used by manufacturers and sellers to distinguish their product are claimed as trademarks. Where those designations appear in this book and Adams Media was aware of a trademark claim, the designations have been printed with initial capital letters.

To protect the identity of my patients and to maintain their right to confidential treatment, I've altered basic facts (names, ages, occupations, and geographical locations) presented in the case histories that follow; I have, however, faithfully preserved the essential elements that made these patient experiences illuminating and instructive. For more information about the guidelines I followed, see: Clift, Mary Ann, "Writing about Psychiatric Patients: Guidelines for Disguising Case Material," *Bulletin of the Menninger Clinic*, Vol. 50, No. 6, pp. 511-524, 1986.

This book is available at quantity discounts for bulk purchases.
For information, please call 1-800-289-0963.

"There is only one good, knowledge,
and one evil, ignorance."

—*Socrates*

Dedication

I would like to dedicate this book to all the patients and their families whom I have treated over all these years. Each and every person has a place in my memory.

■ ■ ■

I would further like to dedicate this book to my esteemed colleagues who have dedicated their careers to educating the future generation of healers. Teaching with this faculty has given me assurance of the high quality of health care providers for generations to come. I would especially like to thank Maryellen McHale, Jane Meehan, and Marilyn Nussbaum for their friendship and support during my teaching career.

■ ■ ■

Finally, I thank my husband, Frank, my daughter, Marlene, and my son-in-law, Christopher, for making the world a better place.

Contents

Chapter Four
Psyched Out by Abuse / 53

Chapter Five
In Denial / 69

Chapter Six
How the Healing Happens / 83

Chapter Seven
Knowing He's Not Alone / 97

Chapter Eleven
Taking Care of You / 160

Chapter Twelve
Coping Skills and Common Obstacles / 172

Part Three
The Legacy of Abuse

Chapter Thirteen
Fatherhood and Children / 186

Chapter Fourteen
All in the Family—or Not / 199

Chapter Fifteen
If He Should Fall / 213

Chapter Sixteen
Long-Term Prospects for Couples / 228

Introduction

The purpose of this book is to enlighten, educate, and, perhaps most important, encourage the woman who is in the delicate, extraordinary, and possibly heartbreaking position of being in a relationship (married or not) with a man who—she comes to learn, or suspects—was abused. As a practicing psychotherapist for almost four decades, and as a college professor for nearly that long, I've had the opportunity and privilege to work with women in that position—your position—as well as with men, like your partner, who endured child abuse. Whether that abuse was psychological, physical, or sexual (and, you will see, Chapter 1 is devoted to discussing the characteristics of each), I found that these men, and their partners, suffered the effects of that trauma long after it occurred.

When my practice began, the feminist movement was in full swing and bringing national (in fact, international) attention to the victimization of women and girls—at all ages and stages of life. As a result of these efforts, psychologists, social scientists, and medical personnel devoted their time—and some, their careers—to studying the effects of female exploitation and the consequences of that abuse from the cradle to the grave. Books were written, seminars were held, and professional associations were formed to inform the public of how females are subjected to, and affected by, abuse and why special social support for these victims was crucial if they were to recover from their trauma. As a result, concerned citizens joined the bandwagon and lobbied federal and local politicians to make resources available to females who were being abused or had been abused as kids. By the 1980s, nearly every mental and physical health care provider was aware that child abuse was a substantial factor in the lives of many of the girls and women seen in treatment.

While the word was out that girls were at risk for abuse, however, the boys continued to suffer without a voice, without recourse, and without a cultural understanding of how commonly they, too, were victimized. At that time, most laypeople—and unfortunately, many mental and physical health professionals—remained grossly, dangerously, and recklessly unaware of boys' exposure to abuse and its effects on their emotional, physical, and psychological well-being. But times were changing and the topic of abuse was about to explode once again upon the collective consciousness of the country.

As you probably know from all the media coverage beginning in early 2002, the world's view about boys and their susceptibility to exploitation began to change with the revelation of the tragic truth about the clergy abuse scandal. John Jay College of Criminal Justice documented the extent of this disgraceful epoch of the Church in the ground-breaking 2004 study *The Nature and Scope of Sexual Abuse of Minors by Catholic Priests and Deacons in the United States 1950–2002*, which confirmed that thousands of children (81 percent of whom were boys, mostly adolescents) were abused by their trusted, respected parish priests. We also know that many in the Church were aware of the problem but turned a blind eye toward the pedophiles and, more tragically, their young victims, over the course of decades. In fact, perhaps one of cruelest ironies of all is that just as the women's movement reached the height of its power in the 1970s, telling the world about how girls were being abused, the abuse of young boys in the Catholic Church surged to its highest levels in fifty years.

Meanwhile, on the academic front, more researchers were studying the frequency and effects of child abuse on both boys and girls. Results of this work demonstrated that boys suffered from abuse just as profoundly, if not more so, than the girls did, and much more frequently than anyone ever expected. In fact, a noteworthy investigation by the Centers for Disease Control and Prevention (CDC), the Adverse Childhood Experiences Study (ACE), released in 2005, confirmed the results of research conducted fifteen years earlier revealing that 16 percent of boys in the United States (that's one in six) are abused in some way. What's more, the study revealed that almost 40 percent of the perpetrators of boy abuse were females.

Today, some experts advise us that the 16 percent frequency figure for boys being abused is inaccurate and too low, suggesting instead it's reasonable to assume that just as many boys are abused as girls (25 percent, according to the CDC). These professionals believe that this underestimation occurs because males under-report their abuse, reluctant to reveal their experiences for all the reasons that are discussed in this book. What's more, some men will not identify their abusive experiences as such, preferring to label the events as "hazing" or "horseplay" (when perpetrated by males) or as early initiations to sex (when perpetrated by females—unless the perpetrator was the mother, in which case the consequences are often dire and damaging if the child is not helped). Now, in the opening decade of the twenty-first century, we know that there are many men out there who are among the walking wounded as a result of their abusive treatment, unaware of how to deal with their abuse in a way that will allow them to lead fulfilling lives, with the ability to trust, be intimate, and have personal peace. My aim in writing this book is to disseminate all the information that's been gathered in recent years to help you, the significant other, understand the dynamics of abuse, from a man's—or a boy's—point of view, and, in doing that, help your mate find healing.

Reading this book, you will learn that no one is exempt from the risk of being abused as a child (though there are factors that make one more or less at risk). You'll learn about the different types of abuse and the pedophiles who perpetrate these crimes, including why they prey upon children, and how they often enter their homes, locker rooms, restrooms, shopping malls, parks, schools, and playgrounds without arousing anyone's suspicion or mistrust. You will gain knowledge about the "grooming" process and how abusers effectively use the "trauma bond" on their victims, forged by intimidation, fear, guilt, and shame, so they keep "the secret" or "promise not to tell"—or else. You'll learn about the biological, psychological, and social effects of child abuse on your partner, giving you firsthand knowledge and further insight into the cause of the current behaviors that you and your loved one might be dealing with as adults. You'll learn all the reasons your mate might find it difficult to have a warm, trusting relationship with you, or anyone else, as a mature man. (Imagine: If your parents or a trusted adult took advantage of you and abused you, you might have difficulty giving your trust to another, too.) You will learn what techniques work best in treatment, and you'll even read about famous victims who have come forward to tell their stories, offering you (and vicariously, your partner) fellow survivors' perspectives about being abused as boys. Finally, you will discover the approaches that will give your mate the emotional, and perhaps get him the professional, support that will make it easier for him to deal with his past and, ultimately, pave the way for a less painful and more gratifying future, for both of you.

Most chapters are punctuated with case studies from my practice, providing you with concrete examples of how abuse issues present themselves in "real life" and, more important, how they can be addressed and resolved by you and your partner in your life, at your pace. As a final technical point, you will notice that throughout the book, I alternate the words *abuse* and *trauma* to refer to the event in your partner's past that caused him injury. Similarly, I interchange the terms *victim* and *survivor* in the text to indicate an adult (like your partner) who has been abused or traumatized. While I recognize that your partner might not see himself as a victim (or as a survivor, for that matter), I use these expressions as they appear in the professional literature on the subject of child abuse and its consequences on the people who experienced it.

For your reference, you'll also find a glossary of psychiatric, medical, and even legal jargon, that bear on the subject of abuse and that appear throughout the book. After the glossary, you'll find a list of the references I've used—in my professional life, generally, and in writing this book, specifically—broken down according to chapter. A list of suggested resources for your use, again separated by chapter for your convenience and ease, follows the references. I want you to know that professionals who work with male victims agree that in most cases (80 percent), with care and emotional, social, and psychological support, your mate will be a "thriver," able to address and resolve the abuse of his past and the concerns and challenges it has caused him and, of course, you. In the meantime, I hope my words and research gathered here provide you and your partner with the first steps toward your journey of healing, with fulfillment, trust, and contentment to follow.

Part One

Defining the Issue, Assessing the Damage

Chapter One

Events That Can Leave a Scar

You probably approach this topic with at least a few preconceived notions of what the term *abuse* entails. However, you might be surprised to learn that researchers have identified a host of household conditions and personal actions—or, in some cases, inactions—that have the potential to be just as psychologically damaging to a child (now your mate) as if his body had been violated. In addition to addressing the significant subjects of physical and sexual abuse, this chapter will explore the range of less commonly considered circumstances that experienced medical, psychological, and sociological experts have identified as particularly damaging to the normal, overall development of a healthy human child (male or female). Although, as the title suggests, this book focuses on helping you (the significant other of a man with a history of abuse) deal with issues and challenges created by your relationship, know that the maltreatment outlined here has the potential to deeply wound both body and psyche, no matter the sex of the victim. All children are vulnerable to exploitive, reckless, criminal, or cruel acts of adults—or even older children—that can, without adequate support and, often, professional help (and we will address both), cause profoundly disturbing, lifelong biological, psychological, and social problems for the youngster concerned. As this youngster is now your mate, you should be aware of the circumstances that informed, or more probably formed, your man's personality, long before you met.

Psychological Cruelty

Not all abuse breaks bones. Some types of abuse can break a person's spirit and sense of well-being. Having a parent or guardian or caretaker continually and consistently diminish a child's worth as a human being or make him fearful of his ability to remain physically safe (thereby threatening his very ability to exist) can, research proves, result in the same kinds of stress and trauma to a child that is commonly associated with physical mistreatment. Similarly, exposing a child to noxious domestic dysfunction can leave him just as defenseless and damaged as if his body had been battered. Let us explore those kinds of actions that cross the boundary from acceptable childrearing to downright toxic behavior.

Verbal Assaults

Although the word *verbal* means "via language," either by the written or spoken word, the most common form of psychological abuse occurs through the voice, when an adult makes a habit of berating, threatening, insulting, making fun of, scolding, or screaming at a child in a manner that is disproportionate to anything the child could have done. (Verbal abuse can occur through the written word using notes or letters to harass, insult, or threaten, but this type of conduct typically occurs between adults, not between a developmentally dependent child and a parent or caretaker.) Certainly, as a grownup, you can appreciate how a big, powerful adult who is in charge of a child's welfare can traumatize him by exploding in volcanic oral eruptions in his presence. Children are vulnerable to stress and have harmful reactions to adult rages (such as increased secretions of stress hormones like norepinephrine, adrenaline, and cortisol that can impair brain development), whether they are directed to the child personally or to a sibling, the other parent, some other family member, or even a pet. In addition to causing psychological tension, an adult's repeated oral explosions can put a child in fear for his personal safety, along with the safety of those he loves and to whom he is attached.

Now, this doesn't mean that your man was abused if his parents occasionally censured him for doing something wrong (even if the reprimand was stern or harsh), or if they lost their tempers once in a while. No one is perfect, and few parents (in fact, few people) have the distinction of remaining calm and levelheaded at all times. Appropriate parental discipline is not abusive. In fact, children need boundaries as they grow up, and failure to establish these rules could be considered parental neglect (a topic covered later). Rather, verbal psychological abuse is marked by its frequency and intensity and, often, by its unpredictability. Who could forget the movie *Mommy, Dearest*, where Joan Crawford's character explodes in fury at her daughter over finding wire hangers in her closet? No one could come away from viewing that scene without feeling the child's utter horror and fear at her mother's irrational and unpredictable rage. In fact, studies show that long-term exposure to a household of emotionally violent behavior contributes to a child's exaggerated "startle" response, among other abnormal emotional and physical effects. Moreover, exposing a child to repeated and arbitrary psychological attacks that insult him and erode his self-esteem (e.g., telling him he's no good, ugly, worthless, stupid, clumsy, or that he won't amount to anything) will, in some cases, make him doubt his right to live and be happy, far past the time of childhood. Verbal abuse and mental cruelty are insidious and destructive behaviors that can, if not checked, destroy a person's life.

Ted is a classic victim of this kind of parental behavior. He was the youngest of four children, all boys. His father was with the Foreign Service and his mother was a doctor who descended from a very privileged family. Ted's family traveled and lived all over the world. Ted spoke three languages fluently. His father and three brothers all graduated from Stanford and were scholars. Ted, however, was told as a very young child not to even consider Stanford because he was the "runt of the litter" and didn't have what it would take to achieve the lofty goals of his father and brothers. Growing up, Ted's mother nicknamed him "Gordo," which became his name in the family. Ted rejected this designation and requested to be called by his real name, but his mother refused. She explained to Ted that he looked like a "Gordo" and that's how she, and everyone else in the family, would refer to him. As young as Ted was, he knew this was not what a loving mother would do or say. He felt the pain of ridicule and derision. Unfortunately, Ted's pain increased as he grew older. When his parents and brothers traveled, he was often sent away to stay with his maternal grandmother. The family's explanation for leaving him behind was that the trips would be wasted on him and, besides, he could have fun with grandmother. (She was in her eighties and lived on an estate with household help who became his friends. That relieved some of Ted's pain temporarily.)

When it was time for high school, Ted was sent to a military academy in another state where discipline was extreme. Ted's family never visited on Parents' Day or any other day. Ted was allowed to come home to visit on some holidays, which he looked forward to, until upon his return home, he was once again made the butt of family jokes. Ted wanted to apply to Stanford, since his SAT's were within the range required for acceptance, yet his parents forbade him to do so, saying that he would never make the grade. Instead, he was allowed to apply to a small, unranked college where his parents told him he would not embarrass himself or the family. So Ted went off to this third-rate school. By the time he arrived, Ted's self-esteem was so damaged that he could not even ask a girl out on a date. Instead, he waited for women to approach him. He became more withdrawn, depressed, and somewhat despondent. He barely made Cs in his classes. (So far, a family-instilled self-fulfilling prophecy was coming true; Ted was becoming the loser he was told he was since he was a young boy.)

When I first saw Ted in my office, he was a well-groomed, good-looking twenty-eight-year-old man, unhappily married to Ann, a very attractive young woman who belittled and disrespected him.

Ted and Ann had met in college and married shortly after graduation. Ted did not want to marry at that point, but Ann insisted, and he acquiesced to her demands. They had a child within the first year of the marriage. Soon after their child's birth, Ted began to act out and display passive-aggressive behaviors. He applied for and accepted a job that was considerably below his talent and education. This embarrassed Ann and her family, who had some status in their community. Still, Ted insisted this almost menial work would be his lifelong employment.

As I treated Ted, I realized that he was extremely bright, although I could not convince him of his intelligence. As we explored his childhood, Ted began to question some of his parents' behavior toward him. Doing so set him free. Ted realized that his parents were wrong to belittle him and treat him with such contempt. Ted's first big step toward becoming the man he could be was to enroll in a course at a local university where he received an A. Next, Ted enrolled in more courses, culminating in an M.B.A. with a 4.0 GPA. Having achieved what he was capable of, Ted gained emotional power and ambition for a better life, personally and professionally. He told his wife that she could no longer abuse him without consequences. Ann rejected his new behavior (and refused to modify hers), and the couple eventually divorced.

Ted is now a senior VP back at the investment firm he'd left when his child was born. He's happily remarried to a woman who does not abuse him, but, rather, appreciates him. Ted is now confident and content with who he is and how he overcame his abusive past (including his first marriage, where, in marrying Ann, he replicated the agonizing but familiar pain of his mother's hostility toward him). He's been able to reach a point in his development where he has released repressed anger toward his parents and even visits them once a year.

If your mate was subjected to a domestic campaign of verbal emotional violence (a pattern of parental yelling, swearing, threatening, or belittling), know that he might have incorporated the messages of worthlessness into his mindset, making them into undesired, but inevitable, self-fulfilling prophecies. While it is true that some kids are able to transcend this type of abuse, many are not, without substantial effort (through reading, writing, reflecting, and support, or in a therapist's office). In any case, now that you are aware of the severe damage that recurring cruel words can wreak on a person's welfare, you have the ability to empathize with his experience and recognize his possible need of help, guiding him to health and restoration through your actions.

Exposure to Dangers

Not only harsh words can damage, but harsh situational experiences (apart from direct physical or sexual abuse) in childhood can also take their toll on a person's developing sense of self and security. In fact, certain adverse experiences in childhood can destroy a person's relation to his body. This disconnect occurs as a child's internal regulatory controls (the limbic system and hypothalamus, charged with keeping the body and brain in hormonal balance and emotional good health) fail to operate effectively due to a constant fight-or-flight state. Consequently, children who live in severe domestic dysfunction suffer the same kinds of physical, psychological, and social damage that you expect from direct corporal contact or sexual abuse, including pervasive anxiety, inappropriate reactions to stimuli (not perceiving danger when it is present, or sensing peril where none exists), and an inability to trust or attach to caretakers and, later, peers. Consider this: In the 1990s, the Centers for Disease Control and Prevention (CDC) and the Kaiser Permanente Medical Care Program, a huge health maintenance organization (HMO) in San Diego, California, conducted a detailed survey and subsequent epidemiological research project on 17,421 middle-class American adults (with a mean age of fifty-seven) who had recently undergone a routine health care checkup. The results of this comprehensive study revealed that two-thirds of them were exposed to adverse childhood experiences (ACE), defined as psychological, physical, and sexual abuse and "severe household dysfunction," before age eighteen. These identified ACE were not only damaging to the individuals as kids but were the likely root of a range of negative physical ailments and psychological problems from which they suffered many, many decades after the ACE occurred. You might be surprised to learn that this study defined "severe household dysfunction" to include:

1. Living in a household with a parent or an adult who was an alcoholic or problem drinker.
2. Living in a household with a parent or an adult who abused and/or used street drugs.
3. Having a household member who was mentally ill or depressed.
4. Having a household member go to prison.
5. Having a household member attempt (or commit) suicide.
6. Having a mother (or stepmother) who was "sometimes, often, or very often" treated violently.
7. Losing a parent through death. (This element was added to the list in 1997, for the "second wave" of survey recipients.)

So, you see, your mate could be suffering from the remnants of severe domestic dysfunction that he never thought of as noxious but that we now know to be as harmful to his long-term emotional health and physical well-being as the more commonly identified forms of child abuse. (For more information about the ACE study, see the resource section at the end of this book.) Some kinds of abuse are rarely identified by the abuser at the time they occur. Instead, symptoms of the abuse appear later in life and cause the abused to seek help. Often, a diagnosis of abuse becomes apparent after a patient's recitation of his family history. This is when many people first realize that what they suffered in childhood was, indeed, abusive.

Take James, who came for treatment with symptoms of depression, underachievment, and an arrest for driving under the influence. James was angry, defensive, and hostile. He told me the only reason he was in my office was that the court ordered him to have treatment or go to jail. James described himself as having a short fuse. When someone upset him, he would "lose it." He believed that he would not be able to keep a job if he didn't own the company (which was not an issue for him, because he did). James stated he often was out of control and was verbally abusive to his employees, both men and women. On occasion, he would resort to physical violence and not really regret it. James explained that that was simply "how he was brought up."

When we explored that statement further, James told me that as a child, his house was always chaotic. If his mother didn't have dinner on the table, it was not unusual for his father to "slap her around," or, at the very least, verbally abuse her. These events happened primarily when his father came home drunk. In defense of his dad, James said that his father started the family business that James now owned, and that his father had always supported his family well. Growing up, James felt he never lacked for anything material. When questioned about his own marriage and family relations, James replied that it was pretty much the same as he grew up with. He felt he turned out okay. Once we had established a solid therapeutic relationship, I began to question how, if given the choice, James would have liked to have grown up—that is, how he would have changed his own childhood and upbringing if he could. He responded that he would have preferred never to have seen his mom hit or crying, and he would have liked to have gone to sleep without fear of yelling and fighting. When questioned about how he thought his own children went to sleep, James began to cry. He said that as a young child he had promised himself never to be like his father, but now he realized that he'd become a carbon copy of his dad.

We began to explore how to change this situation. While James realized he could not change the past, he could change the present and the future. The first step was to openly examine his behaviors and then make changes. James's first step was to join

Alcoholics Anonymous (AA) and ask his family to join Al-Anon. At AA, James found other people who'd had some of the same types of life experiences he did, making him feel less alone. James lost much of his anger and became warmer and kinder to those around him. He found that he liked this behavior better than the behavior he emulated from the father of his childhood.

One evening, James came to my office, anxious to have me answer a question. He heard some of his employees referring to him as a "benevolent dictator," and he wanted to know if he should thank them or be offended. I told him what the term meant and he decided he liked it—after all, he was still the boss, but no longer abused people verbally or physically. James was a changed man, and he enjoyed his new behavior and the way people now related to him.

If linking childhood abuse and household pathology to adult disorders, disease, and early death is not enough to get your attention, the research shows that without positive intervention or active healing, adverse childhood experience sufferers often lead lives (albeit, shorter ones than they should, per the study results) of quiet desperation, using harmful, and ultimately self-destructive, coping mechanisms they have adopted to survive their pain—often as much emotional as physical—on a day-to-day basis. (You'll learn much more about the common maladaptive coping mechanisms used by abuse survivors—and what to do about them—in later chapters.) The point to take from this section is that your man did not have to be hit to be hurt deeply in an emotional way. Knowing, for instance, that your mate's mom was abused can give you insight into why he behaves the way he does, and, most important, how you can help him and your relationship through your knowledge and understanding.

Physical Maltreatment

We arrive at the issue where most people believe that child abuse begins. Violating a child's body, in many instances, will cause physical wounds that will transmute into profound psychological damage that lasts until that child (or adult) receives attention, care, and treatment. Children who suffer physical trauma will often experience the same symptoms as kids who are sexually abused (which we will address in the next section). As you will read, physical abuse involves more than the acts of beating or kicking or punching that you might first imagine. It also includes the grave omissions that parents and caretakers can commit, neglecting the child and his basic needs. As we will explore, in some cases, neglect can result in a child having permanent psychological damage, resisting treatment and amelioration in later life. Keep this in mind as you read this chapter and the ones that follow.

Corporal Abuse

When you read about this topic, the image of a schoolmaster rapping a child's knuckles with a ruler might pop into your head (recall the debates over corporal punishment in schools?). Certainly some of that discipline crossed the line from acceptable behavior to abuse and battery. In older generations people warned about sparing the rod and spoiling the child. Since the arrival of the baby boom generation in 1946, however, that adage of parental wisdom has generally fallen out of favor, replaced by the kinder, gentler insights of Dr. Benjamin Spock and his professional (and proverbial) progeny. Due to their influence, fewer children overall are disciplined with belts and rulers. Still, children continue to be physically abused by their parents and other adults.

This section does not address appropriate bounds of child discipline. Rather, this segment of the book examines the actions that clearly exceed the administration of domestic justice and child-rearing authority. When an adult (or bigger, older human) uses frequent and unpredictable physical force with a child, whether it takes the form of punching, hitting, shoving, slapping, or whipping, that child is placed in emotional as well as physical danger, causing a mental state of fear and panic to set in and pervade his being. As you might suspect, research shows us that the harmful effects of physical force against a child are not limited to situations leaving broken bones and bruised skin. Rather, physical abuse includes the less perceptible, but similarly insidious, circumstances where a child is subjected to repeated, and often random, physical acts of humiliation (having his pants pulled down in front of others and being slapped, for instance), degradation (having his face slapped), and general disrespect concerning his personal boundaries. When a child is subjected to physical abuse at home, instead of being a sanctuary, his home becomes another dangerous place where the child is at risk and must remain vigilant. This constant state of readiness contributes to the anxiety and stress that the child's brain will become wired to expect and experience for the rest of his life if he does not receive appropriate care and intervention. (We will look at the most successful methods of intervention and care later in the book.)

Abandonment and Neglect

You can think of abandonment and neglect as the mirror (or negative) image of physical abuse. In the latter instance, the child is subjected to the actions of an adult or caretaker (or even an older kid) who decides that committing physical violence upon that child is a way of relating, punishing, or teaching him a lesson. In the case of neglect or abandonment we are looking at deprivation. In these instances, the child suffers not only because he lacks the necessities of life (food, clothing, shelter) but also because he is deprived of the care, socialization, and emotional commitment that a child requires in order for his brain to develop and function in a way that allows for growth, maturation, and successful human relationships. What we are taking about is physical affection, vocal stimuli, and emotional and physical security. At each stage of a child's development, he requires not only food and water and protection from the elements to survive, but as a little human he must receive certain tactile and mental stimulation, or his brain will not be wired properly to live among other humans as an adult.

You are probably familiar with the studies that reveal that babies who are denied human touch will actually wither and die for want of affection, even if adequate nutrition and shelter are provided. Moreover, you might have read the studies on so-called "feral children," who were either abandoned in youth to be raised among animals or who were denied human contact and company even though they "lived" (actually, survived) in a residence in an urban area. In fact, one famous case dating back to 1970, that of Genie, a young girl from a suburb of Los Angeles, underlines this point. She was found living in a dingy back room of a house, in a wire cage with no amenities except a potty seat, to which she was strapped during the day. At night, Genie was placed in her cage, like a dog kept in the yard. Her family (parents and an older brother) did not interact with Genie, and by the time she was discovered, this thirteen-year-old girl could not speak and was only the size of a six-year-old. Despite the best efforts of the most caring and skilled professionals (child psychologists and psychiatrists, neurobiologists, linguists, and medical doctors), Genie could not be saved from the permanent damage to her brain caused by her parent's severe neglect. The part of her brain that is used for speech was never activated, losing its ability to learn language. Although Genie had learned to utter many words after she was rescued and began recovering from her horrible life of isolation, her brain had atrophied irreparably so that she would never be able to grasp grammar or syntax or learn how to communicate a thought via language—oral, sign, or written. Naturally, your mate will not have been as abused as Genie was, or you would not be in any kind of relationship with him.

So, I will assume, no matter how uncommunicative your mate might be at times, he does know how to speak, write, sign, or somehow get his point across to you. That said, neglect and abandonment can still have a profound affect on your man, even if it was less traumatic than a feral child's experience. For instance, research on neglected children tells us that they lack the ability to attach appropriately to another human. This attachment disorder can affect relationships in adult life if not addressed and ameliorated. Moreover, a child's ability to empathize—that is, to feel what another might be feeling in a given situation—is thwarted when that child fails to receive the attention required at each stage of development. Of course, the ultimate abandonment is the death of a parent. Although the death might be the result of an accident or disease, the attachment disorder and resulting psychological pain that follow are similar to the parental abandonment caused by neglect. The point for you, as the mate of an abused man, is to be aware that the different kinds of life experiences that cause childhood trauma can last far past the time of the event or the loss. We will probe the issue of attachment disorder in a later chapter.

Sexual Abuse

Since we will be relying upon studies throughout this book as references and resources for further information on the subject of sexual abuse, it makes sense to look at how they define the term. Most researchers describe it as sexual activity between an adult (or bigger or older juvenile) and a child (under age eighteen) who lacks the emotional, social, and often, physical and mental capacity to consent, comprehend, or process the traumatic acts. The sexual activity can involve contact (i.e., touching, fondling, attempted or actual sexual contact of any nature, including but not limited to anal, oral, or vaginal intercourse) or not (i.e., exposure of genitals and/or use or making of pornography). Yet, as we explore this topic, you, as the mate of the man who was abused, must consider that each victim has a different reaction to his abuse. A child's individual temperament; age at onset of abuse; its duration, frequency, and severity; the kind of relationship—if any—between the child victim and the abuser, and the abuser's tactics (e.g., use of physical force, threats, coercion, or emotional manipulation) all make a difference in how he tries to cope with the crisis of his experience.

The Dynamics of Damage

And crisis it is. Although severe household dysfunction and psychological and physical abuse and neglect can cause profound damage to a child, researchers reveal that sexual abuse victims suffer most acutely. In addition to their loss of innocence, these children suffer a breach of their physical integrity through coercion, inducement, or force, possible exposure to disease, and specific psychic wounds related to the abusive sexual activity. Over twenty years ago, researchers Angela Browne and David Finkelhor identified four distinct components of trauma (which are known in the scientific literature as *traumagenic dynamics*) that a child suffers after becoming a victim of sexual abuse. Issues stemming from these dynamics can plague a victim long past childhood, which is why they should be of interest to you, his mate, now.

Betrayal

This stage refers to a child's feeling of being tricked or taken advantage of by the offender and/or not being protected or believed by his parents, caretakers, or guardians, who were supposed to keep him safe from harm and care for him once the sexual abuse occurred, but who instead ignored the child's cry for help or, worst of all, refused to believe him or accept him after the abuse took place.

Powerlessness

This dynamic reflects the child's perception that he is incapable of stopping the abuse (the violation of his body). The child will feel inadequate, shame, or responsibility for his inability to have protected himself somehow. The child typically judges himself harshly for his perceived weakness, which prevented him from seeking or getting help. Unfortunately, many children, especially boys, do not place blame on the offender, whose use (or misuse) of authority, intimacy, threats, force, manipulation, or any other circumstances put the child in jeopardy. A child's sense of victimization increases when he is ignored, disbelieved, or ostracized after disclosing the abuse. On the other hand, this feeling of powerlessness abates when someone believes the child and takes protective measures on his behalf.

Stigmatization

This stage refers to feelings of isolation, shame, guilt, disgrace, and self-blame that a sexually abused child picks up from his environment (family, friends, community and religious connections, and society in general) and incorporates into his own self-image. Thus, the child victim believes that he is somehow "stained" or different from other children because he has been sexually abused. This stigmatization grows in proportion to the child's need to keep the abuse a secret or the lack of support he receives upon disclosure. If, upon disclosure, the victim is viewed as the seducer or "damaged goods," his sense of stigma will intensify. If the child is believed, helped, and supported, or if the child finds out that he is not alone, that other children have experienced abuse, the stigma is reduced.

Traumatic Sexualization

This concept refers to a child's incorporation of developmentally inappropriate and unhealthy views on sex and sexuality due to his abuse. A child, generally unable to understand the implications of what the offender has done to him—sometimes via enticement, affection, and manipulation, and sometimes by force or threat—may adopt the abuser's legally, socially, and morally corrupt sexual beliefs and behaviors. For instance, a child might learn to use his age-inappropriate sexuality to manipulate others into getting his developmentally appropriate needs (i.e., love, affection, tenderness, protection) met. If a child's "traumatic sexualization" is not addressed, the victim often brings his confused and inappropriate sexual attitudes into adulthood, where they can interfere with his ability to have healthy physical and interpersonal relationships.

Having a sense now of what a child victim feels after the sexual abuse occurs, next we examine how boys bear the burden of their abuse differently from how girls do. In many ways, due to our culture and society, boys tend to suffer in silence, which, the experts tell us, is the least effective way of dealing with the crisis of the past to make room for a promising, optimistic, healthy future. The following section will shed light on why your man might still carry the effects of his sexual abuse, long after the occasion of his childhood trauma.

Ways It's Worse for Boys

Everyone accepts the fact that sexual abuse can severely damage a child's self-image, regardless of gender. Yet, as you read in the introduction, much more research and study has been conducted on the effects of sexual abuse on girls and women than on boys and men. Finally, in the mid-1980s, academics and professionals took a serious look at how sexual abuse specifically affects boys. Until the early '90s, most scholars and psychological professionals would tell you that perhaps one in ten, or fewer, boys under the age of eighteen had been victims of sexual abuse. Then, in July of 1985, using the auspices of the *Los Angeles Times* poll organization, four social scientists (Finkelhor, Hotaling, Lewis, and Smith) conducted a national telephone survey in the United States in which 1,145 men and 1,481 women were interviewed. For approximately an hour, each person answered a series of questions about the topic of sexual abuse. The remarkable results of this survey were published in a landmark 1990 article revealing that 27 percent of the women and 16 percent of the men questioned had been abused before age nineteen. (The 2005 CDC/ACE study referenced in the introduction and throughout this book recently corroborated this statistic, that one in six boys is sexually abused.) But in 1990, the Frankelhor paper broke the story that boys in the United States suffer from sexual abuse much more frequently than society, and even academic researchers, had believed. What's more, this study revealed that, though an almost equal percentage of girls (41 percent) and boys (43 percent) reported their sexual abuse to someone within a year, almost as many boys (42 percent) told no one what had happened to them—ever. By comparison, reportedly 33 percent of the girls kept their sexual abuse a secret. Four years later, another study confirmed a primary difference between boys and girls when it came to dealing with sexual abuse. Most girls (61 percent) disclosed the abuse when it happened, but most boys did not (only 31 percent did). Later studies revealed that almost none of the men in the sample disclosed their abuse when it occurred. Why keep this secret? Most psychologists and sociologists believe that the boys' silence stems from the differences between male and female socialization. Although the boys and girls share many of the same short-term consequences of childhood sexual abuse (e.g., shame, self-blame, guilt, fear, betrayal, anger, humiliation, helplessness, isolation, depression, poor self-esteem, anxiety, inability to trust, and alienation from peers and family), male victims must counter their experience against the masculine roles they believe that society demands of them. Instead of being the self-reliant, stoic, strong, forceful boy that he is expected to be, the young male victim must cope with having been powerless, exploited, fearful, submissive, weak, and not in control of his body or his circumstances at the time of his sexual abuse. What's more, if the perpetrator was a male, the boy has to deal with society's general taboo against homosexual activity.

So, in addition to dealing with the abuse itself, the boy usually finds himself confronting profound gender identification issues: fear of being stigmatized by others as homosexual, should he disclose the abuse; or fear of being gay himself (even without disclosure) as a result of having had any physiological signs of sexual excitement (e.g., an erection or ejaculation) during the abuse event. There are other differences in the ways that boys and girls experience sexual abuse. For instance, researchers have found that boys are more likely to be abused by people they know but who are not family members. And, as a whole, boys tend to suffer more frequent abuse events, with more invasive acts (oral and anal penetration), with more force and tissue damage than girls do. Finally, parents of male children reporting abuse tend to minimize the event and thus react less helpfully than parents who deem the abuse significant and seek immediate therapeutic intervention.

Given these facts, one can understand why a young male (your mate) might not have disclosed his abuse to anyone. Instead, in an effort to cope with his experience, he has repressed or minimized the abuse event, as if it never happened or was not damaging to him in any lasting way. We will delve into the long-term effects of child sexual abuse in later chapters. For now, take a look at the often-cited myths of male abuse. These mistaken beliefs about boys and sexual abuse are valuable to remind you of the difficulties your mate probably endured, for he almost certainly believed them as much as anyone, until he reached out and found help—or found you.

Myths of Male Abuse

The following list of seven myths is commonly identified as having come from a presentation that was given at the 5th International Conference on Incest and Related Problems, held in Biel, Switzerland in 1991, and it seems to be informed by the work of Mic Hunter, Psy.D. on the sexual abuse of boys.

1. **Boys can't be victims.**

   Of course they can, and, often are. Boys are children too and can be victimized by sexual predators just as girls are. One of six boys in the United States is abused before his nineteenth birthday, most of them between the ages of six and ten.

2. **Homosexual males perpetrate most sexual abuse of boys.**

   Wrong. First, approximately 38 percent of boy abusers are female. Second, of the 62 percent of abusers who are male, most (98 percent, according to some studies) identify themselves as heterosexuals who are not attracted to adult (read: mature) males. Many predators pursue children (boys or girls) who are small and hairless, who lack secondary sex characteristics and the power in the relationship, and who are, above all, accessible.

3. **If a boy experiences sexual arousal or orgasm from abuse, this means he liked it, asked for it, or was complicit in the abuse.**

   False. Boys, by virtue of how they are physiologically constructed, might experience physical sexual arousal (e.g., erection, pleasant sensations, ejaculation, and orgasm) by virtue of having certain parts of the body stimulated (even when under the most agonizing conditions). These physiological responses are automatic in most males and do not mean that they wanted—or worse, enjoyed—the abuse.

4. **Boys are less traumatized by the abuse experience than girls.**
Utterly false. Studies confirm that boys are just as affected by abuse, only many suffer more acute long-term consequences because of most boys' reluctance to disclose the abuse and seek help.

5. **Boys abused by males are, or will become, homosexuals.**
Absolutely not. Sexual assault does not have anything to do with sexual preference; however, boys who were abused by men or older boys often suffer from gender confusion and sexual dysfunction because they have not received the support they need to realize that something that happened to them does not affect who and what they are.

6. **Boys who are sexually abused go on to sexually abuse others.**
This might be the most damaging myth of all, because it makes the boy feel like he's not only a victim of his abuser, he's now labeled a criminal or potential abuser himself. Researchers have found that most abused boys do not go on to abuse others. Those who do are the ones who were severely mistreated and who never received help or support from anyone.

7. **If the perpetrator is female, the boy or adolescent should consider himself fortunate to have been initiated into heterosexual activity by a more mature woman.**
This myth is ridiculous. We now know that 38 percent of boy abusers are women: sisters, mothers, stepmothers, aunts, and, of course, teachers and caretakers. Just because the perpetrator is not male does not mean that the boy escapes suffering from feelings

of confusion, powerlessness, shame, guilt, betrayal, fear, and anger. In fact, this issue came to a head when a 1998 study titled "A Meta-Analytic Examination of Assumed Properties of Child Sexual Abuse Using College Samples," published in the *Psychological Bulletin*, concluded that boys who had sexual experiences were "not abused" if they perceived the experience as a good thing (consensual sex with an adult of either gender). When the public became aware of this study (as a consequence of a Dr. Laura Schlessinger radio show that aired in March 1999), there was outrage and universal refutation by the scientists who had been working on the issue of child sexual abuse for years. The consensus of most professionals and academics is that adults of either gender should not engage in sexual activity with children. To do so is to be a child abuser.

These myths have played a powerful role in perpetuating the silence that many boys elect to keep, instead of disclosing what happened to them and getting help. Let your mate know that you appreciate what he's been up against, culturally, emotionally, and physically, and that with your support and other help, he can fully recover and thrive. Next we will look at the different types of abusers and their effects on their victims, depending on who they were and what they meant to the child.

Chapter Two

Who Did It Makes a Difference

Having covered the forms of abuse that your mate might have suffered—psychological, physical, sexual—let us focus on what research shows us is the most damaging kind of cruelty: child sexual abuse (CSA). A child from any kind of home and family background can be a victim of sexual abuse. But as you will read, the type of sexual abuse he suffered probably depended on how, where, and with whom he grew up. In this part of the book, we'll explore the type of person who commits abuse, as well as the effects the different kinds of abusers can have upon a victim, your man.

Why Want Sex with a Child?

Before exploring the different types of perpetrators who might have abused your man, and the likely circumstances that provided access to him, we will consider the general characteristics shared by those who target minors for sex. First, let's clear up a basic misconception. Technically speaking, the term *pedophile* has a distinct meaning and is not correctly applied to every case of child sexual abuse. (See the sidebar "Clinical Definitions Describing Sexual Preference" for the technical terms for various deviant sexual attractions.) Nonetheless, for ease of reading, I will use the word *pedophile* to describe those who sexually exploit minors (all youngsters under the legal age of consent).

One of the leading academic researchers in the childhood sexual abuse field, David Finkelhor, Ph.D., has provided an outline to analyze how a person overcomes the modern cultural taboo on having sex with children. As you'll see, Dr. Finkelhor identified four essential elements that child molesters share:

1. The perpetrator finds emotional congruence and gratification from relating to a child in a sexual way. In other words, the abuser's arrested emotional development is on the same level as a child's. Thus, the abuser lacks the ability to relate emotionally to peers or more appropriate sexual partners.
2. The perpetrator finds children physically arousing.
3. The perpetrator is blocked, which means that the abuser is unable to receive physical and emotional gratification from more acceptable sources, like mature adults.
4. The perpetrator is not deterred by the taboo on having sex with kids.

There may be many pathways, from the strictly biological (hormones made him or her do it) to the psychodynamic (poorly developed impulse, or id, control) to the behavioral (learned conditioning), that might lead an abuser to reach the point where the "Finkelhor four" coalesce and he or she takes the first overt action toward sexually abusing a child (see page 73 for the definition of the term *id*). But no matter how the abuser gets there, once she or he has sexually violated a child, and is caught, found guilty, or confesses, the pedophile will rarely take responsibility for her or his actions.

In study after study, researchers find that, as a group, pedophiles tend to deny, justify, and minimize their offenses. If they do deign to admit their actions, they will admit to only one incidence, claiming to have never exploited a child before (often lying, for many pedophiles have multiple victims). Moreover, many pedophiles attempt to excuse their behavior by blaming their actions on depression, loneliness, drugs, or alcohol—anything to escape taking responsibility for what they did. (Remember, many violators are emotionally like kids, blaming others for their actions.) Furthermore, pedophiles generally deny or minimize the damage their actions have caused their victims and their victims' families. Instead of recognizing the harm they have caused, childhood sexual abuse offenders tend to focus on how the abuse charges have damaged them! What's even more alarming is how many abusers are inclined to blame their victims, some going as far as to claim that they were doing their victims a favor by teaching them about sex and even giving their victims pleasure. When asked about the machinations that necessarily took place to make the abuse possible, many pedophiles deny planning the circumstances or manipulating their victims (known as *grooming*). Instead, they claim the abuse was spontaneous and unintentional. Finally, most pedophiles deny that they are exclusively or primarily attracted to youngsters and, perhaps not surprisingly, deny their "denial," their overall minimizing and justifying rationalizations for their crimes.

Now that you have the basic psychological profile of a pedophile (there is no physical profile), let's look at the different circumstances in which childhood sexual abuse takes place. As you'll see, there can be profoundly different consequences to your mate, depending on who committed his abuse.

When Parents Abuse

Being sexually abused as a child can be devastating. Being a victim of parental incest can be overwhelming. Researchers who study childhood sexual abuse tell us that the closer the victim is to the perpetrator, the more psychological damage is done. So it should not surprise you that on the CSA continuum, parental incest has the most profound capacity to permanently harm the victim. When a parent or stepparent sexually abuses his child (or the child who is under his legal protection, such as when a guardian abuses his ward), that child experiences the ultimate distress. Not only is the child violated on a physical level, the very core of his universe is shaken. He has been betrayed by the very people to whom he entrusted his survival. From the child's point of view, if he cannot count on his parents to protect him, how is he supposed to feel safe and supported? Unfortunately, he can't. When a parent is sexual with a child, the resulting role confusion (who's the parent, who's the child?) and boundary uncertainty cause extreme psychic distress, in addition to the other common short- and long-term consequences of childhood sexual abuse: depression, anger, self-mutilation, suicidal behavior, shame, self-hate, substance abuse,

Clinical Definitions Describing Sexual Preference

Take a look at the definitions and etymologies of the terms below:

- **Ephebophilia:** a word derived from combining the Greek words *ephebos* (ἐφηβος), meaning "adolescent," and *philia* (φιλια), meaning "friendship or love." It is now used to describe those who are sexually attracted to postpubescent youngsters (ranging in age from twelve to seventeen years old) of either sex. This term is most commonly encountered in articles about priests, or coaches, or teachers who sexually abuse the adolescents (but not technically "children") in their care.

- **Incest:** from the Latin word *incestum*, meaning "not chaste." Today it refers to sexual relations between people who are too closely related to marry—generally, parent-child and siblings.

- **Pederasty:** a word derived from combining the Greek word *pais* (παις), meaning "boy" or "child," and *erastês*, meaning "lover." Today, the term is used to describe sexual relations between adult men and young men or boys to whom they are not biologically related.

- **Pedophilia:** a word derived from combining the Greek words *pais* (παις), meaning "boy" or "child," and *philia* (φιλια), meaning "friendship" or "love." It is now used to describe those who are sexually attracted to prepubescent children—more precisely, children under age twelve or thirteen.

anxiety, attachment disorders, trust and intimacy problems, sexual dysfunction, and social isolation.

As with other kinds of childhood sexual abuse, there have been many studies on the circumstances in which parental incest most commonly occurs and the particular effects it has on its victims. Let's take a look at what we know so far. First, parental incest violates two primordial taboos (prohibiting sex with children, in general, and sex with your own blood, in particular), yet it paradoxically takes place throughout the world, at all levels of society. Some studies suggest that parental incest occurs more frequently to the young (some studies suggest under age six), to those living in poverty or isolation (or both), and to those living in dysfunctional families with substance abuse or financial, emotional, marital, or even physical instability (e.g., moving often) and stress.

Also, according to some studies, having divorced or separated parents increases the risk of incest, and so does a parent's remarriage. (Although a stepparent is not a biologically related parent, most lawmakers and researchers define stepparent childhood sexual abuse as parental incest.)

There are exceptions to every rule. Just because your mate's parents were ostensibly successful, accomplished, and socially astute doesn't mean they never abused him. There are plenty of cases where doctors, lawyers, politicians, and wealthy businesspeople sexually abused their kids. There are differences, however, between boys' and girls' respective incidences of parental incest. Female children reportedly suffer from parental incest—particularly father incest—at higher rates than boys do. (As you'll learn, boys are more likely to be abused by extended family members, acquaintances, or older, bigger children.) Some researchers postulate that the reason boys are less likely to be abused by their parents, particularly their fathers, is that we live in a patriarchal society where men depend upon their sons to carry the family wealth and lineage forward into the next generation. Therefore, sexually abusing a son (an extension of the father) makes no "sense," especially when the boy is likely to grow into a strong man, while his father declines in age, making the father vulnerable to his son's potential quest for vengeance. In contrast, under this patriarchal theory, girls are devalued and will always be weaker than their father. Violating a daughter is thus easier, and the father's entitlement to take what is his for use and pleasure can outweigh the prohibition on sexual contact with his own child. Still, there are enough studies and reports of father-son (read the memoir *In My Father's Arms*, by Walter De Milly) and mother-son incest to conclude that this crime does occur to boys, albeit less commonly than it does to girls.

Other studies tell us that boys might be just as vulnerable to parental incest as girls are, but due to the same cultural inhibitions that you read about in the preceding chapter, boys simply don't discuss or disclose their abuse as freely as girls do. (Remember, most cultures expect boys to be strong, brave, sexually aggressive, not submissive, and silent about their feelings, fears, and weaknesses.) Frankly, parental incest is among the least reported kind of childhood sexual abuse by both girls and boys.

Thinking about it from the kids' point if view, you can understand why. Disclosing the abuse to a third party (doctor, teacher, spiritual leader, or trusted adult) could literally result in the destruction of the only family unit that child has ever known, albeit dysfunctional and unhealthy. The child might know, or sense, that upon mandatory reporting, the authorities will take the abusive parent away. Meanwhile, the child might fear that the nonabusive parent might be punished or removed as well, for failing to protect the child. In this instance, the child could be facing the frightening loss of both parents and the terrifying possibility of placement in foster care. On the other hand, if the child tells the other parent about the incest, he fears not being believed, being blamed for the activity, or worst of all, being told that the parent's allegiance is with the abusing mate, not the child, who then becomes the adversary and possible threat to the family's very existence. From the kid's vantage point, parental incest places him in a lose-lose situation.

Now that you understand why your mate probably remained at home for as long as he did without getting help, let's explore what happens when a mom or dad abuses a son. First, there is a profound break in the boy's mind between his parents as providers and protectors and his parents as sexual predators. The child's distress is often directly proportional to the severity of the childhood sexual abuse in which his parents engage. For example, children seem to be harmed less intensely by noncontact abuse, such as posing for inappropriate pictures or acts of indecent exposure (by either the parent or child—submitting to visual genital examinations and the like). Children are more apt to be psychologically wounded if there is sexual contact with the parent, like fondling or masturbation. Finally, kids are most disturbed by acts of parental penetration (anal, oral, or vaginal). Naturally, the frequency and duration of the abuse, and the age of the child at the time, will affect the short- and long-term consequences of the parental incest.

Generally, the more invasive and the longer the abuse continues, the more damaging the incest will be to the boy, although the effects will vary from child to child based upon his individual temperament and emotional development. For instance, a very young child, lacking a sense of sexual context, might be unaware that he is being abused, particularly if the parent makes the act a part of his hygiene routine, makes it resemble a game, or somehow rewards the child in the overall process. Still, even young kids sense that daddy or mommy is acting secretly and strangely, which confounds them. Some studies indicate that children between the ages of eight and eleven are most at risk for psychological damage from incest, because they know enough to understand that what is happening to them is wrong, but they are not emotionally mature enough to deal with these acts in a self-protective manner. Older children, ages twelve to seventeen, know exactly what's happening during the incest and may have better coping skills, but they remain trapped by continuing to be emotionally and financially dependent on their abusing parents.

Before we leave the topic, realize that incest is not limited to parents and their kids. Although it receives more attention than other kinds of incest, it comprises only 6 to 16 percent of reported childhood sexual abuse cases. Unfortunately, other family members—aunts, uncles, grandparents, cousins, and siblings—can and do abuse kids to whom they have easy access. In fact, research reveals that in many cases, children who abuse their younger siblings have themselves been abused. The so-called cycle of abuse is primarily seen in the cases of male adolescents or teens who were sexually exploited as kids, and who then act out their own abuse and resulting anger by attacking another child (and generally, their own siblings are most accessible). The good news is that kids who sexually abuse other kids have an excellent therapeutic prognosis if they are given the professional time, attention, and treatment they need. The same is true for their young victims. If not treated, sibling incest can be as damaging to a child as parental abuse—both make for a childhood filled with shame, pain, secrecy, and terror.

Other Offenders

By overwhelming majority—by some estimates, as much as 89 percent of all childhood sexual abuse cases—boys are abused by adult friends and acquaintances, caregivers, neighbors, or authority figures (e.g., coaches, doctors, police officers, principals, scout leaders, teachers, and priests—whom we'll cover separately in the next section). This means that the chances are very good that the person who abused your man was his parents' friend or a person held in some esteem by his family or even the community at large. In fact, gaining this outward trust and friendship is the method many pedophiles prefer to obtain access to their young victims, often right under the noses of their parents or guardians. Looking precisely at how pedophiles operate will give you insight on how your man might have been targeted as a youngster.

First, the abuser places himself in a situation that allows him open access to children (trusted teacher, coach, scout master, or friendly neighbor) and where he is perceived by others as safe and responsible. Next, the pedophile will engage in a practice known as "grooming." For example, the typical "friendly neighbor" pedophile would begin his grooming process by helping your mate's dad start the barbecue or by helping his mom carry the groceries into the house. Next, he'll engage the neighborhood kids by offering to pump up their bicycle tires in his basement or garage or by giving them food or letting them watch TV or play video games at his house. The kids will get used to going to this man's house for help or even fun.

Then this friendly neighbor will focus on a particular boy and make an effort to establish a bond with him. Generally, a pedophile will target a boy who seems eager for attention, is unsure of himself, or is smaller than the other boys of his age. Picking up on the child's emotional or physical insecurities and neediness, the pedophile will reach out to make him (the boy—now your man) feel better about himself. At this point, the grooming moves to the next level. The neighbor will fulfill the boy's apparent need for affirmation and affection by giving him gifts or extra attention, such as asking him to go to a ball game or on a camping trip. It could also be something seemingly innocent, such as inviting the boy to his home—alone—to look at his fishing tackle, workout equipment, or whatever, just to make the boy feel exceptional and appreciated.

Once the rapport is established and the man and the boy (now your mate) have a bond, the man—a pedophile who knows exactly what's he's doing, what he's after, and how to get what he wants—will begin to desensitize the child to physical contact with him. At first, the touching will be incidental and innocent. The abuser will casually stroke the boy's leg, embrace him, touch his neck, hold his hand, caress his head, pat him on the buttocks, or brush the hair away from his forehead. Meanwhile, the abuser is making sure the victim continues to feel special and trusted and cared for. As your mate is systematically being desensitized to touch, the pedophile might ratchet up the sexual content of his actions. The pedophile might begin to talk about sex, share pornography, or even ply the boy with alcohol or drugs to wear down the child's, and perhaps his own, inhibitions.

Once the pedophile makes his first overtly sexual move, the targeted boy is completely ensnared in his neighbor's wicked web of counterfeit loyalty and confidentiality. From the boy's point of view, the two are now bound by their secret of shame and guilt, and he will most likely remain silent about the event in an effort to cope with what has happened to him (especially if the boy felt any physical sensation of pleasure during the abuse). If the neighbor fears that the boy will report the abuse, he will not hesitate to do what he must to preserve the secrecy of his actions. He will threaten to harm the boy, or his family, or even himself should the boy disclose to others what "they" have done.

Often these threats are enough to secure the boy's silence. If not, the pedophile will use any means at his disposal, including blaming the boy or ridiculing him (no one will believe him, or they will think he's gay), to persuade him to keep his mouth shut. Naturally, coercion, force, or bribes (liquor, drugs, porn, or cash) are commonly used to obtain the victim's continued compliance and secrecy. Meanwhile, by this time, the boy, who often feels just as responsible for the abuse as the abuser himself, is easily manipulated by this pedophile, who thus far has played him to perfection. Can you imagine the incredible burden a youngster must bear having been manipulated, betrayed, and then sexually abused by a person who is well known to his family and perhaps even respected throughout the community at large? Now you can appreciate just how vulnerable your mate would be to someone in a position of authority who at first treated him as if he were special, only to deceive him and use him for his own sexual gratification. If you are interested in a fictional depiction of a gripping story about two boys who were sexually abused by their coach, view the 2005 film *Mysterious Skin*, based upon Scott Heim's wonderfully sensitive 1995 novel of the same name.

Under the Eyes of God

Catholic clerics are not the only ones who have violated the young among their followers. There are plenty of cases where the spiritual leaders of other faiths (Jewish, Mormon, Protestant, Muslim, and others) abused their revered power over the pious and have sexually exploited the children in their care. Still, no one, regardless of religious denomination or spiritual belief, could read this book without at least some awareness of what the clergy sexual abuse crisis has meant to the issue of child sexual abuse at large, and to boy victims in particular, who were exploited for decades in shame and secrecy by their trusted parish priests.

In January 2002, the *Boston Globe* broke the clergy abuse scandal by following the case of John Geoghan, a Roman Catholic priest who was standing trial for having molested a boy in a pool more than a decade earlier. In the course of discovery for that case, the *Boston Globe* reporters learned that Father Geoghan had been abusing kids for years and that the Church knew it but kept it a secret. Furthermore, instead of protecting the parish children from a pedophilic priest, the Boston archdiocese elected to transfer Father Geoghan from school to school, parish to parish, giving him ample opportunity to molest over 100 children all around the Boston area. What's more, the *Boston Globe* revealed that the Boston archdiocese had been secretly settling cases with Father Geoghan's abuse victims, as well as others, for many decades, relying upon confidentiality agreements and cash payouts to keep the scandal a secret. When Father Geoghan was convicted of child molestation in early 2002, and many of the formerly confidential Church papers were exposed to the public under the auspices of the *Boston Globe* stories, the scandal received national attention. As a result, more victims came forward from all over the country, indeed the world, to share their stories of abuse and to force the Church to change its policies concerning pedophiles in its midst—finally allowing the victims a chance to put the matter behind them and heal.

Aside from letting light shine on the dark, shameful secret of the Roman Catholic Church's protection of its sexually predatory priests at the expense of the most innocent members of the Church, the clergy abuse scandal highlighted the basic fact of male child sexual abuse—that it happened, that it was common, that its innocent victims needed help to cope with the harm they had suffered, and that the predators had to be punished and kept away from children. Over the past few years, academic research has yielded valuable information to guide our understanding of the unique consequences of sexual abuse in a sacred setting. First, studies reveal that the victims of clergy abuse (at least in the Roman Catholic Church) are disproportionately male. Second, unlike most molesters who self-identify as heterosexual, more than 35 percent of the abusers identified themselves as homosexual. What's more, the victims tended to be slightly older then the mean age of ten for other CSA victims, and many of them were repeatedly abused (whether fondled or raped) by the same priest over the course of months or years. Many victims reported that their abuse took place in the priest's living quarters and that other priests knew what was happening when they were taken to those rooms. Other victims reported that their abuse took place in the churches or school buildings or on camping or spiritual retreats away from home, but others were present and knew, or should have known, what was happening. Many victims blamed themselves for being unable to stop the abuse, or for taking it as long as they did. Surprisingly, many victims of child sexual abuse by the clergy said that they came from warm or loving homes, where both parents were present and engaged in their upbringing. (So much for the broken-home, CSA victim stereotype.)

So what happened to your mate—spiritually, emotionally, psychically, and physically—as a victim of clergy abuse? Well, to start, if your mate was Roman Catholic, realize that a priest is called "Father" and is the representative of Christ in the Church. So, in addition to all the religious issues of good and evil, guilt and shame, sin and salvation, and the power of God, priesthood, and protection—or lack thereof—your mate also suffered a perceived form of incest in that he was abused by "the Father," his priest, and by extension, the Almighty Father. But that's not all; for a child who has been raised a Roman Catholic, the priest is the highest possible authority on Earth, higher even than the child's natal parents. In this way, the priest, a father figure (*the* Father figure), has an enhanced authority position, not only in the child's eyes but also in his family's and his community's. To be abused by a priest, then, is to be the ultimate object of betrayal, not only in the physical sense, by the person but, in the spiritual sense, by the very sanctuary and salvation that that priest represents to the faithful. Therefore, the victim of sexual abuse by a member of the clergy must deal with the fact that the Church, and all that he believed was good, holy, and wholesome, came together to violate him in the worst manner imaginable. In addition to that, the victim must face the usual effects of child sexual abuse: depression, anxiety, shame, poor self-esteem, self-blame, guilt, gender identification and sexual orientation issues, post-traumatic stress symptoms (discussed in a later chapter), dissociation (separating his mind from his body as a means of coping with the experience as it occurs), suicidal thoughts, substance abuse and dependency, eating disorders, difficulty maintaining and enjoying intimate relationships, general sexual dysfunction, and social isolation.

As you'll learn, most victims of child sexual abuse recover from their trauma after they are able to confront what happened to them, generally by disclosing their secret to a caring person, be it a therapist, a spouse, a loved one, or a friend. When, however, a boy is molested by a spiritual leader, the need for secrecy is even more severe than with most cases of incest or sexual abuse by an acquaintance. After all, whom would the boy tell? His parents, who often view the priest as the highest moral authority in the community? The bishop or monsignor who allowed the pedophile in the church to begin with? What is a young boy to do when a priest sexually abuses him and then tells him that he's sworn to secrecy by the powers vested in him by God Almighty? Whom would most people believe, the boy or the well-respected priest? (Remember, this occurred before the problem became widely known and recognized.) Where was that young man to turn for help?

Often, nowhere. He had to suffer in silence. Many men who were abused by their spiritual leader say that they were afraid no one would believe them, and that when they tried to distance themselves from the abuser their parents punished them for not going to church or for no longer wanting to serve as an altar boy for the pedophile priest. In this way, the victims of clerical abuse were captives of their families' religious beliefs, their own faith, and the willingness of the abusers to exploit all the divine power over the devout they knew they possessed. As a result, many male victims of clergy abuse report having suffered severe problems dealing appropriately with authority of any type, anger, trust, and, as you'd expect, faith, in their adult lives before getting help. Scores of victims said that until they told someone who believed them, they were barely able to function, hold a steady job, or have satisfying interpersonal relationships. What's more, having lost their faith in God and religion, these men lacked access to a spiritual source to guide them or help them cope with what happened to them as boys. As a result, many turned to drugs and booze and generally self-destructive behavior to numb themselves to the pain of their past.

We know, however, from recent work, that healing can happen, but it takes courage on the part of the survivor and support and patience from his loved ones. As you will read in later chapters, your mate will realize that he was not to blame for what the priest did to him and that God was not forsaking him or punishing him. Rather, looking at the abuse from a perspective of years and distance, your mate may accept that at a young age, he was unfairly, unjustly, and perhaps unforgivably put in a position to learn that no man is godlike and that he, the victim, can channel the goodness in himself and others to repair his heart, body, and soul from the horrendous, wounding events of the past. Bear in mind that your mate will probably need as much spiritual healing as he will need emotional and physical mending. Later chapters will guide you in your mate's healing process. For a real-life glimpse of what happened to a man and his family when he discovered that the priest who secretly raped him as a young teen now resides just down the street, consider seeing the 2005 Academy Award–nominated documentary film *Twist of Faith*.

Predators and Other Criminals

Although books (and later, movies based on them) like *The Prince of Tides* and *Mystic River* popularize the notion of "stranger danger"—that is, an unfamiliar person lurking in a park, or a criminal breaking into a house to attack a child—statistics from the U.S. Department of Justice tell us that these kinds of attacks on children are very rare. Some figures place this at less than 6 percent of all reported cases of child sexual abuse (this number is slightly higher if incidences of exhibitionism or voyeurism are included). Still, it is possible that your mate was abused by a stranger. If that's the case, it's likely that the incident occurred under threat or use of force and that your man was injured during the attack. On the other hand, stranger abuse is the most reported kind of child sexual abuse, for the impediments to disclosure of incest or acquaintance abuse are not present. Still, there are fewer resources available for boys who are raped or otherwise molested than there are for women, particularly if your mate was attacked years ago. Then there's the trauma of a criminal prosecution and maybe even civil action that could drag on for years. If your mate was a victim of this kind of ordeal, his chances for recovery are excellent, as long as he received or will receive support and perhaps trauma therapy, as we'll discuss in a later chapter.

There is another kind of "stranger" child sexual abuse that can be every bit as harmful as the outright criminal variety, but the perpetrators attempt to dress it up in the high-minded concepts of freedom of speech, freedom of association, and freedom of personal sexual choice. Falling under this category are the groups or associations that promote sexual relations between adults and children ostensibly under the guise of giving the children the "right" to have consensual, cross-generational sexual relationships with whomever they choose. These associations hold conventions and sponsor trips abroad that purport to offer members the opportunity to meet minors who want to have sex with them. One such well-known organization, founded in Boston in the late 1970s, is called the North American Man/Boy Love Association

(NAMBLA). NAMBLA claims its agenda is to educate society on the positive nature of consensual emotional and erotic relationships between men and boys, much as the ancients Greeks and Renaissance men of Europe engaged in the practice and their respective societies accepted and even encouraged the practice. Other associations exist throughout the country—in fact, the world—that purport to have the same sort of agenda, promoting the freedom of individuals to have sex with whomever they want, regardless of the other person's age.

If your mate was involved in an abusive relationship or event arising from a NAMBLA-type club, he is likely to share all the short- and long-term effects, with an emphasis on gender identification and sexual orientation issues. After all, this group, and many like it, focus on promoting homosexual relations and, in fact, have modeled some of their literature on the American and German gay rights movements of the last century. In any event, you will learn how to address your mate's possible sexual identity and orientation issues in a later chapter. For now, we'll turn to the specific symptoms of child sexual abuse from which your mate could be suffering, and how you can identify and deal with them in a helpful, healing manner.

Consider Felix, a thirty-six-year-old male who suffered abuse from birth at the hands of a family member. Referred to me by his primary physician, Felix was attractive, with a well-developed body. He had had four engagements with—by his definition—four different, lovely, fine women. However, after a few months of intimacy, Felix would find himself withdrawing from each woman, even though he did not want to do so. He would find reasons why he should end each relationship, but he did not know why he acted this way.

After six months of treatment, we discovered that the act of intimacy that seemed to end each relationship was when the woman came close to touching his penis. Even discussion of the possibility sent him into a panic attack. Meanwhile, Felix could have other types of sex and considered himself a good lover.

Eventually, we were able to get to the root of his problem. Of all things, it was his grandmother, who often babysat him. Felix remembered her as kind, loving, and warm, always making him feel special. He remembered her, initially, as the stereotypical grandma. But, I noticed, after any discussion of grandma, Felix would hyperventilate and manifest signs of panic. We were able to address the repressed memories Felix had that his grandma would sooth him by stroking his penis, most often with her hands and at other times with soft or silky material. If this tactic failed to calm Felix, she would place his penis in her mouth. Felix endured this incest until the age of six. At that point, he had asked his older cousin if their grandma did those things to him as well. The cousin said no, and he told Felix that what he was describing was "sick." His cousin told Felix to tell his mom what their grandma was doing—and he said if Felix didn't, he would tell his mom. Felix could not bring himself to tell, but his grandma never did that again. Felix believed his cousin "told on her" and she decided to stop the behavior. The topic was never addressed on any level with any adult—within or outside the family—nor did Felix's cousin ever mention it again. Felix knew in his heart there must have been something wrong with the whole thing, but this was his grandma and he believed that she would never hurt him.

Unconsciously, Felix made a pact with his psyche to protect himself by never putting himself in a position where a woman he loved could do that to him again. He had no conscious awareness of these events, yet he developed symptoms that were ruining his life. It took several years in treatment for Felix to give himself to a woman without restrictions. By the way, grandma is still alive and Felix continues to have a relationship with her. Felix eventually married and had a baby boy, whom he never allows grandma to babysit. In fact, he will not even allow grandma to hold his son unless he is present. Still, to this day, no one questions this behavior. Sadly, grandma's sexual abuse of Felix is still the family secret.

Chapter Three

Watching for Symptoms

When a person suffers severe trauma in childhood, he attempts to cope with his experience as best as he can. Regrettably, many a youngster's short-term, self-protective survival strategies become something else as he grows into adulthood. Unfortunately, as you know from Chapter 1, defensive coping mechanisms (even involuntary ones) born from childhood abuse are often maladaptive and can cause as much damage to the person's overall emotional, physical, and social health in later life as the initial abuse. In this chapter, we will examine the issues of stress, coping mechanisms, and resulting traits, views, and characteristics that many child abuse survivors share.

Remember as you read this material that your mate's abuse did not have to be sexual to be damaging and traumatic and to cause long-term, unhealthy symptoms to arise. If, as a child, your man was exposed to intense suffering or distress—whether from psychological, physical, or sexual assaults—you are likely to see remnants of his coping efforts in the way he acts, reacts, and generally behaves as an adult. Once we explore the experiences and traits of child abuse survivors (i.e., how they think about themselves and relate to others and the world), we'll spend the following chapter looking at different underlying psychological patterns that are found in many abuse survivors, and how to deal with them.

Your Man's Brain on Stress

It's possible that many of your man's difficulties (e.g., anxiety, depression, hostility, obesity, personal relationship problems, physical risk taking, sleep disturbances, social isolation, substance abuse and dependency, and suicide attempts) are directly related to how his brain chemistry was affected by the stress of the abuse he suffered as a kid. Since the late 1990s, scientists have studied the effects of extreme stress on the human body. Groundbreaking research by Bruce McEwen, Ph.D., provided evidence of just how damaging major stressors can be, long after the events themselves have passed. Dr. McEwen's work proved that when a person, such as an abuse victim, is exposed to intense stress, his body will react in a predictable way to protect him in the short term. Specifically, in response to external circumstances and internal cues, the brain will cause the release of certain hormones, neurotransmitters, and

Understanding Brain Chemistry

Here are two helpful definitions:

- **Hippocampus:** Shaped like a seahorse, it's a small structure found deep in the forebrain. We have two, one in each hemisphere of the brain. The hippocampus is part of the limbic system and its primary function is to encode memories so they can be stored in the brain. It is constantly forming new neurons throughout life. It gets its name from the Greek words *hippo*, meaning "horse," and *kampos*, meaning "sea monster."

- **Limbic system:** About the size of peach pit, it's a system of neural structures deep in the brain that regulates one's sense of smell, primary drives (sex, hunger, thirst, aggression, pleasure, pain, fear, greed), feelings (i.e., affective states including emotions like joy, amusement, sorrow, and contentment), memory, and motivation. It also controls the body's endocrine (hormonal) and autonomic (involuntary) nervous systems (governing muscle movements, like breathing, heartbeat, and digestion).

other chemical signals that mediate the body's stress response. These biological chemicals will initially help a person concentrate, boost his immune function, and generally allow him to summon a fight-or-flight response (restrict blood flow, increase heart rate, inhibit digestion, and increase energy reserves) to help the individual survive the perceived crisis.

So far, so good, but take a boy and expose him to constant or repeated stressors in early life and the consequences are not constructive. McEwen's research demonstrates that the boy's brain chemistry and function will be altered and he'll lose the ability to regulate his internal stress response in an adaptive (i.e., an effective and protective) manner. Instead, his hormones and other body chemicals will flow constantly—or inappropriately—and his body will no longer be helped by their presence—or lack thereof—in the bloodstream. Instead of boosting memory and concentration, these stress-related chemicals will diminish both. Instead of improving immune function, the person will succumb more easily to infection and disease. Instead of prepping the body for efficient, self-protective action, the person will accumulate abdominal fatty deposits and arterial plaques. But that's not the worst of it. Not only will these chemicals suppress the body's ability to think clearly and remain healthy, Dr. McEwen's research shows that these internal stress mediators unleash a series of events—including gene expression and suppression—that result in significant changes in the brain's actual structure. Too much stress over too long a period causes the hippocampus to atrophy (shrink), possibly permanently.

Knowing that your man's abuse could've not only caused his brain chemistry to change but also affected the very size of his brain, what now? The upside to these findings is that medications are available that can ease your man's symptoms and help restore the balance to his brain and overall emotional health. (We'll address this aspect in a later chapter on healing.) For now, let's take a closer look at the abuse and the fallout (including biochemical changes) that typically manifests in an adult man who's survived.

Anxiety All Around Him

Almost every abuse survivor suffers from a form of anxiety, be it the occasional but paralyzing panic attack, an overall feeling of unease with the world at large, or a specific phobia, such as of dark places, small spaces (claustrophobia), or people and public places in general (agoraphobia). People with anxiety have a preoccupation with danger and are burdened with thoughts of impending doom, sometimes turning into full-blown paranoia. Anxious individuals tend to see the world as a hazardous place, fraught with perils and pitfalls, and they view human interactions with worry, suspicion, and distrust. In fact, anxiety causes many of the problems with interpersonal relations that abuse survivors experience, for they have difficulty attaching to others or showing any dependence on anyone (even a healthy interdependence with a mate). On the other hand, anxiety can have the opposite effect, causing overdependence on others and a clinginess that can smother a mate or a friend. No matter which route it takes, from underattachment to overattachment, anxiety prevents many abuse victims from reaching their potential in the work force due to their inability to relate appropriately on a personal level with coworkers, subordinates, and superiors.

Other common anxiety symptoms are avoidance, withdrawal, numbing with substances, physical exertion (including compulsive exercise and sex), eating disorders, or risk-taking behaviors (or some combination thereof). These activities, particularly alcohol or drug use, can provide temporary relief from the abuse-induced pain, but they are ineffective as long-term coping strategies. Science tells us that these survivors are merely doing what they must to function, compensating for the fact that their neurochemistry has been altered and no longer serves to protect them from the psychic ache of anxiety. Knowing that disruptions in normal brain chemicals like corticotropin-releasing factor (CRF) and serotonin levels are directly related to intolerable feelings of anxiety, depression, and stress can help you understand your man's actions. So, until he receives more permanent help from therapy, medication, and emotional support, being aware that your mate may be doing drugs or getting drunk in an effort to relieve his immediate emotional distress or cope with his overwhelming anxiety might just give you the strength and will to see him, or even yourself, through, at least in the short term.

The Angry Young Man

It's a cliché; it's even a Billy Joel song. In fact, some would say that the "angry young man" is an archetype in modern—or postmodern—Western culture. While that may or may not be true, the anger I'm talking about is quite different and stems, once again, from a childhood experience that left your man feeling weak, unprotected, betrayed, and helpless. Many child abuse victims, particularly males, exhibit anger as a primary symptom of their inability to stop or prevent their terrible experience from happening. This anger often takes the form of sudden rages, erratic mood swings, aggression, resentment, violent tantrums, and overall hostility toward anyone who comes too close and, paradoxically, anyone who doesn't come close enough.

Depressed and Despairing

Some will tell you that when anger is turned inward, it becomes depression. But other causes, like the imbalance of the brain chemicals serotonin and CRF, are also implicated with clinical anxiety and overall stress. One thing is clear: Most abuse survivors endure bouts of depression, with many fighting depression and its fallout for most of their lives, until they receive help dealing with their childhood trauma. Since it is a major consequence of abuse, let's take a closer look at it.

There are many indications of clinical depression, but not every depressed person exhibits every one. Still, your mate's change in mood and conduct will be all too clear to see. Watch for forgetfulness, difficulty concentrating and making decisions, loss of interest in people and activities that once brought pleasure, inappropriate feelings of guilt or worthlessness, withdrawal from friends and family, decreased sex drive (libido), weight loss or gain, inability to sleep or sleeping too much, hyperactivity or slow motor movement, inability to find hope for better times ahead, and thoughts of helplessness, death, harming oneself, or suicide. In order to separate depression, in the clinical sense, from malaise or having a blue streak, these symptoms must last for more than two weeks and interfere with the person's normal functioning.

Dysthymia ("mild depression" or "chronic depression") is a condition that is similar to clinical depression but less severe. Symptoms of dysthymia include irritability, brooding, joylessness, morose behavior, and feelings of inadequacy and despondency. Unlike depression, however, those with dysthymia are still able to function somewhat normally, if not happily, for months, sometimes years. Generally, the treatment for dysthymia and depression are similar: personal support, therapy (either group or individual), psychotropic (having an effect on the brain) medications, and, when appropriate, hospitalization.

Finally, though not technically meeting the criteria for depression or dysthymia, many abuse survivors suffer from a despairing resignation, a worldview that is negative and downward-pulling. John Briere, Ph.D., the director of the Psychological Trauma Program of Los Angeles County and USC Medical Center, has written extensively on the topic of trauma and depression (as well as other disorders) and has identified *cognitive distortions*, or CDs (distorted beliefs), common to victims of child abuse and other traumas. He designed a test (in psychological terms, a "scale") to assess the negativity of a person's outlook and how his or her beliefs might be interfering with "optimal functioning." Specifically, Dr. Briere tests for:*

- **Self-Criticism**—low self-esteem and self-devaluation, expressed in the tendency to criticize or devalue oneself

---

*Source: Material reprinted with permission from the description page for Dr. Briere's Cognitive Distortion Scales (CDS), *www.johnbriere.com.*

- **Self-Blame**—the extent to which the respondent blames himself or herself for negative, unwanted events in his or her life, including events outside the respondent's control
- **Helplessness**—the perception of being unable to control important aspects of one's life
- **Hopelessness**—the extent to which the respondent believes that the future is bleak and that he or she is destined to fail
- **Preoccupation with Danger**—the tendency to view the world, especially the interpersonal domain, as a dangerous place.

If your man meets the criteria for any of the depressive syndromes, remain vigilant and be ready to get him professional help. Although depressive disorders respond well to treatment, they can devastate a person and his family if ignored.

Zoning Out

This section is not about the act of having a daydream or fantasy. Rather, it's addressed to the act of mentally removing oneself from one's physical environment as a defensive way of dealing with stress, fear, or danger. As you'll read in the next chapter on personality disorders (which can underlie the symptoms we're examining in this chapter), many survivors, particularly survivors of child sexual abuse, coped with their abuse as it occurred by emotionally detaching themselves (or at least their conscious selves) from the traumatic event, becoming spectators of their own bodies as they were being abused. While dissociating from a traumatic event can work well as a short-term coping mechanism, it can seriously interfere with life as an adult when it becomes a way of dealing with any circumstance that appears menacing to the victim (now, your mate), when in fact there is no actual danger.

In its worst case, dissociation results in dissociative identity disorder (DID), formerly known as multiple personality disorder (MPD), a.k.a. the "Sybil" problem. Milder forms of the disorder are present when a person loses track of time, gets lost on the way home, or is unable to account for where he is or how long he's been away. None of these symptoms is helpful in a relationship, especially if your mate is out late and literally can't account for where he's been and with whom. Still, when handled appropriately, generally in therapy a person can learn to harness this protective escape mechanism, allowing it to kick in only when it's absolutely necessary (that would be under a real threat of psychic terror or profound bodily injury to himself or another), not when it's time for intimacy or even less threatening life events like a job interview or a family dinner. For an excellent account of dissociative identity disorder attributed to child sexual abuse, check out Robert B. Oxnam's book, *A Fractured Mind: My Life with Multiple Personality Disorder.*

Problematic Social and Sexual Relations

Most of the symptoms that abuse survivors endure make it difficult to function on a day-to-day level, but some are less obvious, though no less challenging to the victim and those around him. First, as a consequence of abuse, including the constant invalidation of one's feelings as a youngster, many victims—particularly men—will question what they feel and think in relation to the abuse. Often, they erroneously believe that they were somehow complicit with the abuser. Prolonged self-doubt and self-blaming (or being blamed by others) for something that was beyond one's control eventually leads to a disconnect between what the person is feeling and what that person allows himself to feel. Over time, the result of this self-denial is a man who suffers from impaired self-reference and eventually what the professionals call a self-identity problem.

Though not as obvious as the symptoms of depression, dissociation, anger, or anxiety, the inability to know oneself, to have insight into who one is or how one feels, can cause enormous stress and ultimately interpersonal conflict when the victim must deal with other humans who don't understand why he refuses, or is unable, to communicate feelings. The name for this condition is *alexithymia*, from the Greek words meaning "not having words for emotion." (*A* means "lack," *lexis* means "words," and *thymos* (θυμος) roughly translates as "spirit" or "breath-soul.") Technically, the term refers not so much to someone who passively and aggressively remains silent (we'll explore defense mechanisms in a later chapter), but rather, to someone who can't describe or identify his feelings and emotional arousal states, lacks insight into himself or others, and instead expresses himself (and his distress) through psychosomatic (induced by the mind on the body) ailments (e.g. a stomach ache or a pain in the chest). Having a mate who lacks insight into who he is, who doesn't know and can't tell you what he's feeling, is as frustrating for you as it is unhealthy for him and the relationship. Thankfully, however, there are excellent treatment modalities for this problem, and, if given the time and attention required to learn another way of relating, your man's prognosis is excellent. We'll take this matter up in a later chapter.

Finally, as you can imagine, a man who has survived abuse, particularly child sexual abuse, can suffer as an adult from sexual dysfunction. These symptoms can be manifestations of your mate's unresolved feelings of shame, conflict, guilt, self-hatred, anger, confusion, and perhaps revulsion when confronted with the issue of sex and intimacy. No matter what the cause, the issue will have to be dealt with and resolved to your mutual satisfaction for the sake of your relationship. In this final section, we'll explore some common survivor sexual behaviors, from the excessive to the minimal to the nonexistent.

Generally, people's sex drives will differ on a continuum from high to low, depending on their ages, health, culture, values, and vitality. When, however, someone's need for sex interferes with his ability to live a normal life and have healthy relationships, his sex drive has entered the realm of pathology and requires intervention. Inappropriately sexualized at an early age, some male survivors have an insatiable need for sex, regardless of the context—that is, the time, place, or person. If they were women, they'd be diagnosed as having *nymphomania*, but since they're men, they are said to suffer from *satyriasis* (so named for the Greek satyr—part goat, part man—that lived in the woods, drank, reveled with the god

Dionysius, and had sex with as many creatures as he could find). Commonly referred to as a *sex addiction*, this hypersexual activity is really a compulsion in which a person performs an act regardless of its consequences. Like any other addiction or compulsion, the addict is after the feeling that the agent (in this case, sex) gives him, not the interaction with the agent (or sex partner) as a distinct entity. A person with a sexual addiction is not out to have a relationship with those he beds. Instead, he's trying to replace a painful feeling (a remnant from his abuse) with a more pleasurable feeling. When interviewed in a clinical setting, these men say they have little interest in sex combined with intimacy. Rather, it's the physical release of orgasm that they desire. Interestingly, there are many documented cases of male survivors of child sexual abuse who have sexual addictions without partners. Instead, their sexual fantasies and urges involve obsessions (intrusive thoughts) and compulsions (actions regardless of consequences) that are sometimes based on the kind of abuse they suffered as children—whether humiliating, sadistic, or masochistic—and that can only be satisfied through masturbation, sex with objects, or self-abuse (not a euphemism for masturbation, but a phenomenon in which the man must hurt himself in order to climax). In these examples of paraphilia (from the Greek words *para* (παρά), meaning "beside," and *philia* (φιλία), meaning "friendship" or "loving") the men focus their sexual desire on circumstances or objects, not loving, affectionate partners.

On the other side of the spectrum from satyriasis and paraphilia, your mate might have little interest in sex for either psychological or physical reasons, based on his abuse experience. His low sex drive, hypoactive sexual desire disorder (HSDD), could manifest in a variety of ways: impotence (also called *erectile dysfunction*); an inability to have an orgasm, called *dyspareunia* (literally, "difficult coitus," a condition when a man—or woman—experiences physical pelvic or genital pain in connection with the act of intercourse, before, during, or after); or an overall aversion to any sexual act, thought, or touch.

So there's the gamut, from too much to nothing; male survivors exhibit a panoply of sexual behaviors, like any other humans. For you, his partner, the good news is that many sexual matters are successfully navigated by a couple with the help of a competent therapist—and a lot of self-work for your partner with your loving, patient support—as you'll see in later chapters. The sexual patterns that resist treatment and may cause permanent problems in a relationship, and even with the law, are addressed in the latter part of this book.

Here's an example of how sexual abuse can cause sexual problems in adult life for both the abused partner, and the one who was not abused. Sandy was a forty-one-year-old mother of three children, all under age ten. She presented a picture of sadness. When I interviewed Sandy, I found she was warm, bright, and very much wanted help. She told me that she was unable to satisfy her husband's needs and had agreed that her husband deserved better than she had to offer. He was very upset with the varicosities on both her legs since the birth of the children. She wanted to have them attended to, but the care of the children would interfere. She had also promised him she would lose thirty-five pounds within the next three months. When questioned about other problems, which she hinted at but needed help to confront, I realized that these complaints were only one part of the problem.

She felt inadequate as a wife because her husband had various desires he insisted she fulfill but that she could not perform, one of which was to stick his scrotum with sewing machine needles during the sex act. Another was to tie very fine thread around his testicles to arouse him. She could not bring herself to comply with this and other similarly sadistic requests. He told her that any good wife would do this if she truly loved her husband. She could, with difficulty, do some of the other acts (e.g., change her clothing in front of the bedroom window at night with the lights on so as to be viewed by her neighbors if they should happen by), and even though she was upset by doing this behavior, she acquiesced to gain the "good wife" title.

Sandy felt so inadequate that she agreed to allow her husband to date twice a month, as long he did not see the same person more than twice. She would budget money from her household allowance so that he could go to nicer restaurants and not have to settle for less. Sandy's husband made many other requests, but you get the general idea of the kinds of abuse that were at play for both partners in this marriage.

At this point I requested to see Sandy's husband, and he agreed to come to a session. Richard was a well-groomed man. Dressed in chinos and a plaid shirt, he would be considered aesthetically quite pleasing to the eye. Richard was eager to address the problems in his marriage. My initial statement was that the problems were as much his as his wife's, and they would both need treatment. Sandy would first need to address her feelings of guilt over her inability to perform behavior that was not within the norm, and then she would need to address her decision to allow her husband to date. Sandy's self-esteem was gone, and she had to work on regaining it. Richard was not at all surprised and agreed. Then he surprised me: "When we talk about my childhood," he said, "this may all make sense." He admitted that he needed help.

And so he began: Richard was raised by his mother in Philadelphia. He never knew his father, and his mother told him that he could have been fathered by one of many of her partners. His mom had lots and lots of male friends who would come to visit— sometimes five or six in one night, but never more than one at a time. When his mom had lots of visits, she was very generous and bought Richard just about anything he wanted. He said his mom seemed happy at these times. Richard told me that, sometimes, as a boy, he could hear some of what was happening in the room with his mom and, after a while, he couldn't stop himself from listening. Richard told me that he learned a lot about how to do things in bed and what made people shriek with pleasure. Then, Richard remembered that he was about six when he learned what the word *prostitute* meant, and he was not much older when he realized his mom was one. He realized that other children were not permitted to play with him or even go near his house. He said that he grew up managing his mother's affairs.

Eventually, Richard recounted that his mother began to climb into bed with him on some nights and do things that she said would relax him, but that was not the effect it had on Richard. Before he knew it, he was his mother's sexual partner when the men had stopped "calling." By this time, Richard said his mom had gained weight, had varicose veins on her legs, and just gave up trying to take care of herself. Richard told me how he promised his mom he'd stay with her for life and take care of all her needs. His mom reinforced the notion that it was Richard's responsibility to take care of her, since she had always taken such good care of him.

Richard recalled that this situation continued until his first year in high school, when he met the girl of his dreams and fell in love. He told his mom. After that, things were never the same. His mom would treat him the same way she treated some of the men from the past, and she would have Richard perform all kinds of acts on her. Sometimes she would "charge" him—sometimes money, and sometimes it was in chores or errands. Furthermore, Richard's high school love was not allowed to go near him. Richard understood why. He felt like the scum of the earth and knew that everyone talked about him. He felt worthless and was sure that no nice girl would ever want him. To get away, Richard applied for, and received, a scholarship at a college far enough away from home that no one would know him or anything about his mom. He met Sandy in his second year. She came from a nice family from the other side of the country. She and Richard began to date, and he never looked back. Richard and Sandy married right after graduation with the traditional bells and whistles.

Finally we got to the core of the matter. "Now you know why I feel the way I do about women," Richard said. I responded by telling him that I knew he'd been abused, but did not know why he would chose to carry on the cycle of abuse with Sandy when he tried so hard to put his past behind him and seemed conscious of his conduct. At that point, Richard began to weep and asked if I could help him to be a good husband.

We began treatment with two visits per week, working on how Richard felt about his mother and the fact that he now recognizes that the behavior was bizarre and abusive. He also had to deal with the fact that he never really had a childhood. As his mother's caretaker (and lover), Richard was "parentified," assuming the role his mother should have been playing. He was never able to make normal peer connections and learn to play and just be a kid. As an adult, Richard never learned how to integrate with people on a social or intimate level. Yet, Richard was ready and willing to deal with all these issues. The first thing he decided to do was to share some of his background with Sandy, who had no knowledge of his history. This was a great start for Richard and a major leap of faith on his part, trusting that Sandy would stay and work things out with him. For months we worked on confronting his past and addressed the sexual and intimacy issues of the present related to his abusive past. With effort and the support of his wife, Richard became a caring, compassionate man with no need to replay the acts of his childhood. He now sees his prior behavior as symptoms of abuse (in which he would re-enact the mother's sexual behavior as a grown man in an effort to control it, which he could not do as a boy). Richard was able to replace all dysfunctional behavior with new, healthier sexual conduct. And, as Richard got better, so did Sandy's self-esteem. She lost fifty pounds (to satisfy her *own* needs, not her husband's) and she became her husband's "date," rather than allowing him to date other women. Richard has learned to socialize, and for the first time in his life he has joined a club and is active on the board of directors.

Chapter Four

Psyched Out by Abuse

Having reviewed some of the physical and emotional symptoms that you might see in a mate abused in early life, now we'll take a look at their likely underlying psychological causes. This information will help you help your mate understand and resolve why he acts in destructive or painful ways, and learn how he can help himself heal and live a happier life, for both your sakes.

The Consequences of Trauma

Many studies have concluded that trauma, including abuse, can and often does cause long-term emotional harm to the victim, especially if he never receives help and support to process his experience. This emotional harm finds expression in the different traits and conduct—anxiety, anger, depression, and the like—discussed in the prior chapter.

But, you might wonder, how exactly did your mate's early life experience with abuse result in his symptoms or behaviors in adulthood? Psychiatric professionals would explain that a person's unresolved and often unconscious emotional conflicts can affect his conduct in many ways. To begin to understand how, let's consider two popular (though not technical) terms that are probably familiar to you from their frequent usage on talk radio and TV shows, and in movies, magazines, and certain newspapers. The first is *neuroses* (plural of *neurosis*), and the second is *psychoses* (plural of *psychosis*).

You've certainly heard, perhaps even used, the term *neurotic* to describe someone who is slightly off the beam of normal. Not dangerous, not crazy (another term that psychiatric professionals definitely don't use), just a bit odd or perhaps a few bubbles off plumb. If you picked up a textbook from the last century, it would tell you that the neuroses describe a cluster of mental disorders (e.g., anxiety, compulsiveness, hysteria, depression, nervousness, and obsessiveness) without hallucinations or delusions that have no organic or physical cause in the body, but that nevertheless interfere with a person's ability to lead a normal life.

The term *psychoses*, on the other hand, refers to mental conditions, still without apparent physical basis in the body (i.e., not caused by virus, bacteria, genetic components, tumors, disease, or injury), that involve a break from reality, fragmented thought, and bizarre speech and conduct. A psychotic, unlike a neurotic,

Schizophrenia

Many psychotics suffer from a condition called *schizophrenia*—literally "split or shattered mind," from the combination of the Greek words *schizo* (ςχίζω), meaning "to split," and *phrenos* (φρενός), meaning "mind." Schizophrenia, a mental disease affecting 1 percent of the world's population, is thought to have a genetic root and has a relatively early onset (between ages fifteen and thirty). Schizophrenics distort reality (often through hallucinations and delusions) and are unable to differentiate between the internal self and the external world. They have bizarre thoughts, incoherent speech, strange behavior, repetitive movement, flat affect (no emotional tone), indifference to personal appearance and hygiene, and are socially withdrawn (but not generally aggressive, as many mistakenly believe). Some studies show that stress can trigger a schizophrenic episode in those with a genetic predisposition to the disease.

is considered very sick and probably cannot function at all without help. Although it wouldn't be politically correct, a layperson might describe a psychotic as "mad" or "insane."

Depending on the individual's symptoms and circumstances, his neuroses or psychoses—whichever he has, and generally, you have one or the other—will fall into one of the following categories: acute (sudden and severe but of short duration, usually in response to an extreme stressor); chronic (lifelong, often due to genetic or neuro-biochemical reasons); or episodic (occurring over a period, then receding, only to return again, often triggered by external stressors and a predisposition based on genetic or neuro-biochemical weakness).

Although the expressions *psychotic* and *psychoses* remain serviceable, few if any contemporary clinicians or academics use the word *neurotic* to describe people in their practices or peer-reviewed papers and literature; yet both terms remain instructive and inform the current nomenclature for psychological function and dysfunction embodied in a book called the *Diagnostic and Statistical Manual of Mental Disorders* (DSM). The DSM, based on statistical models, was written by a panel of American Psychiatric Association (APA) professionals and is published by the APA. The manual contains references to a range of mental disorders, brain defects and injuries, and medical conditions (from mild to moderate to severe), but it does not list "neuroses" or "psychoses," per se. We'll review this bible of psychological diagnoses in the next section to gain an understanding of what psychological conditions might undergird your partner's behavior, the challenges he faces and why, and, most important, what help he needs according to current psychological practice.

The DSM Made Easy

Though not the only book to detail psychiatric conditions and symptoms, the DSM is the text most institutions, researchers, and mental health practitioners (e.g., clinical psychologists, counseling psychologists, psychiatric nurses, psychiatrists, psychoanalysts, occupational and rehabilitation therapists, social workers, and therapists) rely upon for collecting data, making clinical diagnoses, and when necessary, classifying visits (or hospital stays) on insurance forms to facilitate payment or reimbursement for treatment. In addition to classifying mental disorders and medical conditions, the DSM lists the criteria for each condition and describes each ailment in a text section containing its family patterns; culture, age, and gender prevalence; and associated disorders.*

Clinical Disorders

The next section will focus on the syndromes (major depression, dissociative, and post-traumatic stress disorders) that we know are common to trauma survivors.

Depression as a Disorder

Depression is a problem for many childhood abuse victims. Although people use the term to describe someone who is feeling blue, to have major depressive disorder (MDD) is quite a different thing, wherein an adult is "abnormally" depressed or suffers from an uncharacteristic loss of pleasure and interest in life nearly every day for more than two weeks. Plus, at least five of the symptoms you read about in Chapter 3 (i.e., weight increase or decrease—when not trying to lose weight—sleeping too much or too little, moving or speaking too fast or too slowly, low energy and libido, abnormal guilt or self-blaming for matters outside one's control, inability to concentrate or make decisions, pessimism, and thoughts of dying

---

*While the DSM can provide clarification for a layperson, the book is meant to be used by people with special training and experience. Therefore, it is appropriate to read the DSM for more information about your partner or to see for yourself exactly what the doctor or therapist or counselor is referring to in the course of your mate's treatment. However, you should not use the DSM text to diagnose your mate or yourself, because the manual was not designed for that purpose. Still, as a reader of *this* book, it is reasonable for you to review what the DSM says about the conditions and disorders that researchers tell us are most likely to affect child abuse survivors, cause dysfunctional symptoms, and affect intimate partners.

A Summary of Dissociative Disorders as Defined in the DSM

- **Dissociative amnesia:** This is when a person selectively, yet unconsciously, forgets people, places, or periods of time, which is generally related to a traumatic event or time of life

- **Depersonalization disorder:** This disorder is most common for abuse victims. It's the feeling of being detached from one's body or living in a dreamlike state in which the real world seems at a distance from one's conscious experience of self. Related to depersonalization is *derealization*, which is a term that refers to a person who perceives other objects or even people to be unreal or distorted, yet is aware that his perceptions are false (if he didn't recognize his perceptions as false, the experiences would be defined as delusions or hallucinations, which would be a marker for schizophrenia).

- **Dissociative fugue:** This is when a person picks up and takes off and doesn't know who he is or where he's from, but begins to live a new life in a new place, as a new person.

- **Dissociative identity disorder (DID):** Formerly known as *multiple personality disorder* (MPD) and made famous by the book and movie *Sybil*, DID is a condition wherein a person has more than one identity (normally between 2 and 12, but it can be as many as 200) and each identity (or "alternate") has its own personality (some are not even human!) with unique characteristics, including names, genders, ages, educations, languages, memories, and even physical ailments. Each of these identities, or alternates, lives inside the individual and reaches the surface of his consciousness at different times, depending upon external circumstances and internal cues.

- **Dissociative disorder not otherwise specified (NOS):** This diagnosis is a catchall for individuals who have dissociative symptoms but don't fit into the other categories.

and suicide) must be present during this same period. Additionally, to have major depressive disorder, a person's depressive symptoms cannot be caused by bereavement (it's normal to suffer depressive symptoms when grieving a loss), drugs (street or otherwise), or organic disease (e.g., adrenal, cardiopulmonary, or renal diseases, AIDS, cancer, thyroid dysfunction, or vitamin deficiencies).

If your mate meets the DSM criteria for major depressive disorder, he has many treatment options, including hospitalization, if necessary, or outpatient therapy (a topic we'll explore in a later chapter) with assorted antidepressant medications.

Dissociation and Abuse

You read in the last chapter about how victims of child abuse learn to protect themselves in a number of ways that, though effective for survival in the short term, don't serve them well in the long run. One of them was what we called "dissociation," learning to distance—or dissociate—oneself or one's consciousness from one's physical (external) circumstances, particularly harrowing or traumatic ones. Underlying your man's propensity for zoning out could be one of the five kinds of dissociative disorders.

These disorders take several forms, depending on the symptoms, yet all are marked by a person's compartmentalization of traumatic experiences or events in such a way that they are isolated from that person's normal consciousness but may recur and cause the person psychic pain. When the compartmentalized memories reassert themselves, usually on account of stress, they cause the person to suffer amnesia or, in the most severe form, an entire identity change.

Consider Dave, a forty-five-year-old dentist who had a successful practice. He was married to another successful dentist. They attended all the social events in their town and even hosted many of them. They had one daughter, who was involved in soccer and seemed well adjusted. When I asked Dave the reason for his appointment with me, he said he really didn't know, but his therapist suggested he continue treatment over the summer, and he was following his suggestion. I asked the reason for his therapy and what his symptoms were. He told me he sometimes finds himself in strange places and doing things he doesn't remember. He said that he would find clothing in his closet that had obviously been worn, but not by him. He stated that he felt like he was leading a secret life—but one over which he had no control and found out about only when he got in trouble.

The trouble was his wife's threat to leave him if he didn't straighten out. He was at a loss, not knowing what he needed to fix. He had read about multiple personality disorder (now referred to as dissociative identity disorder) and discarded that as a lot of nonsense. But now he needed help. He discussed his relationship with his wife and child with no difficulty. He loved them both very much. He was not, however, happy with his career choice. He found being a dentist unsatisfying and boring. Dave said he knew that he was not the only dentist who felt this way, saying that he'd read that dentists have the highest suicide rate of all the professions; yet they are among the highest-paid professionals.

When I asked Dave about family history, he was very resistant. He said he didn't want to open old wounds. I suggested that the wounds might have to be addressed to go forward. This was the first time I saw "Dean," who was his alternate personality (an "alt"). Dean came across the desk with an angry look that I had never witnessed with Dave, and he asked me who the hell I thought I was to make him go back to the slime he had arisen from. I asked who he was and he said he was Dean, telling me not to make the mistake of calling him by "that wimp's name." I told him I didn't understand and asked for his indulgence to explain what he meant. Dean told me that he knew all about Dave, but that Dave knew nothing about him. He said the only fun Dave ever had was what Dean gave him. Dean told me that he got Dave a different "flavor" girl every chance he had. I asked Dean why Dave was so hesitant about his past. He said, "Well, lady, you would be too if your old man sold you off to any man or woman who would pay for you."

Dean explained that he grew up in a small community where his father was known as the town pimp. He also said that the father made a good living at it and always had food on the table. I noted to Dean that it sounded as if he were defending the father. At that point Dean said it wouldn't take much more for him to slap me across the room.

When I asked Dean about his mother, he told me that she was "a dishrag that the father threw around." He said Dave just cried and acted like a baby until he took over. I asked him to tell me about it. He said he loved Dave and couldn't stand to watch him suffer and was afraid he would kill himself; that's when he came on the scene, to protect Dave. He got him out of that town with some money he stole and signed him up in high school across the county line. He worked odd jobs and finally graduated and got into a fine university. (Remember, this is Dave speaking through "Dean.")

Dean went on to explain that for a long time Dave didn't need him because he was doing just fine, until "that bitch he married started to make him a nervous wreck." That's when he (Dean) came back to help him. He told me that he would always protect Dave. I suggested that perhaps it was time that Dave learned to protect himself. Dean replied that if that happened it would be like killing him (Dean). I told him my goal would be for Dave to become aware of Dean and for one of them to eventually become dominant, and that Dave would most likely be the survivor.

Therapy continued until the fall, when Dave's original therapist returned. During that summer, I spent just a few more sessions with Dean, but most of the time I was with Dave. It was during one of our later sessions that Dave told me he had become aware of Dean, and although he thought he was helpful, he felt he had to get rid of him and lead his own life. Once Dave realized he had an "alter ego," he was able to deal with his past. His father had died, so he had to address his rage in therapy, where he could get help without regressing to a point where he needed Dean to help him. At the end of the summer during our last session he thanked me and said he was sure Dean would thank me if he was around, but he didn't think that would be happening. To date Dave is still practicing dentistry and is married to the same woman, and his daughter is in medical school.

Dissociative disorders are not caused by injury or any other organic causes, like infection or disease, and they must interfere with a person's personal, social, or professional life to qualify under the criteria of the DSM. Finally, as with major depressive disorders, dissociative disorders are very common to abuse survivors—particularly CSA victims—and are amenable to therapy (group and individual), as well as certain antianxiety (like Xanax) and antidepressive (particularly drugs like Paxil, Prozac, and Zoloft) medications.

Survivors and Post-Traumatic Stress Disorder

Many trauma survivors show symptoms of anxiety. One of the most common anxiety disorders to affect abuse survivors is something called post-traumatic stress disorder. According to the DSM, post-traumatic stress disorder (PTSD) affects individuals who've felt intensely fearful, helpless, or horrified (or some combination thereof) after witnessing or experiencing a traumatic incident or event in which they, or someone in proximity, were threatened with death (or someone did die), serious injury, or violation of bodily integrity. To qualify as post-traumatic stress disorder, however, there must be intrusive symptoms in which the person re-experiences the traumatic event, typically in the form of flashbacks, nightmares, or severe physiological or psychological distress when exposed to activities, people, or circumstances—like sounds, scents, or sights—that remind him of the event. In addition, to have a diagnosis of post-traumatic stress disorder, the individual must try to avoid people, situations, or feelings reminiscent of the trauma. These evasive behaviors include trying not to think about the event, being unable to remember the experience, a blunting of all emotion (referred to as *numbing*), and having a negative view of life. Finally, the person with post-traumatic stress disorder must be agitated or suffer what the DSM calls *arousal symptoms*—that is, being unable to sleep, startling easily, and being over-reactive to noises, hypervigilant or alert to any stimuli, no matter how harmless, having difficulty concentrating, being irritable and sometimes even violent.

As you might have read, post-traumatic stress disorder is common among combat veterans as well as survivors of violent crime, natural disasters, the Holocaust, and chronic child sexual abuse. It can appear within three months of the trauma, or later. Unfortunately, the disorder is often associated with other problems like drug or alcohol addiction or dependency, depression, guilt, obsession, and physical (somatic) or sexual dysfunction. Fortunately, professional treatment (particularly cognitive behavior therapy and eye movement desensitization and reprocessing therapy) and medications (the antidepressant Serzone, the antipsychotic drug Zyprexa, and the antianxiety drug Xanax) can help reduce flashbacks and depression and ease the anxiety associated with PTSD.

Take into account Jeff's story. He was a fifty-year-old police captain who appeared at my office without an appointment. He was trembling and in obvious need of help. Though not responsive to my questions, Jeff was willing to tell me what had happened. His first statement was, "I almost killed my daughter." He went on to say that his daughter often disrespected his wife, and that this time, he heard the fighting and thought he was back in Vietnam and his daughter was the enemy. He stated he had killed many young women her age during the war, and he thought for a time earlier that evening that he was back there. In reality, Jeff did not actually harm his daughter, but he felt confused, disorientated, and afraid that if a situation like this ever arose again, he might. Jeff told me he was scared to death because he couldn't tell the difference between his home and a war zone. Another instance in which Jeff couldn't tell the difference between his home and a war zone was as a child when his father would come home drunk and beat Jeff and his brother; as children, they always referred to his parents' home as a "war zone." Now Jeff thought he was really at war, only this time it was in his own house. Jeff and I talked about flashbacks and post-traumatic stress disorder. Jeff thought he knew all about it, but he never thought it could overtake him to this degree. He feared that if his son had not been home, he would be arranging for his child's funeral, not talking to me. I suggested that Jeff have someone hold his gun temporarily and that he commence treatment. He began therapy with the department psychiatrist and is now a lieutenant and leads a support group for sufferers of post-traumatic stress disorder.

Personality Disorders

Unlike the clinical disorders discussed in the preceding section, personality disorders (sometimes called *character disorders*) are more invasive and persistent. A personality disorder (PD) can be defined as a cluster of fixed traits (ways of thinking, feeling, relating, acting, and reacting) that a person exhibits as he or she meets with various personal and social circumstances. Put simply, people with personality disorders think, feel, see, and react to social situations predictably, inappropriately, and at odds with the cultural norm. Their inappropriate thoughts and behaviors are entrenched and enduring and interfere with their ability to function in personal and working relationships and in society at large. Most people with personality disorders are oblivious to their part in the repeated social or interpersonal conflicts that they regularly encounter and, instead, blame their circumstances on others. From the health care provider's point of view, personality disorders can be a challenge to treat. Being the partner of a mate with an undiagnosed and untreated personality disorder can be difficult to endure. The ten personality disorders listed in the DSM (antisocial, avoidant, borderline, dependent, histrionic, narcissistic, obsessive-compulsive, paranoid, schizoid, and schizotypal) can be categorized according to shared traits and symptoms. For example, individuals with paranoid, schizoid, or schizotypal personality disorders generally seem strange or bizarre to others. On the other hand, individuals with antisocial, borderline, histrionic, or narcissistic personality disorders seem unstable, highly emotional, and drawn to drama. Finally, people with avoidant, dependent, or obsessive-compulsive personality disorders seem edgy and anxious and appear to be wound very tightly. As you read the following description and criteria for borderline personality disorder—the personality disorder most commonly associated with abuse survivors—think about your man's behavior and consider whether his actions might be influenced by a personality disorder, and if so, how to get help for him for the healing to occur.

On the Borderline

The name for this personality disorder comes from the fact that many, many years ago psychologists thought people with this disorder were "on the borderline" between neuroses and psychoses (or schizophrenia). Now clinicians believe that borderline personality disorder (BPD) is more closely related to major depression than anything else (with identity, emotional, and relational disturbances as additional symptoms). Studies prove that of all the personality disorders, borderline personality disorder is the most common among abuse victims, particularly childhood sexual abuse survivors. Although no one can say with certainty why there is such a strong correlation between borderline personality disorder and childhood sexual abuse, some researchers theorize that the abused individual, as a child, developed borderline personality disorder in an effort to cope with his traumatic experience, his home environment (and inability to securely attach to a caretaker), and his intense feelings of shame, invalidation, and worthlessness.

As adults, people with borderline personality disorder have it hard. Although they can initially appear warm, bright, amusing, and well adjusted, it's often impossible (without professional support) for the person with borderline personality disorder to keep up a functioning façade in the long run. Due to their lack of self-identity and emotional control, many borderline personality types are unable to maintain stable relationships of any kind—social, personal, or professional—until they receive help. Without a firm sense of who they are, individuals with borderline personality disorder often feel empty, which results in an intense fear of abandonment. This fear of abandonment can make a person with borderline personality disorder act extremely needy and dependent one minute, but given their rapid mood changes, be raging and angry the next. Adding to their difficulties, borderline personality types tend to engage in *splitting*, a maladaptive defense mechanism whereby they regard a person—a loved one, family member, friend, or boss—as either all good (valued) or all bad (devalued), without the ability to consider any possibility in between. What's more, people with borderline personality disorders have a problem with object constancy, which means that they lack the ability to retain a context for people when they are no longer present, and for incidents once they are in the past. For instance, the way the borderline personality disorder judges you most recently (as either good or bad, valued or devalued) is how he believes you are, notwithstanding the many years you might have known each other, or how many other kinds of experiences you might have shared.

People with borderline personality disorder often are attracted to self-destructive conduct, and some may cut or burn themselves (self-mutilation), binge and purge, or threaten or attempt suicide. Adding to their self-defeating bent, people with this disorder can be impulsive and careless. They are known to have promiscuous sex, do drugs, drive recklessly, gamble irresponsibly, shoplift, and engage in whatever risky behaviors they can find. But that's not all. Many with borderline personality disorder are paranoid, with symptoms of severe anxiety, depressive, and dissociative. Sadly, individuals with this disorder are in so much psychic distress that they are very likely to have problems with drug or alcohol abuse as they try to cope with their pain. It's not unusual for an individual with borderline personality disorder to be diagnosed with antisocial personality disorder (APD) as well.

These people are difficult to treat and are often dismissed from therapy due to the very symptoms that make them borderline. Take the story of Harry as an example, a forty-four-year-old married man with two teenage boys. He had a position as an executive vice president of a major New York City firm and he earned a large annual salary, plus bonus. He was fired from the position, and he was having difficulty dealing with it. Harry's wife, an accountant, demanded he seek treatment. Harry had been in treatment once before when he had an affair, and his wife again insisted he get help as part of the agreement to continue in the marriage. That therapy had lasted a year and a half, and Harry had done well. Though fired from almost every job he had, he always managed to find a new one with the help of his brother-in-law. But this time was different. His family refused to help because they felt he took advantage of their good will and influence and that he embarrassed them with his inappropriate behaviors. Harry was on his own. For a borderline, this is trouble.

During our first session, I learned that Harry was fired because he had ordered eyeglass holders to be fitted for the wall in the executive bathroom. Harry, like many of the executives, wore glasses and would wash up before a meeting. He thought that everyone would be delighted with this decision. (Remember, borderlines take events very personally, and they become enraged easily without thinking or caring about the consequences.) Well, Harry's boss entered the executive men's room and didn't like the holders. He called Harry into his office and asked whose silly idea it was to affix what he considered vases on the wall. Harry admitted it was his idea and tried to argue the point with his boss. The argument continued, until Harry's boss finally said, "I will make this easy. Either they go or you go." Harry responded that the issue was one of principle and that he would clear out his desk. Harry was escorted to the door and, within fifty minutes, was once again out of a job.

When he arrived home he told his wife what had happened and she tried to convince him to appeal to his boss and apologize. She informed him that her brother had said when he got this job for Harry that it would be the last time he'd bail him out. Harry's reaction to that was to then ban his wife's brother (and her entire family) from his house; they were "no longer welcome." (This is a manifestation of borderline "entitlement.") Harry was also "splitting" by denying the wife's brother access to his home, even though this brother had been the source of employment and assistance in the past. Like all borderlines, Harry viewed everything and everyone in life as either good or bad, black or white—never shades of gray. Living with a borderline is like walking on eggshells minute to minute. You never know if he is going to be nasty or nice, nor does he. It all depends on his perception of the world.

When I began treatment with Harry, I of course asked for some family history. He knew he was a diagnosed borderline and said he thought his mother and father also had the disorder but were never diagnosed. Harry said he hated living in his house as a young boy. He spoke of the dysfunction in his house, about the fights his parents would have, which would become physical. On those occasions, Harry would try to intercept. Instead of welcoming his help, both parents would chastise him. Remembering his home life, Harry told me that he never knew if he was right or wrong to try to save his mother from his father's fists or the furniture he sent flying. Harry felt he acquired his borderline disorder from his family, and I agreed.

Harry continued treatment. Eventually, I saw his wife as well, to try to have her understand how she at times would enable his behavior. Treatment was successful because Harry did have some insight into his behavior (many borderlines never get this far, even in treatment). Besides, Harry wanted his boys to have a better chance in life than he had. (They already did; neither boy was borderline. Fortunately for Harry's family, if you have one parent who is stable, the children of a borderline parent can be saved from the terrors of the borderline life.) Harry and his wife remained in treatment for over two years until Harry found a job in New England for less money, with a smaller firm. Harry had developed better coping abilities, which he said he could use now with some degree of comfort. I received a postcard from Boston at the next holiday season, and that has continued through the years.

The Good News

Although borderline is just one officially designated personality disorder, it happens to be one with a good prognosis, given proper treatment. To make the point, I'll compare the borderline to the antisocial person (the commonly called *sociopath*), a personality disorder that has one of the poorest prognoses. The two share a few overlapping symptoms, but are different at their core. For example, the borderline has a conscience, so he can be helped in therapy, whereas the sociopath lacks a conscience. The borderline, having a conscience, feels guilt and remorse for his unacceptable behavior and is very anxious. In comparison, the antisocial person has little or no remorse for his behavior and doesn't learn from past experience. Also, the antisocial person has no real anxiety unless he feels direct danger to himself. As a result, while most people afflicted with antisocial personality disorder are nearly impossible to treat successfully, many borderlines can learn how to handle their behavior through varying levels of therapy and support. Although your relationship might be more volatile than others if you are involved with a borderline personality, take comfort in the fact that there is hope. As you'll read in the following chapters, your partner's prognosis can be positive, with proper guidance and support.

Generally, there is hope where there is caring and understanding, and sometimes good pharmaceuticals can help when things seem out of control. Given proper therapy, rehabilitation, and medications, many individuals with psychological dysfunction learn to function and lead joyful, productive lives, controlling their symptoms and in some cases even enjoying full or partial remission of their disorders. The key, as you will see, is helping the person to address his underlying trauma, deal with the residual conflict he harbors, if any, and learn a new way to cope with his thoughts (cognitions) and feelings (emotions). Naturally, learning how to cope with stress helps the individual to control his behavior and his emotional output. Finally, having a supportive network of family or friends or both is critical to continued mental health and emotional stability.

Chapter Five

In Denial

The fact that you picked up this book indicates that you must already know—or suspect—that your man was abused as a kid. Let's go a step further and assume that now, having read about certain symptoms and clinical and personality disorders, you recognize one or more in your man's behavior. Understandably, in a heartfelt, proactive effort to help your mate and enhance your relationship, you address these subjects in casual conversation (not a confrontation or a showdown) with your mate. Then, afterward, you are surprised or disappointed (or both) that despite your best intentions, you got nowhere with him. Instead of the welcome reception and productive dialogue you expected, your partner stared at you with incredulity (or resentment?) and told you that he didn't know what you were talking about. Pressed further in response to your well-intentioned observations of troubling symptoms or gentle inquiries about disturbing conduct, your partner might have firmly declared, "I'm fine. Nothing's wrong," ending the discussion. This type of reply is what is known in the psychological business as *denial*, an ego defense mechanism (or simply *defense mechanism*, for short).

In this chapter, we'll focus not only on defense mechanisms and their triggers but also on what you can do when your mate employs these coping strategies to stop you from helping—or, in his mind, to stop anything from hurting—him. You will discover the approaches that will help you give your mate the emotional, and perhaps get him the professional, support that will make it easier for him to deal with his past and ultimately pave the way for a less painful and more gratifying future, for both of you.

Unconsciously Coping

As you embark upon the journey of living with a mate who was abused, it might help to bear in mind that your man has been dealing with his abusive past for most of his life, or at least a good chunk of it. You, on the other hand, have known about the issue only for as long as you've known him, or perhaps even less than that, if he just recently told you about his ordeal. Also, unless you were abused (and if you were, there's a later chapter on what you might be going through as your partner addresses his abuse), you really don't know how your mate feels now, or felt then, about his experience. Frankly, even if you were abused, your reaction to your situation was no doubt different from your mate's reaction to his. (Remember, boys have different social expectations to deal with. Consequently, he may have processed his experience differently from how you processed yours.)

In any case, no matter how empathetic you are or whether you have personally experienced abuse, since you weren't there when he was berated, beaten, neglected, or sexually abused, you can't know how your man's temperament (his innate disposition, whether calm and shy or loud and outgoing, or anything in between), his environment, and his own habits of resiliency or helplessness (what you could call his *developing character*) combined at that point in his life and emotional development to make his childhood trauma whatever it was to him. What you can be sure of is how he's acting now, physically, mentally, emotionally, and spiritually. If he rebuffs your efforts to help him deal with his past, chances are he's employing unconscious coping strategies developed years ago to shield him from unbearable distress. Although these strategies protected him in the past, they can hinder an intimate—or any kind of—relationship in the present and possibly block his opportunity for full recovery and freedom from pain in the future.

Freud's Big Idea

Before we delve into the nitty-gritty of defense mechanisms, you have to be familiar with the Freudian concepts concerning the conscious, preconscious, and unconscious mind, as well as his theories about the id, superego, and ego. First, a brief sketch about psychoanalysis and its father, Sigmund Freud, might give you a feel for the material. Freud was a medical doctor who practiced psychiatry and lived (mostly) in Vienna in the second half of the nineteenth century and died in London in 1939. Some argue that Freud's greatest contribution to Western culture was his insight that the mind (as in "psyche," not "brain") had three levels of operation: the conscious (the material we are aware of at any given point); the preconscious (the material you can be made aware of, with little effort, through memory, such as recalling a song's title or a book's author); and the most crucial, per Freud, the unconscious (the deep, dark, hidden material—like traumatic events—that you are not aware of because it's buried, but which still influences your thoughts, feelings, impulses, and actions). Interestingly, Freud's conceptual breakthrough occurred as he

"Phaedrus," by Plato (circa 360 B.C.E.), translated by Benjamin Jowett

I divided each soul into three—two horses and a charioteer; and one of the horses was good and the other bad: . . .The right-hand horse is upright and cleanly made; . . . his colour is white, and . . . he is a lover of honour and modesty and temperance, and the follower of true glory; he needs no touch of the whip, but is guided by word and admonition only. The other is a crooked lumbering animal . . . of a dark colour . . . the mate of insolence and pride, shag-eared and deaf, hardly yielding to whip and spur. . . .

treated upper-middle-class white women for an ailment that was then called *hysteria*, but which would now be called *anxiety* or a *nervous condition*. After listening to these female patients, Freud discovered that many of their "nervous" symptoms were related to (you guessed it) sexual abuse in childhood—generally, incest. Freud determined that these women had repressed their incest memories. Still, these traumatic memories wreaked havoc upon the women, even though they remained in the unconscious, far beneath the level of everyday awareness. When Freud enabled these patients to access their repressed incest memories through psychoanalysis (generally via dream interpretation—dream-work—or free association), they were able to address their anxiety and alleviate their symptoms.

Moreover, as you probably know, in addition to the conscious, the preconscious, and the unconscious, Freud gave us the id, the ego, and the superego to explain the complexity of human behavior and personality. Many academics have theorized that Freud's triumvirate bears a striking resemblance to the three-part "soul"

The Dangers of Superego Interruptus

The superego takes about seven or so years to mature. When something occurs that prevents the superego's complete or correct formation, the person in question typically develops an antisocial personality disorder (APD). A person with full-blown antisocial personality disorder (a so-called *sociopath* or *psychopath*) can lie, murder, cheat, and steal without feeling a single pang of remorse because he lacks a conscience (a superego). Though not nearly as prevalent as borderline personality disorder among abuse survivors, antisocial personality disorder has been found in children whose parents sexually brutalized them at a young age. If this condition describes your mate, you will need support (we'll address this in the next part of the book) and he will need professional help, and perhaps medication, to help him adjust to a lawful life with you and the rest of the world.

set forth in Plato's "Phaedrus" dialogue, describing a bad black horse, a good white horse, and a charioteer who must mediate between the two (interestingly, the Greek word for soul, ψυχή, translates as "psyche").

In any event, Freud's id (Phaedrus's "black horse") lies deep with the unconscious mind and represents our primal survival instincts for food, water, shelter, sex, avoidance of pain, and immediate gratification of whatever we want—the so-called *pleasure principle*. The ego (Phaedrus's "charioteer"), the only conscious part of the psyche, moderates among the unconscious id, reality, and later, the superego, allowing us to function—at least theoretically—in a healthy, well-adjusted manner according to external demands (i.e., the real world in which we live, hence, the *reality principle*). The last to develop is the superego (Phaedrus's "white horse"), the part of our unconscious that represents our conscience (what makes us want to do the right thing) and our ego ideal (what makes us want to be the best we can); it generally represents the identification with, or incorporation of, our parents' or caregivers' ethical concepts.

When our conscious ego can't resolve the conflicts created by our unconscious impulses (both the id's "bad" and the superego's "good"), we feel anxiety. To reduce the tension and protect our ego, we employ defense mechanisms—like repression or denial, among others—to keep the unbearable thoughts, feelings, memories, or desires away from our awareness. Unfortunately, when we use defense mechanisms to rework reality or minimize the situation, we reduce our ability to function effectively and solve the problem at hand. Plus, as Freud's work taught us, a person's unresolved unconscious conflicts will continue to—in keeping with Phaedrus's equine metaphors—rear their ugly heads until the individual finds a conscious way to confront them.

Dealing with Defense Mechanisms

Although Freud found that regression and denial were the two primary defense mechanisms his patients used to ameliorate their anxiety and reduce their tension, subsequent psychologists (including his daughter, Anna Freud) have identified others, sometimes called *secondary defense mechanisms*, that do the job as well. Many are offshoots of denial and repression. Most are unconscious, and all are irrational and used to bend our anxiety-producing awareness just enough to be tolerable, but not enough to lose touch with reality, as in psychosis. See if you recognize any of them in your mate's behavior (or your own?).

- **Aggression**—acting out in a hostile way that polite society would not accept. This behavior can be active or passive. For example, if your partner strikes you, it's overt or active aggression. If he tells you how pretty you were "when you were young," this is still aggression, but it's called *covert*, or *passive aggression.*

- **Avoidance**—the act of removing oneself from another. This can be achieved emotionally or physically. Your partner may choose to sleep in another room or not be able to respond to your verbal needs. This mechanism gives him the emotional ability to distance himself.

- **Compartmentalization**—the act of separating parts of oneself from awareness of other parts and acting with separate sets of values. For instance, a man cheats on his wife, yet he is a co-leader for a couples' support group.

- **Compensation**—when a person "makes up for" something with other behavior. Let's say your partner does not meet your physical needs, yet he brings you flowers or buys you jewelry, to "make up for" his inadequacy in the bedroom. This would be an example of compensation.

- **Countertransference**—when a therapist's own repressed feelings are brought to the surface in reaction to the patient's experiences and emotions. The therapist must be aware of this issue while treating patients.

- **Denial**—a mechanism that allows us to refuse to accept the reality of a situation. It is the major mechanism used by substance abusers, alcoholics, gamblers, and pedophiles. If your partner is an alcoholic, he might say that he drinks only occasionally and can stop anytime he wants to. The truth is, he cannot stop without help. Don't confuse denial with lying. Lying is conscious behavior, while denial is unconscious.

- **Displacement**—directing anger or other negative feelings toward a person or an object that is unrelated to those feelings when they cannot be aimed at the appropriate person or object due to fear of recrimination. Usually the person using this mechanism will select someone or something of lesser value in his mind, to diminish the possible repercussions of his actions. For instance, if your partner is angry with his boss and he says nothing at work, but he comes home and takes it out on you or the kids, or perhaps hits the wall or kicks the dog, that's displaced anger.

- **Emotional insulation**—withdrawal in some form to protect oneself from hurt. For example, a person who claims to be shy may be using this mechanism to avoid socializing.

- **Fantasy**—our mind's way of taking us to a more pleasurable place to give us freedom from an uncomfortable situation. If your partner angers you and he doesn't seem at all bothered by your scolding reply, it may be because he is using fantasy to take him to the golf course—perhaps even making a birdie.

- **Humor**—a mechanism that masks anger or hostility. This mechanism fools many people, because in general, we consider humor to be happy, light, and fun, but much humor is based on making fun at someone's expense. The humor we consider helpful and light is not directed at someone's inadequacies or shortcomings. When your partner falls and he says, "I went boom," this is healthy humor. If you have weight issues and he falls and laughs and says, "Good thing I fell and you didn't or we'd need a new floor," he's being sarcastic and aggressive. This "humor" is not funny; it's mocking and derisive.

- **Idealization**—giving someone or something greater value than it deserves, like placing someone on the proverbial pedestal. If your partner does this to you, it may feel good; but when you fall off that perceived pedestal, it can be devastating. It doesn't necessarily mean you did anything to warrant that change in view. Rather, it might mean that your partner has changed his view of you or the situation for the moment.

- **Identification**—a process that occurs throughout our growth and development in which we take on inner emotional qualities, as well as some imitated outer characteristics, of those to whom we are attached. We all use this mechanism at some time in our lives. It starts out when we are babies and we identify with our mother (or caregiver) and her smile or her look. Then we identify with our father and other people in our environment. We acquire the good and the bad qualities of those with whom we identify. Therefore, if your partner grew up in a dysfunctional family with stress, aggression, and perhaps physical abuse, it would be natural for him to respond to your family situations in the same manner.

- **Introjection**—taking on the qualities, wants, likes, or dislikes of another who is emotionally important to us. Perhaps you are religious and your partner was abused by a member of the clergy, and, as a result, rejects all religion. Unconsciously, you too begin to divorce yourself from your own religious belief and tend to follow your partner's lead, to make him comfortable. Remember, this is all done unconsciously. You will not realize this unless it comes out in therapy.

- **Passive aggression**—when a person hurts, offends, or obstructs another but does so in such a way that it is not clear whether or not the harm was intentional. Suppose your partner is angry with you and he places his coffee cup on the work papers you spent hours completing. Then he accidentally spills the coffee on those papers. You know that the act of placing the coffee on the papers was the possible passive-aggressive act, but you will never know for sure.

- **Projection**—the unconscious process whereby we place or cast our own objectionable or unacceptable thought onto another.

Here's how it works: Assume your partner has unconscious urges to go into fits of rage, but instead of dealing with his anger, he asks you why you are so nasty and angry all the time, projecting his emotional urges (anger, in this example) onto you. Note that you may be completely innocent of any behavior that resembles the nastiness or anger of which you're being accused.

- **Rationalization**—a mechanism that allows us to salvage our ego when we are in pain. We come up with an unconscious, plausible reason for relief from the anguish we may be feeling. For instance, your partner would like to be your lover and share special adventures with you; however, due to symptoms remaining from his childhood abuse, he cannot fulfill this ambition. This is extremely disconcerting to him, so his unconscious gives him the freedom to blame you for his flaws. He may say that you don't use deodorant or shave your legs, or he may give some other implausible reason why his failing or inadequacy is not his fault.

- **Reaction formation**—this is when an individual unconsciously exhibits behavior that is the opposite of what he witnessed as a child. This means that if your father-in-law was an alcoholic or beat his wife and kids, your partner would not ever want to taste liquor or raise his hand to anyone.

- **Regression**—when a person goes back to a former stage of development where he was more content and secure. If your partner should become hospitalized, don't be surprised or frightened to see him act childlike or cry and seem somewhat immature. If he responds more like your four-year-old than how you think an adult male should, try to understand that his regression is driven by his unconscious need for safety.

- **Repression**—a mechanism that protects us from situations that we find emotionally intolerable and, typically, so hurtful that we cannot bring the memory to our consciousness without the help of some form of analysis. If your partner was molested and has symptoms, but has no memory of what happened, this is repression at work. With treatment, he would have the opportunity to explore his unconscious memories and begin to deal with the issues with the help of a trained and experienced analyst.

- **Somatization**—the mind's unconscious conversion of emotional distress into physical distress. For example, if your partner has to go to therapy, where he is dealing with painful issues, he may develop a migraine headache or an upset stomach. Keep in mind that these illnesses are real, but they originate from the mind's unconscious processes.

- **Sublimation**—when a person takes impulses that are socially unacceptable and finds an outlet for them through an activity that is acceptable to mainstream society. If your partner has anger and rage due to the abuses he endured as a child, he may have urges to literally pummel and beat other humans. He could "sublimate" those urges into becoming a professional boxer—or, some might say a butcher or even a surgeon.

- **Suppression**—the mechanism that allows us to put hurtful situations or feelings out of our everyday thoughts. This is usually less painful material than the matters we repress, which we cannot even begin to deal with unless somehow released from our unconscious. Suppressed material can be brought forth without therapy. Upon some soul-searching, your partner may be able to bring to his awareness some of the events that are causing him such pain. (It's best to have a professional mental health care professional guide you through the process of dealing with suppressed material.)

- **Transference**—the feelings a patient attributes to the therapist, who may come to represent various people in the patient's life (e.g., parents, wife, teacher, abuser, siblings, relatives) at different times during the therapeutic process. In this way, transference allows your partner to work out issues he is dealing with in an emotionally safe, nonthreatening, professionally directed environment, hopefully resolving them while in treatment.

- **Undoing**—the method a person uses to try to make things right when he feels he has done wrong. If your partner has abused the family, he may come home with tickets for everyone to go to Disneyland, to make up for his unacceptable, abusive behaviors. The idea of undoing is that it will supersede the person's "bad" behavior.

- **Withdrawal**—the process by which a person removes himself—either physically or emotionally—from a situation that he finds unacceptable. Assume that you and your partner have not been getting along lately due to the stresses related to his childhood abuse, so he takes a job that involves traveling overnight 90 percent of the time. He has now physically—and perhaps emotionally as well—removed himself from the stressful household. Withdrawal provides a temporary fix at best, merely postponing the inevitable situation that must be addressed.

While reviewing the preceding list of defense mechanisms, realize that some people, abuse survivors included, will turn to drugs or alcohol to achieve the same effect—that is, ego protection from the anxiety, guilt, insecurity, lack of self-esteem, shame, or whatever loathsome and intolerable thoughts or feelings they might have as a consequence of prior traumatic experiences.

The Effects of Stress

Knowing now that traumatic childhood experiences and events buried deep in our unconscious can continue to influence our desires, thoughts, feelings, and conduct, imagine what an abuse survivor, like your partner, must endure as he tries to juggle all the normal tasks (i.e., living in the modern world of work and personal demands) in addition to what he suffered as a youngster. Actually, research has confirmed that stress (whether objective or subjective) is a factor that can make the difference between a functional person and a dysfunctional person, depending on his innate emotional makeup and his unconscious psychological burdens. We know for instance that too much stress can exacerbate the symptoms of a person with borderline personality disorder. Similarly, stress can increase clinical disorders like anxiety, depression, and dissociation and can even cause psychotic episodes in people who are susceptible to them. Since stress can be so damaging, let's take a closer look at how and why that's so.

In the mid 1960s, Thomas Holmes and Richard Rahe, medical doctors at the University of Washington School of Medicine, studied the effect of various life events on an individual's mental health. They developed a numerical "risk factor" for each incident based on its severity. The doctors concluded that if a person accumulated 200 points (in "life-change units") in a single year, he or she would have a greater chance of suffering from anxiety and depression. This predictive grading model became known as the Social Readjustment Rating Scale (SRRS). The following table lists the first ten (meaning the most stressful) of forty-two incidents listed on the SRRS chart.

The Social Readjustment Rating Scale (SRRS)

Life Incident	Change Units
Death of spouse	100
Divorce	73
Marital separation	65
Jail term	63
Death of close family member	63
Personal injury or illness	53
Marriage	50
Fired from job	47
Marital reconciliation	45
Retirement	45

Source: Holmes and Rahe: "The Social Readjustment Scale," reprinted from *Journal of Psychosomatic Research*, 11 (2): 213–218, © 1967 with permission from Elsevier Inc.

Beware that any one of these single stressors could be enough to affect your mate's healthy coping strategies, causing him to regress and rely on the maladaptive, but tried and true, defense mechanisms that enabled him to survive in the worst of times.

While the SRRS assesses the effects of big life changes and the stress they can cause, many people are just as apt (and some studies tell us, even more likely) to suffer stress from the daily accumulation of smaller-scale difficulties that regularly irritate and worry modern man. These daily stressors fall into three general categories: conflicts (discord and friction between a person and the world around him); frustrations (people and things that interfere with a person's needs or goals); and pressure (chronic demands and daily concerns relating to money, jobs, relationships, kids, health, loneliness, performance, and too much to do in too little time). Although anyone can be overwhelmed with the daily hassle of twenty-first-century life, someone like your partner (who was placed under so much stress at a young age, and by such harrowing circumstances) can be especially vulnerable. So, if you know your mate is experiencing a high stress level, be prepared for his fallback position (a problem we'll explore in the next section). But no matter how psychologically comfortable for him, your mate's reliance on defense mechanisms can stand in the way of effective communication, at least, and his fundamental functioning and contentment, at most. So what do you do when you encounter his denial or projection? Read on.

Defusing the Denial

Now that you are aware of your partner's defense mechanisms, what can you do with this knowledge? Hang tight. Bear in mind that mental (or defense) mechanisms are often a healthy way to cope with painful emotional events or feelings. We all use them to allow our psyche to process painful subjects. As a mate, you don't want to try to destroy these useful tools and leave your loved one with no way of coping. Defense mechanisms are unhealthy only when they are used to excess or when their employment interferes with normal functioning. In some instances, when reality is so painful you just can't deal with it immediately (e.g., the sudden death of a loved one), denial is a useful coping tool. It allows a person a period in which to regroup and gather forces to handle reality when it does sink in. Also, keep in mind that defense mechanisms are unconscious. You don't just say to yourself, "I think I will deny [whatever]." Denial, when necessary, will happen without your (or your partner's) intercession.

So don't get angry at the defenses your mate must use to keep his psyche protected. Remember, this is a kind of first aid for his mind, a temporary relief of emotions too difficult to address at that moment. The hope is that with help and a sense of security, your partner can increasingly rely on his conscious ability to problem-solve and not have the unconscious need to emotionally protect himself in the first place.

Chapter Six

How the Healing Happens

In the prior chapters, we charted the biological, psychological, and social waters upon which many male abuse victims tread. You know that a lot of these men have unhealthy habits (addictions to work, food, alcohol, drugs, sex, gambling, shopping, etc.), some have clinical disorders, others have personality disorders, and the majority even if free from the preceding afflictions— employ ultimately self-defeating defense mechanisms to deal with current life issues and protect their egos from painful thoughts, feelings, and impulses associated with the abuse they suffered as kids. In this chapter, we'll explore, as the title states, how the healing happens.

Releasing the Pain

For many childhood abuse survivors, healing means confronting the causes of their pain and taking back their power. For instance, when a victim goes back to that time in his mind, he realizes that, as a powerless child, he could not prevent the abuse, and no matter what he thought or did then, he did not deserve what happened to him. Generally, the awareness of himself as a vulnerable child permits the victim to appreciate that he did the best he could in a terrible situation under awful circumstances. At the end of this often painful psychological process, the survivor finally figures out that the guilt, shame, and self-loathing he's been carrying with him all these years really belong to his abuser, not to him. This eureka experience is what is known to professionals as *empowerment*.

From your reading so far, you might expect your mate to achieve empowerment with little difficulty. Of course he'll recognize that the abuse wasn't his fault, that he's not the one to blame, and that he's not alone in his experience. Sadly, psychological wounds don't heal that easily. The problem is, when a child is abused, he forms certain thoughts (cognitions), feelings (emotions), and behaviors as a result of the experience. Soon, these infantile and maladaptive patterns of coping, thinking, and feeling become ingrained in his mind as core beliefs. Eventually, they color not only how he views himself, but also how he sees others and the world in general. These patterns do not go away overnight or without immense courage and a mountain of self-work.

So how do you help set your mate free from the effects of childhood abuse? First, he must have an inkling that there's a problem. Either you, or someone close to your partner, must penetrate his defense mechanisms and succeed in making him understand that there are matters needing his immediate attention. Or, failing to convince your mate that he needs help, perhaps you told him you're not happy with the status quo and he's agreed to do something about it to appease you. (In this later case, it means your mate hasn't faced his past or its current effect on him in any meaningful way, so expect a longer time for recovery.) Whichever your circumstance, once your man has agreed to take action toward change—for your sake or his—you have to know where to turn.

Seeking Help

Your mate's first move toward a healthier existence will be choosing (with your input, focused on his needs) what method of help would best suit him. There are many forms of support available for your mate to begin his course of self-knowledge, healing, and renewal. In some instances, a trusted ally (pastor, fellow-abuse survivor, friend, or you) who provides calm, steady encouragement and caring is all he will need to find a better way to live with his past, himself, and others. Sometimes, a more structured approach is desirable, in which case support groups run by community, religious, twelve-step, or abuse-survivor organizations (covered in the next chapter) are the perfect means to help a man recover from the pain of childhood trauma.

Generally, however, if a man has built a wall between the abuse he suffered and his current behavior, he will benefit most from having a skilled psychological practitioner help him sort out what's happening now, how it relates to the past (maybe, depending on the kind of therapy he receives), and how to overcome the trauma to lead a happier life. Unfortunately, many male survivors of childhood abuse lack the financial resources, the insurance coverage, or the desire—for reasons we've discussed—to talk to anyone, much less a stranger (even a qualified professional), about very personal and often intensely disturbing matters. For these men, there is another tried-and-true method to purge from them the distress of youthful trauma: writing.

The Power of the Pen

One of the best ways for an abuse victim to gain release from the emotional prison of his past is by keeping a diary or journal, or just scribbling a running commentary in a bedside notebook. You might doubt the power of something as prosaic as a pen to help your partner work his way through the pain, down to the essence of what ails him; but how else can I put it? It works. Don't just take my word for it. Consider the findings of James W. Pennebaker, Ph.D., who has conducted numerous studies and written books and academic articles about the therapeutic and restorative aspects of writing down one's deepest, darkest secrets, fears, experiences, and feelings. Specifically, Dr. Pennebaker found that "high disclosers," those who revealed in their writings the traumatic events that they had suffered, were less likely to get sick, had improved immune systems, and enjoyed overall better physical and emotional health than those who didn't write about such personal matters ("low disclosers").

After Pennebaker and others found a correlation between disclosing powerful emotions and healing from traumatic experiences, many psychological health care providers suggested that their patients take up expressive writing (art therapy, too) as an adjunct tool to their normal psychotherapy. The real beauty of writing, however, lies in its effectiveness whether or not an individual is seeing a counselor. A person, or more to the point, your mate, can write about what he's feeling, going through, fearing, needing, wanting, remembering—whatever he wants, wherever he wants, whenever he wants. Furthermore, in keeping with the notion of empowerment, it's up to him whether his writing remains private or he shares his material with anyone or everyone. When writing, your mate is in complete control of the entire process: from the kind of writing he does (keeping a journal or log, blogging, or writing an autobiography, a poem, or a novel), to how he does it (whether by paper and pen or pencil, typewriter, or computer), and where he does it (whether in social isolation or while commuting to work on a crowded rush-hour train).

But there's more. Writing often helps people develop their thoughts and opinions about a subject, be it a time, place, person, or experience. Many writers say that they don't know what they think until they write it. In a similar vein, writing will allow your partner the personal freedom to process his innermost thoughts and feelings about his childhood, the people who were involved, and how these people and places affect him now. What's more, if your man decides to share his work with others (such as in a group setting or on a blog—even if anonymously), it can help other victims overcome their own traumatic experiences. In this scenario, not only does the listener or reader gain the writer's (your mate's) perspective and understanding, for each victim it also reinforces the fact that he is not alone—that others have been where he is and have transcended their trauma, to lead full, productive, comfortable lives, free from the emotional baggage of childhood abuse. If you think your mate could benefit from the writing experience, buy him a copy of Pennebaker's 2004 book, *Writing to Heal: A Guided Journal for Recovering from Trauma and Emotional Upheaval*, and see what happens next.

Mourning Lost Innocence

Although writing can help your partner process the suffering of his past, expect some fallout from the feelings he'll be experiencing as he works his way through the issues that caused him so much distress as a child. For instance, men tend to feel anger and rage in the early stages of their trauma recovery, so don't be surprised by an increase in those intense emotions as he begins to deal with his abuse in his writing. Similarly, expect to see signs of grief and sadness surface later in the process, when your mate, realizing that he can't change what happened to him as a boy, mourns the innocent childhood he was denied.

Sometimes, after releasing his feelings in writing, a survivor will feel a need to write letters (that he doesn't necessarily send) to the person or people who abused him, or to those who failed to protect him or believe him when he told—or tried to tell them—about the abuse. These letters can, for the most part, be a healthy exercise in your partner's recovery, for they offer him an opportunity to rid his body, mind, and soul of poisonous emotions and bitter resentments toward his perpetrator, the perpetrator's protectors (like the cardinals, bishops, and priests who know of the abuse by certain Catholic priests), or even his parents (or caretakers) for not saving him from the abuse in the first place. (We'll examine the legal options against abusers and their protectors in the next chapter.)

The Pros of Seeing a Pro

Although it's possible that your man will reach his potential with your help, and perhaps a cathartic journal, where he's able to make sense of his childhood and exorcise old devils from his psyche, sometimes only a trained professional will do. For instance, if your mate is seriously depressed or contemplating hurting himself or others, you must get him to a hospital for urgent treatment. Short of psychological emergencies, however, how can you tell if your man needs professional help? Generally, if he seems to be getting worse (i.e., suffering more, making life more unpleasant for either or both of you, is missing work, is falling under the weight of addiction), it's time for professional psychiatric help.

Not only will a professional be able to provide your partner with counseling to allow for better functioning as a man and a mate, he will also be able to prescribe (or make sure he sees a person who can prescribe) medications that can, at least in the short run, alleviate some of the worst symptoms abuse victims share: anxiety, depression, mood swings, and flashbacks. In addition, after ruling out medical reasons (e.g., low thyroid function, cancer, pulmonary disease, or brain injury) for your partner's psychological issues, a professional can order psychological testing to give your mate a clearer picture of what exactly ails him. For instance, the properly scored results of a Minnesota Multiphasic Personality Inventory-2 (MMPI-2) can give the psych professional valuable information and insights into your partner's personality, behavior, and coping styles, including any likely clinical or personality disorders. Other subjective and projective tests can unlock your mate's unconscious, offering rich veins for the therapist and your mate to mine in their sessions. (See the sidebar "Types of Psychological Tests" on pages 90–91 for more details.)

Psych 101

Although I've used the term *psych professional* in a generic way, there are many different approaches to therapy. Three basic schools of thought, founded by Viennese physicians Sigmund Freud, Alfred Adler, and Viktor Frankl, form the primary branches of treatment from which others forms of therapy have sprouted. Freud, whom we discussed in the prior chapter, founded the school of psychoanalysis. Therapists who identify themselves as "Freudian" or "Neo-Freudian" believe the tenet that humans' unconscious causes many of our difficulties and that the pleasure principle (composed largely of our sexual impulses) is our primary motivating factor. In psychoanalysis, the so-called *talking cure*, the therapist follows the patient's lead, allowing him to direct the session, in which free associations, dream interpretations, slips of the tongue, and self-reflections allow the patient to unearth the unconscious issues that are causing problems. Many patients feel that having the benefit of a skilled, concerned psychoanalyst helping them discover their psyche's secrets over a course of years is as reassuring as it is therapeutic.

Alfred Adler, a physician and former Freud follower in Vienna, founded the next school of therapy, called *individual psychology.* Unlike Freud, who thought that human behavior was influenced by fragments of the mind called the id, the ego, and the super ego, Adler said that the human was whole, or integrated, and that his drive was not centered on something physiological like sex. Instead, Adler believed it was based on an inferiority complex and the desire to strive for perfection, or superiority. (Some refer to this as the "will to power," a term borrowed from the German philosopher Friedrich Wilhelm Nietzsche). Twentieth-century psychologists founded other forms of therapy from Adler's model. Most agree that humanistic psychology, as espoused by Carl Rogers ("client-centered" therapy and encounter groups) and Abraham Maslow (hierarchy of needs, self-actualization, and peak experiences), grew from Adler's ideas about striving for perfection and the integration of the mind.

Another Adlerian child, cognitive therapy, became popular in the middle of the last century. Today it's often joined with behavioral therapy (remember the Russian physiologist Ivan Pavlov and his "conditioned" dogs?) to give us a very popular type of treatment called *cognitive-behavioral therapy* (CBT). Unlike psychoanalysis, this therapy tends to last, at most, twenty sessions. Instead of probing the patient's past for unconscious clues to his present dysfunction, practitioners of cognitive-behavioral therapy focus on his current thoughts (cognitions), feelings, and conduct

Types of Psychological Tests

Here are the most popular personality tests and what they do.

Objective Tests:

- **Revised Eysenck Personality Questionnaire (Revised EPQ):** This test measures the three traits (i.e., extraversion, psychotism, and neuroticism) described by Hans Eysenck in his theory of personality. This test also measures emotionality, tough-mindedness, and sociability. It is used in relation to substance abuse. Fifty items are tested in a yes or no format. It is administered to individuals or groups. It takes about ten minutes.

- **Beck Depression Inventory (BDI-II):** This test is for people from age seventeen to eighty, and it assesses somatic and affective patterns related to depression. It also measures cognition in relation to symptoms of depression. It has a twenty-one-item self-report format.

- **Millon Clinical Multiaxial Inventory-III (MCMI-III):** This test measures twenty-two personality styles and clinical syndromes. It is used for people seeking mental health testing or psychological treatment. The test has ninety-five items and is used on people from age seventeen up with at least an eighth-grade reading level. It takes about thirty to forty-five minutes to complete.

- **Minnesota Multiphasic Personality Inventory-2 (MMPI-2):** This is a standardized test used to sort out behavior that indicates the possibility of pathology. It is based on self-reported responses ("true," "false," or "cannot say") from a series of 567 questions that address a person's feelings, behaviors, and attitudes, as well as overt symptoms of psychopathology.

- **Neuroticism, Extraversion/Introversion, Openness to Experience Personality Inventory (NEO-PI-R):** This is used to assess five facets of personality: neuroticism, extraversion, openness to experience, agreeableness, and conscientiousness. This test is suited for adults and measures differences in personality traits, but it is not intended to diagnose psychiatric disorders.

- **Trauma Symptom Inventory (TSI):** This test is used to assess acute and chronic trauma, such as effects of child abuse, rape, and assault. It is also used as a measure for post-traumatic stress disorder, as well as other symptoms of traumatic events. It consists of 100 items, is self-administered, and takes about twenty minutes to complete. The person tested should have at least a fifth-grade or better reading level.

Objective-Subjective Tests:

- **Kinetic Family Drawing:** Used for children, this is a projective test administered with the goal of gaining insight into the child's relationship to and status in his family. The child is asked to draw a picture of his family involved in some activity. The test's protocol dictates that the tester leave the room and return only when the picture is complete. Based on what the child has drawn, the tester will look at the style of the drawing and then make an interpretation or assessment.

- **Thematic Apperception Test (TAT):** This is a projective test used for children and adults. The subject is shown thirty-one picture cards and is asked to describe the activity in the cards, revealing emotions or conflicts of the personality. This test has been used for mental status examinations.

- **Rorschach (Inkblot) Test:** This test is used for both treatment and diagnosis of a range of psychiatric conditions. Used for all ages, it has no time limit placed on it. The subject is asked to interpret ten psychodynamic pictures. As a projective test, there are no right or wrong answers. Scores are based upon the patient's responses.

(behavior), seeking ways to make them healthier. As the term *behavioral* suggests, the clinician considers how the patient reacts to various circumstances ("stimuli"). If his reactions are inappropriate or destructive, the counselor works with the patient to change his responses. As the term *cognitive* suggests, the therapist helps the patient explore the cognitions (thought processes and impulses) that might have led to the behavior that needs to change. (See the sidebar "A Therapy by Any Other Name" on pages 94–95 for more details.)

Logotherapy, founded in 1938 by Viktor Frankl (another neurologist-psychiatrist), is the last of the three Viennese schools of therapy. Taking its name from the Greek word *logos* (λóγoς)—meaning, in the philosophical sense, the divine rationale behind the universe—logotherapy's premise is that humans are motivated by a "will to meaning," not perfection or power, as in Adler's view, or pleasure, as in Freud's. According to logotherapy (also known as *existential psychology*), life intrinsically holds meaning, no matter the circumstances of the moment. Dr. Frankl, perhaps more than any other psychiatrist, is the perfect poster boy for his viewpoint. As explained in his must-read book *Man's Search for Meaning: An Introduction to Logotherapy*, Frankl has "walked the walk," having spent three years in concentration camps (Auschwitz and Dachau, among them) in the early 1940s. Frankl's haunting experiences as a Holocaust survivor provide poignant examples of the dignity of the human spirit and the fact that a person can transcend the bleakest of situations to find meaning in one's own existence.

In practice, logotherapy is an active, directive therapy used to treat crisis, depression, phobias, anxiety, and obsessive-compulsive disorder, among others conditions. It is considered existential because it emphasizes humankind's freedom of the will and the responsibility for one's actions that accompany this concept. Frankl's therapy is based on the idea that humans have a spiritual dimension in addition to our physical and psychological dimensions, and that we all have a will to meaning, which if frustrated results in a spiritual (noogenic) neurosis. Frankl also endorses the stoic concept, the notion that we each have the ability to turn a terrible situation into a more meaningful one, so long as we maintain a positive attitude. Logotherapists may also use something called *paradoxical intention*, whereby the therapist will ask the patient to wish for exactly what he fears, with the idea that this will relieve him of his symptoms. *Deflection* is yet another tool used in logotherapy. The therapist diverts the patient's attention away from his problems and presents him with something more meaningful in the world. Finally, *orientation toward meaning* is another logotherapy technique, wherein the therapist will try to open the patient's visual field to explore his meaning and values.

Trusting a Therapist

Although the therapeutic approach is important, the most critical element of your mate's treatment is his commitment to the process in general and his rapport with the therapist in particular. To be successful, therapy requires a relationship of respect and trust between patient and practitioner, as well as the patient's willingness and ability to be honest, receptive, motivated, and prepared to explore emotional places left previously untended (due to denial, repression, or any number of defense mechanisms). Exposing all levels of one's being—personal and professional, conscious and unconscious—will not always be comfortable or gratifying. There will be setbacks when your partner will have to endure his discomfort, keep the faith with his counselor, and allow the therapeutic process to run its course. (If it were easy, everybody would be in therapy and perfectly functional).

During these difficult times, your mate might need your firm encouragement and a gentle assertion that he remain committed to the process, whatever therapeutic approach he and his therapist use. But no matter what you do, your partner has the final word on his treatment. You might be able to drag a mate to counseling, but you can't make him think it's worthwhile or do the difficult work that's necessary. No matter how supportive you are, your mate is the only one who can face what he must and fix what

Several different therapeutic approaches are included under the cognitive-behavioral therapy (CBT) umbrella. For additional information, see *www.nacbt.org/historyofcbt.htm.*

- **Dialectical Behavior Therapy (DBT):** This therapy is used in the treatment of borderline patients. Based on the knowledge that those who suffer from borderline personality disorder have hyper levels of arousal, are quick to anger and rage, and have emotional outbursts, patients are taught how to deal with their maladaptive behaviors and are given affirmation for adaptive behaviors. Patients are also asked to attend weekly group therapy, where they learn useful interpersonal skills and how to regulate their emotions. Ideally, the patient learns how to identify problems and adopts skills to resolve those problems. Meanwhile, the patient is encouraged to seek advice and support from the therapist between sessions, and the therapist is expected to be available for him.

- **Eye Movement Desensitization and Reprocessing (EMDR):** A controversial method of treating emotional trauma, anxiety, stress, and other symptoms, some deem this therapy to be fast, effective treatment for past and present trauma, particularly post-traumatic stress disorder. The therapist uses hand motions inches away from the patient's eyes in a rapid swing while directing the patient to healthy thoughts. The rationale behind this treatment is that trauma causes a pathological change in the brain (a blockage) and that eye movements are the body's natural way of desensitizing a person to the trauma memory.

- **Rational-Emotive Behavior Therapy (REBT):** A form of cognitive therapy that teaches people to identify their problems, beliefs, and maladaptive behaviors and replace them with positive adaptive behaviors. REBT therapists use many different emotional and behavioral tools to reduce disturbing feelings. These tools include rational-emotive imagery, assertiveness, and risk taking.

- **Rational Living Therapy (RLT):** A form of cognitive-behavioral therapy that stresses the skills of the therapist, as well as the patient's self-counseling skills, and uses motivational interviewing strategies as a tool. This therapy uses cognitive development, social psychology, and linguistics but does not accept the concepts of self-esteem and self-confidence.

- **Schema Focused Therapy (SFT):** This therapy combines a number of different approaches for treatment, including cognitive, behavioral, psychoanalytic, and interpersonal theory. Premised upon the belief that some people have negative and self-defeating patterns—*life traps*, or *schemas*—that impede goals and frustrate needs, the goal of this therapy is to make the patient aware of these negative thoughts, feelings, or behaviors and to help him understand and ultimately break them, while developing healthy cognitive replacements.

- **Traumatic Incident Reduction (TIR):** Used in the treatment of trauma, particularly post-traumatic stress disorder, the length of treatment is dependent on the patient and how long it takes him to reach a point of resolution—or some degree of comfort with the trauma. The therapist will instruct the patient to select a trauma he wishes to deal with and then directs him to view his trauma as a videotape, which can be rewound as needed. This protocol is repeated until the patient shows diminished negative emotions and some degree of comfort with the trauma. The patient's goal is to gain insight into the trauma or himself—or both.

he can to feel and function better. As any therapist will tell you, while a person is not to blame for things that happened to him as a child, when he makes choices as an adult, he must live with the consequences. Your partner is ultimately responsible for his actions (such as showing up for appointments, being candid, and working on whatever he needs to—many cognitive-behavioral therapists give homework assignments between sessions). Your man's basic challenge is to gain acceptance of his unchangeable past, find comfort with his present (or make the necessary moves to attain it), and hold hope for a future with better times and healthier functioning. (More on your responsibilities versus your partner's is found in Part II.)

Finding Meaning in the Meantime

Your partner's recovery might be quick, or it might require years of intense inner work. Whichever, many childhood trauma survivors say that they begin to feel better when they look beyond their own painful pasts, in an effort to make the world a better place—not necessarily better in a monumental way, but in a more personal, immediate, and intimate way. Even if your mate doesn't go for Frankl's logotherapy, the belief that every moment in life is inherently valuable and meaningful can provide the motivation to do something helpful in the community or beyond, like volunteering to work with needy children or sharing his abuse experience with others in a support group. The direct power of his actions, reaching out and making a clear difference to someone somewhere can boost your man's self-esteem and help him battle ailments like depression and anxiety as he tends to his own emotional recovery. Besides, being kind, considerate, and helpful can improve anyone's morale in the present, no matter the horrors of their past.

Chapter Seven

Knowing He's Not Alone

As the preceding chapters describe, the abused boys who grew to maturity (your mate included) have had to endure the emotional fallout of their childhood trauma—whether psychological, physical, or sexual—for many years. Moreover, because these wounds often shape how these men interact with others, their abuse has, in many cases, gained a life of its own, affecting the victims' families and relations, thereby allowing the cycle of emotional harm to continue hurting innocents. While the first part of this book addresses how you can help your mate free himself from the bondage of past abuse (and the next part focuses on you, the intimate partner of a man who was abused as a boy), this final chapter of Part I will reassure you that your mate is far from the only man who is dealing with the detritus and damage of abuse. Unfortunately, the fact of your mate's childhood trauma does not make him unique: rather, it connects him to the growing web of ultimately thriving males abused as youngsters.

Celebrities Who Suffered

As you know now, recent studies confirm that one in six boys is abused in the United States. Other research confirms abuse estimates to be relatively constant worldwide. While I could quote pages of statistics and conclusions on the prevalence of abuse, nothing gives an issue more proper attention than a celebrity who comes forward to say, "I'm in the club, too." Do you remember how Oprah's admission of her own childhood sexual abuse empowered others, particularly women, who were sexually abused as kids to come forward and face their own abusive pasts? On one 1993 show, Oprah even discussed the fact that her weight problems might stem from her abuse. (The connection between morbid adult obesity and childhood abuse was later confirmed by the work of Vincent J. Felitti, M.D., and his colleagues in the Adverse Childhood Experiences Study.) Oprah's bold public disclosure of a private, delicate matter gave her fans the feeling that if she could overcome her abuse, they could, too. They were not alone. They were not stained for life. Most important, with Oprah as the model, they saw that they too, with proper support, could overcome their childhood experiences of shame, pain, guilt, and silence and become whatever they were meant to be, in spite of their abuse (maybe even because of it?).

There's no doubt that Oprah's televised acknowledgment of her own abuse served as a valuable, vicarious catharsis to those in her audience who were similarly affected, but it merely marked the beginning of Oprah's efforts to help victims and prevent future abuse. Putting her influence to work in December 1993, Oprah succeeded in having President Clinton sign the National Child Protection Act (NCPA, or the "Oprah Winfrey Act") into law.

Stopping Abuse: The Oprah Effect

Under the NCPA, procedures were established for child care providers to perform national background checks on potential workers. The goal was to enable an employer or organization to check a person's fingerprints against this national registry and prevent criminals from obtaining jobs or volunteer positions with access to kids, the disabled, or the elderly. In 1998, the NCPA was amended and strengthened by passage of the Volunteers for Children Act (VCA).

Through her compassion and national prominence, Oprah managed to raise people's awareness about the truth: Child abuse is common and its symptoms are pervasive and long-lasting. You might wonder why I would be talking about a famous woman's abuse story in a book about how to deal with your mate's past abuse. There are two reasons. First, Oprah's story helped unlock the secrecy of abuse by taking the shame and stigma away from victims and placing the blame and outrage on the perpetrators. Second, she encouraged other public figures, male and female, to do as she had done and share their own abuse survival stories. Naturally, some men had come forward about their childhood trauma before Oprah, but you just can't discount the salutary effect her revelation has had on so many. So, hats off to Oprah for putting her formidable power where her emotional pain was.

Now, you might ask, who are the men who were abused? In late 2005, Laveranues Coles, the talented wide receiver for the New York Jets, revealed he was sexually abused between the ages of ten and thirteen by his stepfather (who was jailed for the offense). In 1997, former Boston Bruin Sheldon Kennedy shared that as a teen he was raped over a period of many years by his junior hockey coach in Canada. Other prominent male abuse victims include actor and author Martin Moran; Emmy Award–winning daytime drama director and actor Dan Hamilton; comics Drew Carey and Louie Anderson; poet and writer David Ray; physicist, author, and former president of American University Richard E. Berendzen, Ph.D.; global advisor to presidents and diplomats, Asia expert, and author (of the 2005 bestseller *A Fractured Mind: My Life with Multiple Personality Disorder*) Robert Oxnam, Ph.D.; and notable literary lions John Irving and Richard Rhodes.

Both Irving and Rhodes have written about their abuse. In the summer of 2005, Irving used the medium of a novel, *Until I Find You*, to expose his childhood abuse experience. Rhodes, on the other hand, chose a direct approach many years ago by writing *A Hole in the World: An American Boyhood* and cowriting and editing *Trying to Get Some Dignity: Stories of Triumph over*

Childhood Abuse, with his wife, Ginger Rhodes. For an in-depth (literally, that's the name of the TV show) analysis of Richard Rhodes and his work, log on to the BookTV Web site at *www .booktv.org/InDepth/archive_2000.asp*. There you will find the link to watch the three-hour interview in which Rhodes discusses his abuse, among many other interesting topics, including the fact that Viktor Frankl's book, *Man's Search for Meaning* (mentioned in the last chapter), changed his life. (Not a bad endorsement for a book, considering how much Rhodes has overcome and how successful and productive he is, personally and professionally.) So, from Oprah to famous male literary, sports, and entertainment figures, your mate is in good company as an abuse survivor; and you, as Part II describes, can play a special role in your man's renewal and search for contentment.

Generations of Church Victims Revealed

I intentionally omitted one famous sports figure from the preceding section because his abuse was so typical of the multitudes of boys and girls exploited by priests (and other religious leaders) over the last century, and probably before that. In the spring of 2002, sports broadcaster and former major league baseball player Tom Paciorek announced to the press that a priest named Gerald Shirilla sexually abused him (and three of his brothers) over a course of years when they were growing up in Detroit, attending Catholic high school. As an illustration of the so-called "trauma bond" that connects perpetrator to abuse victim, Shirilla continued to abuse Paciorek after he graduated from high school and even had the nerve to officiate at his wedding several years later. (Paciorek's marriage broke up after eleven years because of his inability to love or be faithful.) Paciorek explained how the priest, also his teacher, had won the confidence of the boys' parents and used that trust to gain intimate access to their sons (Father Shirilla abused four out of the five Paciorek boys). None of the boys spoke of the abuse because they were ashamed, embarrassed, and, typical of young boys, just preferred to keep the matter a secret. Besides,

Paciorek was convinced no one would believe him if he did tell someone. (See the sidebar for Paciorek's own words as he told his story to the *Detroit Free Press* in March 2002.)

While it might take a man like Paciorek forty years to be able to discuss his sexual abuse, others are never able to disclose it. Meanwhile, the Catholic Church has, as of the summer of 2005, paid over $1 billion in civil settlements and judgments to those victims who have had the courage to come forward and tell their stories. Estimates are that the Church will pay more than $5 billion to victims all over the world by the time the scandal has run its course. If you do the math, you can deduce that thousands of people have been sexually victimized by the Catholic clergy alone. (Remember, it's not just the Catholic clergy who exploit their positions of trust and authority to satisfy their base needs at the expense of the most vulnerable in their care.) Just as the heading of this section indicates, generations of Church victims have, indeed, been revealed.

"Tom Paciorek Breaks Silence," Detroit Free Press, March 22, 2002, *excerpts:*

"When you're a kid and you're not able to articulate, who's going to believe you?"

"The church back then was so powerful, there's nothing that a kid could do."

"When you grew up in that time in a strict Catholic atmosphere, it was pretty much known that anybody who wore a habit or a cloak represented Jesus on Earth. You were powerless."

"I couldn't tell anybody because of all the shame and guilt and humiliation. . . . I just figured, maybe it will end. When I got home at night after being dropped off, I can remember specifically that he had just inserted his finger in my rectum. I remember getting out of the car and having him drive away and thinking, 'How sick is this?'"

Seeking Redress from the Abuser

It's interesting to note that it took Paciorek forty years to publicly discuss his abuse. (In 1993, Paciorek filed a formal complaint with the Archdiocese of Detroit, but he went public after he learned that the Church eventually shuffled Father Shirilla into another parish.) If macho pro baseball players didn't want to face their abuse for forty years, can you imagine how the typical man feels about it? The general reluctance of men to dredge up old pain and come forward about the clergy abuse they suffered no doubt caused a delay in the ultimate breaking of the clerical scandal until January 2002, when people across the world—including, eventually, Pope John Paul II—simply had to take notice and demand change. Unfortunately, the problem of clerical abuse of children in their care has been ongoing for decades, and there's the rub. As many victims would soon learn, in the majority of states, for the majority of cases, criminal prosecution was no longer possible because the statute of limitations had lapsed. In fact, since the story hit the media in 2002, many victims have been retraumatized by the realization that their tormenters were carefully harbored by the Church throughout the years and were now able to simply walk away from the matter, as if nothing had happened.

So that's the bad news. If your mate doesn't report the abuse to the police within the time allotted by his state's statute of limitation for criminal prosecution, his abuser cannot be prosecuted. (The limitation is typically within two to ten years after the victim

Filing a Report, No Matter What

Even if the statute of limitations in your jurisdiction (state, commonwealth, or possession) has expired and your mate's abuser can no longer be prosecuted for what he did, suggest that your partner file a complaint with the appropriate archdiocese and the local police department. It might not serve his (or your) need for justice, but it might just save another child from suffering the same fate.

turns eighteen, unless he lives in South Carolina or Wyoming, where there are no criminal statutes of limitation, or Kentucky, West Virginia, Alabama, Maine, Alaska, or Rhode Island, where the criminal rules of repose are more favorable to children and sexual assault victims).

The good news is that there's always (almost) a civil remedy, which is how all these victims you've been reading about have recovered money damages. You might wonder why the civil law allows a victim to sue an abuser when the penal code does not permit prosecution. The difference lies in the fact that when the state is involved in a prosecution of a criminal matter, the law in effect on the day that the crime was committed must apply. So in the case of abuse that occurred on March 3, 1983, whatever the statute of limitations was on that day would govern how long a person could be held accountable for that crime. This is not always the case when a civil matter is at stake. Unlike a criminal prosecution (when a state is the party trying to take away the liberty or life of a person for having committed a crime), when a person sues another in civil court, it's all about money damages, equitable restitution, and social deterrence. So, the rules concerning how long one person can privately sue another can change after the fact (ex post facto) if the people—through their representative government—think it's appropriate.

That's exactly what happened in several states after the church abuse scandal broke in early 2002. California, for example, passed a law lifting the civil statute of limitations for one year, allowing abuse victims to file suits against the institutions or employers (the Church) that negligently or intentionally hired or protected their abusers. In this way, even if the abusers couldn't go to jail due to the expiration of the criminal statute of limitations, at least the victims could sue the Church for having placed them knowingly or negligently in dangerous proximity to their abusers. Other states had different approaches to giving their citizens a chance to civilly sue those who caused them harm.

So, what good does suing the Church—instead of the abusing priest—do your man? In short, it could provide him with a sense of justice, not to mention cash, in the event you win or the defendant (Church) settles your case. Here's how it goes: Most institutions that own or operate facilities that accommodate people, like camps, churches, hospitals, orphanages, or schools, have commercial insurance policies to protect them in the event of negligent conditions or conduct on their premises that wind up hurting someone and exposing these institutions to expensive lawsuits. In the clergy abuse suits, victims alleged that the Church's negligent handling of their abusing, pedophilic priests resulted in foreseeable and actual harm to the children in their care (the victims, now plaintiffs).

Seeing where this was going, many archdioceses settled these suits and used their insurance proceeds to pay the victims. When there wasn't enough insurance money to cover the costs of settlement, some archdioceses were forced to file for bankruptcy protection, while others closed churches and schools, mortgaged or sold properties, or borrowed from parish accounts to raise needed cash.

How does this information help you? It informs you that your partner should see a lawyer if (1) you think your mate meets whatever legal criteria is necessary in your state to file a civil suit, and (2) he is the type of person who would emotionally benefit from having his day in court. If you and your partner choose this route, make sure you pick an attorney who knows the ropes. Try to see someone like Raymond P. Boucher in California, Roderick MacLeish, Jr., or Mitchell Garabedian in Massachusetts (the latter portrayed by Ted Danson in the 2005 Emmy-nominated TV movie *Our Fathers*, based on David France's book *Our Fathers: The Secret Life of the Catholic Church in an Age of Scandal*), Kenneth Millman in Pennsylvania, or Windle Turley in Texas. Like anything else, suing the Church or anyone else on behalf of sexual abuse victims is a specialty, and you need a lawyer with experience. Finally, even if suing is not your man's cup of tea, some parishes will offer to pay for the cost of your partner's therapy, including any treatments, rehabilitations programs, or medications he might need to overcome his abuse-induced trauma and lasting symptoms.

Support Just for Him

Finally, before we turn to you, this last section is to let you know that there are plenty of organizations just for men like your mate. They include the National Organization on Male Sexual Victimization (*www.malesurvivor.org*), Survivors Network of Those Abused by Priests (*www.snapnetwork.org*), and Voice of the Faithful (*www.votf.org*), among many others. These are national organizations with many local chapters. If there's no chapter in your area, someone can direct you and your partner to local resources. Many therapists find that support groups are a wonderful avenue for the abused boy, now a man, to see others who've been where he has been and who are there to support him, as he supports them, through the difficult times, to ultimate recovery. Have your partner check out these sites on the Web and see if he doesn't feel immediate comfort and relief.

Understanding Group Therapy

If your mate is game for something more personal than a Web site, group therapy might be ideal. Group therapy is intended to help people with all types of problems, anything from interpersonal relationships to educational issues. Given our topic, we will focus on psychotherapy groups. Groups are particularly suited for people having difficulty with issues like self-esteem, sexual relationships, anger, trust, and intimacy. Here is how it works: Your partner can ask to join a group. He can attend a group while undergoing individual therapy, or just attend a group. Your mate might join a new group or an ongoing group, depending on what he's looking for and availability. Groups are usually ten members or fewer. One or two therapists will be the leaders or facilitators for the group. The meetings are usually held once or twice per week, and during them members share personal issues with the others in the group, with the assurance of confidentiality. The therapists do not present topics for discussion. Rather, group members themselves decide what they will address each meeting. Each member may or may not enter the discussions, depending upon what's going on in that session.

Group therapy represents a microcosm of the world in which your partner lives. As a participant, he can share feelings, emotions, thoughts, fears, hopes, or whatever is apropos to the meeting, and he'll receive feedback from the group. In any event, the group feedback will give your partner an idea of how his behavior affects others. He will also have the opportunity to discuss his personal issues with the group and garner strength and support from fellow members. The dynamic nature of the group can help your man discover improved problem-solving techniques and change his maladaptive conduct into healthy behaviors. A dynamic similar to the "transference" found in individual therapy may arise; your partner will probably find that some group members will come to represent his family or other important people in his life. In group, he might be able to work out emotional issues that he was unable to address with the actual people involved. Here are a few final items for your mate to consider when thinking about joining a group. First, he should confirm that the group leader (or leaders) is qualified. He should inquire about their training, experience, and professional associations. For instance, he could contact the American Group Psychotherapy Association (AGPA) to verify anyone's group-leading credentials. Or you can ask for the leader's qualifications from your group referral source. It is a good idea to interview the group leaders to make a personal assessment before committing to a group. Also, it would be a good idea to ask about the fees and the protocol for missed meetings. If your man can find a leader he can work with, having a group can help him through the difficult times in life, giving him that extra bit of strength that makes life more manageable.

Part Two

A Partner in His Healing

Chapter Eight

Looking in the Mirror

You have just read seven chapters about the repercussions of your mate's abuse. We addressed the kinds of conduct that can scar your partner long after the acts themselves were committed. We explored how such abuse could, without the proper support, intervention, and guidance, negatively affect your man for the rest of his life, as he relates to the world at large, his work, his family and friends—and critically, from your point of view— his loved ones. We discussed how your man can—with your help and the help of other caring individuals, both professional and lay—overcome the trauma of childhood abuse and look forward to a productive life of wellness, function, and, most important, rewarding personal relationships. Now in this part of the book, let us turn our attention to you, the significant other.

What Attracted You to Him

At this point, you are familiar enough with the symptoms and psychological effects of abuse to realize that your mate is a heroic, if not perfect, person to have survived his secret childhood anguish. Despite his private hell, his suffering, confusion, helplessness, and misplaced feelings of shame, isolation, humiliation, worthlessness, and guilt, your guy was able, by whatever means, to overcome these obstacles and place himself in the position to find you or to be found by you. Let us examine the qualities that drew you to each other. You don't need any advanced degrees to know that maintaining intimate human relationships is a challenge under any circumstances, with anybody. And, as you now know from Part I, many abused men (though of course not all) have trouble with trust, becoming intimate, staying bonded, and maintaining—at least before they've healed—a healthy, loving sexual relationship. So, given all those challenges, you might wonder why you became involved with your guy, when there were plenty other men out there (84 percent, according to the most recent study) without the extra emotional baggage brought about by abuse. The answer might surprise you: Chances are good that your man developed some noble coping skills—much as he developed the poorer ones that need attention—as a consequence of his brutal life experience.

Notwithstanding the symptoms and behaviors that can make having an intimate relationship with an abused man so demanding, researchers have found that abuse victims (actually, survivors) often develop skills that many other men lack or don't develop until advanced age. For instance, adults who have suffered abuse as children are more likely to have grown up in circumstances that required them to become self-reliant (their ability to trust others was diminished by the abuse), flexible (they had to adapt physically and psychologically to survive the abuse), and protective (they learned to be concerned for the well-being of others, such as a parent or a sibling, making them exceptional guardians).

Furthermore, research reveals that many abused boys, in an effort to overcompensate for the anger they feel as victims, will become nonaggressive as men. To a woman, this passivity may be interpreted as (and, in fact, may be) reserve, tenderness, and kindness. These traits are particularly attractive to a woman who is looking for a submissive mate or someone who does not value brash, macho, or predatory male behavior. Other research confirms that some abused men cope by becoming ambitious go-getters in an effort to escape the trauma of their abuse or the confines of their dysfunctional domestic environments. These achievers will study hard. They will work hard. They will do whatever is possible to control the areas of their life that they can, overcompensating for the fact that, as exploited children, they had no control over their bodies or their circumstances. For the abused man, mastery of a trade, a profession, or a skill can be a vital means of gaining pride and overcoming his remnant feelings of helplessness and powerlessness as an innocent victim. In most cultures, an industrious man with a sensitive side is considered a real catch. No wonder you fell for him.

Once you have become involved with an abused man, it can take weeks, months, or even years for him to share the secrets of his traumatic childhood. Sometimes you'll learn of his painful past during quiet moments together, after viewing a TV show on the issue or after reading a story about child abuse in the newspaper. You might never have suspected your man was abused because he's already addressed it and dealt with it in a healthy way. Or perhaps you made him feel safe and secure enough to reach out, to seek help for the first time. Or maybe he's simply testing the depth of your caring and commitment to learn if you will still accept him and love him after you have heard what he's been through and what he has had to cope with since he was a boy or young man. Whatever the impulse that caused the subject to come up, your loving, accepting, calm, steady, sympathetic response is critical to your partner's well-being. (Don't overreact, minimize, deny, or ignore your man's experience; instead, listen.)

Sometimes your eureka moment as the mate of an abused man will not be so serene. Many partners first learn of their mate's

Delayed Disclosure—Burying the Memories

Perhaps you will learn of your partner's abuse when he does: when something in his life triggers his repressed memories—such as your child reaching the same age that your mate was when his abuse began.

history through shocking circumstances accompanied by a destructive event: the discovery of an affair, an act of self-violence, a sudden break from reality, an extreme and irrational temper tantrum, a substance abuse "bender," or incidents of this nature. The relationship is thereafter thrown into crisis, requiring a confrontation commonly resulting in a revelation of the root of the bad behavior—your mate's past abuse. Though painful, these traumatic episodes can precipitate the beginning of the healing process described in the first part of this book, ushering in a period of healing, growth, and a profound deepening of your pair bond. After helping each other cope with what has happened to your man, you can often attain a loving, tender relationship, more stable, intimate, and satisfying than anything either of you could have previously imagined.

Your Own Red Flags

It is just as possible that you weren't charmed by your wounded mate's good points, but rather were drawn to him by his flaws (which you can now identify as pathological symptoms of abuse). If, upon reflection, you think you were first attracted to your guy's faults—his moodiness, his alienation, his emotional unavailability, his remoteness, his inability to commit—rather than his attributes, the next question becomes: What are your issues and how do they interact with those of your man to affect you, together, as a couple? After all, your mate's healing will not occur in a vacuum. You and your psychological makeup will be an integral part of your partner's recovery and will have a powerful influence on whether your union can make it through the challenges ahead. In order for both of you to come out of this process healthier than you were when you entered it, you must know where you were coming from, emotionally and psychologically, when you first became a couple. Therefore, to be useful—both as a helpmate and as an individual trying to move toward a healthy, loving, intimate relationship with your man in your own right—you must be honest about your own life experiences, motives, and actions. Let's take a look at some of the possibilities that could have affected your thoughts, your behaviors, and your ultimate partner selection when you were out there looking for a life mate.

The Love Imprint

If you have lived on the planet for at least twenty years, you no doubt have heard the term *imago* (the Latin word for "image") in connection with how we select our romantic partners. Here's the thumbnail version: Forget tall, dark, handsome, smart, strong, stable, ambitious, loyal, kind, and sexy—the conscious attributes many would list for a mate. According to imago relationship therapy (IRT), first espoused by Harville Hendrix, Ph.D. (and made ubiquitous by his book *Getting the Love You Want* and the subsequent endorsement by Oprah), we select our romantic partners unconsciously, based on how closely they fit the image of our childhood caretakers (usually parents)—both positively and negatively (unfortunately, "negatively" has more of an influence on us)—and the emotional wounds they created in us. According to Hendrix, our childhood wounds needn't have been caused by bad parents or traumatic events—like the psychological, physical, or sexual abuse that your mate suffered. Rather, these wounds occur even in supportive and nurturing family environments because no matter how well meaning the parents, they cannot possibly meet every insatiable need of a child. In other words, we are all among the walking wounded looking for ways to get the love and emotional attention we were denied from our parents (or primary caregivers).

To begin the healing process, an imago therapist will work with a couple to help them figure out each one's respective unmet needs (wounds) and then work to understand how and why his or her mate corresponded to them in the first place. For instance, if a woman received the message that she was to be orderly, organized, and conforming, she might realize that she selected her mate because he was an artist who represented that creative part of herself that was suppressed, denied, or neglected. Whatever childhood wounds a person has, Hendrix believes that individuals select their partner to re-enact them, and, ultimately, attempt to heal them. Unfortunately, unless the person is aware of his unconscious motivations, what at first was beguiling as the "imago match" becomes irritating, and ultimately, unacceptable. Getting back to our example, the artist's freewheeling attitude and lifestyle (including, perhaps, substance use, abuse, or dependency) becomes viewed by his more rigid mate as irresponsible and juvenile. This is when imago relationship therapy steps in to assist the healing process, allowing the individuals within the couple to evolve so that each can give the other the love that he or she wants and needs.

How does this theory affect you, the partner of a man who was abused? Well, it might give you insight into your own childhood wounds, whatever they may be. If your mate is emotionally distant (as a symptom of his past abuse), you might learn that his aloofness re-created a wound from your past, representing your dad's formality toward you, making him all but irresistible to your unconscious. On the other hand, if your mate is a free spirit, he might have represented the uninhibited aspect of your nature that your caregivers frowned upon and you suppressed. Overall, understanding why you selected your partner, and vice versa, and learning to communicate and heal each other's wounds will, according to Hendrix, lead to a "conscious marriage," wherein each partner works to resolve future conflict in a way that is supportive and nondefensive, leading to a loving, safe alliance between the partners and a deep, abiding pair bond. For more on this therapy check out Hendrix's Web site: *www.imagorelationships.org.*

Were You Abused?

One of the factors that could have affected your life choices, including mate selection, is your own history of abuse. If you are conscious of your situation—that is to say, you know that you were abused—you can, with the proper help, reflect on how your wounds from the experience have influenced your intimate relationships. You are able, if you choose, to consider whether your own experiences as a victim habituated you to resume (or maintain) the destructive pattern, placing yourself in situations that were either dangerous or likely to result in your continued abuse or exploitation. Or, again, with the awareness of past sexual abuse, you can consider whether—if you still feel unlovable, unworthy, and full of shame—you consciously or unconsciously selected a partner who would not or could not give you what you need the most: loving, affectionate, consistent emotional support and tender, reliable, physical intimacy.

What do you do if you think you have been abused but are not sure because you lack a clear recollection of exactly what happened? I am referring now to childhood abuse that was (or might have been) forgotten and buried deep within your unconscious mind. How is it possible to have suffered something as potentially damaging and life changing as sexual abuse and not even remember it? Well, as you read in Part I, there are coping mechanisms (e.g., denial, dissociation, repression, and suppression) that the mind employs when it is unable to process and retain a conscious memory of an experience without inflicting substantial psychic pain and emotional (and sometimes physical, or "somatic") discomfort on the individual. In these circumstances, the mind will use various coping mechanisms to protect the individual from the pain for as long as it is possible or necessary.

Sometimes, a person's emotional or physical circumstances shift in such a way that the repressed material must be addressed, or the person's ability to function will be impaired in some way. When this change occurs, an individual might experience nagging feelings that something is terribly wrong. Or, a person will become aware of a vague sense that something "bad" happened, but can't put a finer point on it. For instance, a person might find herself avoiding certain friends or family members; she might become uncomfortable in some places or situations for no known reason; or, she might spontaneously begin to suffer intrusive nightmares or recurrent images without any readily identifiable cause. There are plenty of trained therapists who can assist the patient in unearthing whatever is causing such symptoms, whether it is past trauma (like abuse) or not.

Danger arises, however, when a person with a hazy feeling that something awful happened to her in the past seeks help from the wrong source (one who is not properly trained—or worse—has a serious mental problem of her own). In this case, instead of receiving qualified psychological treatment to determine why the patient suddenly feels uncomfortable with certain people or is experiencing nightmares, she receives iatrogenic (from the Greek words *iatros* (ατρός), meaning "healer," and *genno* (γεννώ), meaning "giving birth to" or "induced by") suggestions that she was in fact abused, regardless of the truth. If you think you might have been abused as a youngster but are not sure, you are best served by seeking help from an experienced, qualified mental health professional who lacks an agenda of her own concerning the issue.

Repressed Abuse Memories Versus "False Memory Syndrome"

Some of the most heated, downright emotional, yet academic battles have been and continue to be fought over the issue of recovered memories versus implanted, or suggested, "false memories." What we do know is that if a child is severely stressed by a trauma, his or her brain chemistry is affected. As you recall from Chapter 3, stress can even damage the hippocampi, the structures that assimilate auditory, spatial, and visual cues and are largely responsible for coding memories for later retrieval. So it's not surprising that someone would have difficulty recalling abuse if the hippocampi were damaged as a consequence of chronic or severe stress. Moreover, as you know from Part I, repression, denial, and dissociation are major factors in an abuse victim's survival arsenal. Therefore, it's not surprising that someone would "forget" what happened to her in an effort to ensure her survival or to protect herself from the psychic pain of abuse, only to have these memories resurface spontaneously in later life. Having a qualified therapist help unlock unconscious memories can provide the first step in a person's healing. (Freud did this and "cured" his female patients of their "hysteria.") So, under the right circumstances, with the appropriate therapist (who is empathetic and positive toward the patient yet neutral toward the abuse issue), psychotherapy can allow for the release and reassessment of the patient's experience, whether it was abusive or not.

The other side of the argument is that when a person is abused, he will remember it or there will be corroborating evidence of the abuse in addition to the "recalled" memories. If not, there are many reasons to doubt that someone could come up with an abuse allegation out of the blue. Researchers who distrust the reliability or veracity of later "recalled memories" cite the problem of practitioners implanting memories of abuse through suggestion when they have a bias toward finding abuse in their work with patients. Furthermore, they believe that memory-invoking techniques like hypnosis or giving a patient sodium amytal ("truth serum") are notoriously ripe for manipulation by the unscrupulous practitioner. Those on this side of the academic divide (allying themselves under the "false memory" banner) believe that false memories of past abuse (occurring after implanting, brainwashing, or suggestion by a third party) cause particular damage to the patient, who will sometimes break all ties with family members after having the "false memory" of abuse, causing isolation and further turmoil (lawsuits, writing of false memoirs, etc.). In fact, the "recalled memory" issue is so divisive that the APA professionals working on the matter could not agree on a common stance (see for yourself: *www.apa.org/pi/memories_report/section7.pdf*).

If you think you were abused, make sure you see someone who will help you find your truth, not suggest one for you. If you were abused as a child (whether you have always had memories of the abuse, or whether they came to you later, legitimately), you should identify your own wounds as a victim, deal with them, and resolve them in a healthy way. Otherwise, you will find it nearly impossible to help your man (whom you might have selected due to his own symptoms) overcome his own abuse trauma. Although you and your partner will have similar experiences and feelings that

Memory Terms

Researchers working with the filtering, coding, storing, and retrieving of long-term memory have a jargon all their own.

Explicit (also "declarative") memory: This type of memory is based on facts ("semantic memory"), experiences, or events of a time and place ("episodic" or "autobiographical" memory) and can be deliberately and verbally ("declaratively") recalled. Explicit memory is conscious and is retrieved from the temporal lobes and related regions of the cortex. (Memory is fragmented, stored in different areas of the brain, and must be reconstructed in the process of recall.)

Implicit (also "procedural") memory: Implicit memories are subconscious (just below consciousness); they are affected by repetition and are stored in the cerebellum and amygdala (part of the limbic system that deals with emotions and basic behaviors one would associate with the id). This type of memory involves learning, coordination, sensitization, and conditioning. Tasks or reflexes based on implicit memory seem automatic and cannot be explained verbally (they are nondeclarative). Implicit memory is employed when a person responds to emotional stimuli (such as "cues" or "triggers" that remind him of the abuse he suffered), exhibits conditioned reflexes, or performs complicated motor skills, like swinging a golf club (so-called "muscle memory").

Suggestion: The notion that an individual can influence another's memory of the past by using questions or statements that evoke events or images, which can distort or recall, or even create a false memory, later reported as fact.

Memory recovery techniques: These are procedures used by therapists to assist a person in retrieving long-term memory. They include assisted age regression (placing the patient in an altered state of consciousness, allowing him to recall life a younger age); body memory interpretation (where the mind tries to recall what the body could not forget); dream interpretation; free association; hypnosis; interviewing the patient under sedation ("truth serum"); keeping a journal; or writing with the nondominant hand.

might ease the pain at having been a victim of abuse, you will also share the same needs. Neither one of you will be able to meet the other's needs without, in most cases, professional treatment and, in all instances, an external support network, allowing your mutual healing, understanding, and behavior changes to occur.

Codependent "Savior" or Empathetic "Survivor"?

As you might expect, there are different ways of looking at a situation, and in this section we'll explore two of them. First, let's define the premise. You are reading this book because the man you love was abused. If his childhood abuse hasn't manifested itself in symptoms or relationship difficulties, wonderful. It means that your partner is within that 80 percent of victims who are able to fully recover from their traumatic experiences and live healthy, vital, satisfying lives. Perhaps he healed before you met him, having learned how to cope with his early life misfortune. Or maybe you were there with him as he underwent his healing process, and now you're reading this book as background, to confirm what you had suspected or as a complement to what you've already learned by living through the experience.

On the other hand, you could be reading this book because your man is not doing so well. Whether in crisis mode or not, he's in need of help, you recognized it, and you picked up this book as a place to start learning what you're dealing with and how to assist him. That's terrific. This book should provide you with enough information to put you and your mate in touch with the appropriate resources while giving you an education about what your partner has been through and what you might encounter—both as individuals and as a couple—as he deals with his abuse and as you deal with him and your part in the relationship. For now, however, I want to explore several theories on why you selected a man who might have addiction or substance abuse problems (as many abuse victims do, before they address the pain that underlies their numbing actions). If your man is not burdened by addiction, you don't have to read this section. Remember, however, that food, work, sex, gambling, and shopping can all be addictions. It might affect someone else you know or love.

Having established the premise that your mate was abused and is perhaps suffering from addiction, let us look at what might have been going on in your psyche that led you to choose a mate with these challenges—or symptoms from "wounds" (in the words of Hendrix). As promised, we'll explore two models that could provide you with insight and wisdom about your behavior when you selected a man who, you knew or should have known, had either addiction or abuse issues. First, let's review the more common of the two theories: codependence. Basically born of the famous twelve-step program, Alcoholics Anonymous, and its analogue, Al-Anon, the term *codependency* arose in the last quarter of the twentieth century, when academics began to write on the role of mates in the addiction process. Early studies revealed that the mates (generally, women) of alcoholics or addicts shared specific traits:

- They focused on their mates, to the exclusion of themselves.
- They neglected their own needs and goals.
- They made their mate's needs, goals, hopes, dreams, even leisure pursuits, a priority over their own.
- They were out of touch with their feelings.
- They assumed control and responsibility for the actions of others, particularly their mates.
- They had maladaptive coping mechanisms: repression of most feeling, dysfunctional denial of circumstances.
- They derived their sense of satisfaction from their mate's perception of them.
- They could not set appropriate limits with mates and, often, others.
- They devalued their self-worth and questioned their judgment.
- They engaged in enabling behavior, making excuses for their mate's bad conduct (e.g., drunkenness, abusiveness).
- They lived on the defensive to protect the peace.
- They tended to have complaints of physical ailments.

What's more, researchers found that these women had commonalities in their families of origin. Many had an alcoholic (or substance abusing) parent. Others had a rigid, authoritarian mode of interpersonal communication with little affection and irrational rules of behavior (if daddy's in a good mood, then I'll be okay and safe—which is irrational because the child is not in control of daddy's mood). Many were shame-bound concerning religious, economic, or social matters within the family, which then placed a premium on secret keeping. These types of families of origin taught the codependent women in them to make peace, deny their feelings, and do whatever they had to do to avoid conflict and the consequences of disturbing the problem parent or threatening the existence of the dysfunctional family system. As a result, these women were disproportionately drawn to men with serious problems (drinking, for instance) that their peers (that is, women who did not have troubled families of origin) would consider inappropriate mate material. Once the codependent women married their partners, they simply continued living the way they had in their own families of origin: keeping the secret, enabling the bad behavior, repressing most of their feelings, and "helping" others to the detriment of their own self-interest. If any of these facts ring a bell for you, there are many avenues for help, for both you and your mate, including the twelve-step programs like AA and Al-Anon, but also programs specifically designed for codependents, like Co-Dependents Anonymous.

Thus, codependency would be one explanation for your attraction to a mate with issues that could, if not treated or attended to, cause you enormous heartbreak, at the very least. There is another, more woman-friendly theory about why women behave the way they do in their relationships. The self-in-relation theory was born at the Stone Center at Wellesley College in the 1980s. Instead of pathologizing the qualities (nurturing, caring for others, promoting family well-being over that of self) that women in Western cultures learn from their socialization and lower status, the self-in-relation theory gives women credit for their empathy and need for social connectedness. In fact, this theory suggests that unlike boys in our culture, who gain their sense of self through separation from the family ("individuation") and autonomy, girls develop their identify and sense of self through their relationships with their mothers and, in later life, connectedness to others through relationships. Moreover, according to the self-in-relation theory, women continue to develop and understand who they are through the dynamic of relationships, and in this way even conflict in those relationships is an occasion for deeper understanding and growth for the individuals involved. So, all in all, where the codependence model might make you feel lacking—as if something's wrong with you for exhibiting the prized "female" attributes of caring and nurturing and maintaining the relationship with your partner—the self-in-relation theory suggests that you're simply doing what your culture demands a woman do in order to develop and thrive (even survive) in a society that does not reward strong ("pushy"), independent ("selfish"), assertive ("bitchy") women. Given these truths, however, the goal is to recognize that while you might be socially and psychologically wired to care for others more than you care for yourself, you will be healthier if you learn to strike a balance between self-care and selflessness. We'll revisit these concepts in a later chapter, when we deal with the issues of when it's appropriate to give and when it's not, while you're in the relationship.

The Intersection of Codependency and Abuse

I see many couples who have both elements: codependency and a history of abuse. Read Martha's story to see how these aspects can affect a couple. Martha was a bright, energetic young woman, the youngest of her three siblings. Though bright and pretty, she always felt the need to compete: at home with her siblings, at school, and even on the athletic fields. Though often successful in all three venues, Martha never felt like a winner. Her father would tell her she was good "for a girl," not at all what Martha needed or wanted to hear. (She needed to hear that she was great without any reservations.) Martha went on to a highly selective women's college. There, she met a young man who she felt would change her life—and she was right. Matt was a handsome man from a well-known family with political influence. She was intrigued with Matt and impressed with his background. Martha could never quite put her finger on the reason, but when she and Matt got together, she often felt like she was his caretaker. It didn't make sense to her. After all, Matt was a leader in his class at an Ivy League school and was expected to go into politics, a family tradition.

As their relationship developed, so did Matt's dependence on Martha. Although Martha was disturbed by his almost total reliance on her, at the same time she felt affirmed and empowered by the feeling of indispensability and her ability to meet his every need. Martha would anticipate Matt's desires, making sure he was happy and well cared for, but Matt seemed to take her for granted. Either he didn't realize how much of a burden Martha shouldered on his behalf, or he didn't appreciate it. Whichever, Matt never acknowledged Martha's devotion; he just seemed to expect it. (Later, Martha noticed that it felt similar to the time that, as a child, daddy never gave her the acknowledgment she craved—it was always "good daughter," never "great daughter.")

Martha, a scholar who'd graduated at the top of her college class, was offered a fellowship in biology at a prestigious teaching hospital. Martha was thrilled, but she declined because she knew Matt depended on her, and somehow that seemed more important to her than pursuing her interest in science. She decided that Matt would be the breadwinner in the family and she would take care of all his needs—emotional, physical, and anything else he and his family deemed necessary. Still, by bending over backwards to please "daddy" (now in the form of Matt), Martha had abdicated her ambition to fulfill Matt's needs, fulfilling none of her own.

Martha carried on like this for years until discovering that Matt had had an affair. Heartbroken (hadn't she given up everything to please him?), Martha insisted that the couple enter therapy to save their relationship. Matt agreed. During the course of marital therapy, Martha learned that Matt was abused as a child and had secretly been in treatment for this abuse—and its effects on him—for years. Matt's secret treatment had not been too successful, however, because he could not bear to relay the facts, or even acknowledge the events of his past, to his wife until the marital crisis occurred and therapy intervened.

In time, Martha learned that Matt had been abused by a member of his family's staff and never confided in anyone about it. As a youngster, Matt's family began sending him for therapy because he became less social than he had been as a little boy, and he seemed to be less active than the family expected him to be. No one in his family probed any deeper into Matt's apparent change in temperament and activity level, and life for everyone in Matt's family—except for Matt, who suffered in isolation—just went along as before.

Then he found Martha. Martha learned during their counseling that she had brought Matt some relief from the emotional pain he had endured most of his young life. Now, years later, when he began treatment in earnest because he was in danger of losing her, he was able to communicate his feelings honestly and openly for the first time. He loved Martha and did not want to hurt her, but he was angry with her and the rest of the world because of how he suffered for all those years. Matt finally addressed what he never dared to approach before. During treatment he realized he shut down many of his drives and emotions and began a dysfunctional way of coping in order to survive emotionally. Martha fit into his world perfectly because she had a need to take care of someone (Matt) at the expense of her own needs and emotions. Together they formed a perfect codependent relationship—one fed on the other's unhealthy emotional issues, and neither was happy or fulfilled. Now they had to learn how to separate their unhealthy patterns and start a new phase in their relationship where each could be independent, yet still interact with the other in an intimate, but beneficial way. During two years of therapy, Martha and Matt revisited old memories and old emotional pain that each had suppressed. After summoning the old psychic injuries, then dealing with them and resolving them, Martha and Matt, as a couple and as individuals, could function in a healthy way.

Now they are able to communicate directly and respectfully with each other and others, without sugarcoating the message to make their feelings, needs, or opinions meet other people's expectations or approval. Martha and Matt take care of themselves, individually, and each other by choice—but not from a neurotic need born from mutual childhood wounds. Presently, they enjoy a fulfilling relationship and are discussing—for the first time in their ten-year marriage—the possibility of having a family.

Chapter Nine

Your Relationship—His History

If not dealt with, your man's abuse will continue to influence every aspect of his life: professional, spiritual, emotional, intellectual, and, probably most pertinent to you, personal. Of all the areas shaped by his past, your partner's personal relationships are the most profoundly affected. Unlike the other fields of human endeavor where one can be successful regardless of sensitivity and emotional dexterity, it's nearly impossible to have a satisfying intimate relationship with a partner who has difficulty allowing his lover access to his inner world—particularly if he lacks access to it as well! No doubt, with his motivation and your encouragement, better days lie ahead. But what do you make of the present and your man's past? In this chapter, we'll explore why your partner's childhood abuse can continue to have such a profound affect on your life together as a couple, and in the meantime, how to manage the foreseeable challenges. Before we analyze the details, let's review the reasons childhood trauma wreaks so much havoc on its victims' adult relationships.

Making Peace with His Past

You know from the first part of this book that people who suffered abuse as kids can suffer a lifetime of fears, fixations, and ailments if they are unable to find—and accept—the support and reassurance that they deserve. Without help, victims are at risk of developing health problems, ranging from all manner of physical disease to clinical and personality disorders (like post-traumatic stress disorder and borderline personality disorder, respectively) to an overall, nonspecific depressive pall over their entire existence, punctuated by intense feelings of shame, guilt, self-loathing, and low expectations of life, themselves, and others.

In fact, prior to your arrival on the scene, your partner might have accumulated an entire set of emotional (and perhaps physical, not to mention biological) baggage from the life he's led, attempting to cope with his pain as best he could. What baggage, you ask? Well, we've mentioned the emotional symptoms and psychological complexes and disorders. As for the physical problems, we know from the studies based on adult survivors of abuse that they are—compared to nonabused adults—more likely to suffer from somatic ailments like hypertension, coronary pulmonary disease (CPD), obesity, substance abuse, cancer, and even, according to some findings, an early death from suicide or accidents (caused by the risky behavior many victims adopt after their abuse). Unfortunately, just by the very nature of his trauma, your mate might carry, or be a candidate for, early, latent, or even patent disease, which can have a direct effect on his (and by proximity, your) day-to-day experience of life.

Think about it. If your mate suffers from heart disease, he might have difficulty performing the simplest household tasks—from cleaning the basement to performing in the bedroom (more about sex in a later chapter)—due to the very physical fact of his poor circulation. If your mate suffers from obesity or alcohol dependency, he might be sluggish or tired most of the time, leaving you with the lion's share of responsibility for the routine stuff that makes up a couple's life, such as chores, driving errands, and child care. In fact, it's possible—even likely—that your mate's physical symptoms were what initially set off your alarms bells, making you think that something was wrong and he needed help. The good news is that early detection, early treatment, and even better, prevention, can put your mate back on the road to healthy living and a long life. But until the new physical and psychological habits have taken hold, you'll have to accept the way he is for now, encouraging him by focusing on how much better the future for both of you will be as a result of his initiative (perhaps at your urging) to seek help and change his outlook.

As if the emotional and physical aspects of your mate's abuse weren't enough for a woman to deal with, there's another category of really complicated stuff that can make life almost too thorny to tolerate. I'm talking here about previous personal attachments. Clearly, it's possible that your mate was seriously involved with someone or even married (and maybe had children) before meeting you. Due to alimony, child support, and custody issues, the "ex" can be a factor in his life (and thus, yours) for a long, long time. While not at all uncommon in the twenty-first century, it's possible that the stresses attendant to divorce and its fallout could be an especially aggravating factor for your mate as he tries to transcend his painful personal history. If you're lucky, and the ex is relatively stable, well-adjusted, and free of emotional problems, you shouldn't encounter any more difficulties than the next person who has to deal with an ex.

If, however, the ex was (or worse, is) an addict, a user, or a person with obvious psychological problems who wants her issues to be your issues, you will have to act. The best solution to the dilemma posed by an intrusive, disruptive, disturbed former partner is to point out the problem to your mate and, together (perhaps with the help of a counselor), set some boundaries between the both of you and her, to protect the integrity of your family unit, your sanity, and your mate's ultimate well-being. While you and your man are trying to help him work on his trauma issues, you don't need a pest from the past disrupting his present life with you. A standing legal obligation from a prior relationship, if legitimate, should be met. If however, the ex's actions reveal a desire to continue an abusive or destructive relationship with your mate after they've parted, you have a right to put a legal end to it. See a domestic law specialist in your state for options on how to stop unwanted, unwarranted, and extralegal harassment from a former partner or significant other.

Finally, but on an entirely different emotional level, it's possible that you are raising, or partially responsible for rearing, a child born to your partner before you were together. If the child was alive to see your mate experience difficult times (drinking to excess; psychological impairment that would've affected the child, such as raging or skulking depression; or physical altercations within the family) be alert for the child's own trauma issues. He or she might have problems adjusting to a new family or a new, functional dad. (Even if the dad is healing and doing better, from the child's point of view, he will be different from the dad that he or she was used to. He might not be as lenient as before, and the child might resent the new him, not to mention you, the new stepmom figure.)

Sadly, these kids could very well trigger old, painful feelings in your mate. Yet your mate's child (or children) could be great motivating factors for him to get help and change his life. Either way, realize that the kids from your partner's past were probably affected in some way by the same symptoms in their dad that disturbed you, too. On a more hopeful note, sometimes having a new person like you on the scene to begin an open, healthy dialogue about the way things are (versus the way they were in the bygone, pre-you days) can go a long way toward dispensing with shame and secrets and healing everyone's old wounds. (We'll talk more about how to get on with your mate's family of origin and your mutual children in a later chapter.)

Why It's So Hard for Him

Interpersonal relationships in general, but particularly romantic or intimate ones, often pose the greatest challenges to abuse survivors. And if you think about it, it's a perfectly natural reaction to having been victimized by someone close to you. If your mate was abused by a stranger (the least likely scenario), then his abuse issues will, on the whole, emanate more from the trauma of the actual attack rather than from the dilemmas posed by the abuser's betrayal and breach of trust. If, however, your partner falls within the 90-plus percent of victims who were abused by someone known to them or their family, then he's likely to have difficulty letting his guard down, for fear of future betrayal, not to mention his personal security.

As a consequence of being wary of trusting and feeling safe in close relationships, many abuse survivors share a persistent difficulty forming steady, stable interpersonal attachments (i.e., they have trouble bonding). Furthermore, feelings of inadequacy, worthlessness, shame, depression, fear, low self-esteem, powerlessness, and inability to properly interpret circumstances and people make any interpersonal relationships a challenge for many survivors. But just as no two people are alike, each man has his own take on how to deal with the effects of his childhood trauma. For example, some victims, very much aware of how they were deceived, used, and abused in the past, become controlling and manipulative in their own adult relationships in an effort to protect themselves from the possibility of further exploitation.

Other victims react in an opposite way. Feeling inferior to others, they develop an excessive concern with what others think of them, and they are sensitive to criticism (i.e., they suffer from "interpersonal rejection sensitivity"). Fearing a negative response from their partners, some victims will suppress their emotions (both positive and negative) or fail to assert their own needs in the relationship, leading to frustration and distance between partners, not the desired closeness and satisfaction. Other victims will dispense with all emotional entanglements and resort to promiscuity (no attachments, just sex), avoidance, or isolation, due to their discomfort and awkwardness with delicate situations and emotions.

Although this might not be true for your mate, many victims who have not worked out the psychological remnants of their abusive past believe that it's better to feel safe and in control than sorry and defenseless (a combination that didn't work out well for them in the past). While living by that motto might protect a person from the vulnerability and inevitable messiness of human attachments, it also precludes them from experiencing the tenderness and ultimately healing transformation possible through a loving, intimate, and conscious connection with another.

Unfortunately, the psychological theories concerning how and why it's hard for abuse survivors to have rewarding, close personal relationships as adults have been tested and borne true. Here are the disturbing (but not insurmountable) facts. Unlike peers who were not abused as youngsters, adult survivors report less overall satisfaction from their intimate associations. Upon reflection, this finding should not surprise you. Why would your partner want to be susceptible to being used—again—by someone whom he trusted and perhaps even loved and adored? Why would he want to re-engage that part of himself that was so severely betrayed by another who exploited his need for love and approval by abusing him? The answer is that he would not, without a lot of inner work and reassurance.

Research and clinical experience confirm that your mate's emotional deliverance (and the salvation of your relationship) will come from his understanding that his past will not repeat itself,

Why It May be Hard for You

In order to help your mate heal, you have to be aware of any intolerance you might hold, consciously or not, about the fact that your mate was sexually abused. You must be a source of positive support to be of any help to your mate. Any thoughts about how the abuse might have "tainted" him in any way (made him less of a man) will be just as harmful to him now as the abuse was then. So, if you still harbor any preconceived, incorrect notions about the abuse your mate suffered despite all you have read thus far, you need your own counseling to deal with it.

unless he consciously or unconsciously wills that to happen. Moreover, your partner will have to learn that you, his loved one, will not participate in any self-destruction on his part. Somehow, he will have to recognize that your desire for emotional and physical intimacy with him is entirely different from his abuser's exploitive interest in his body. Once your mate gains insight into the reasons behind his behaviors and feelings, and believes that allowing you to become close will not cause him harm or make him weak, he will eventually let you in. As the partner, you unlock the healing process by gaining your man's trust, making him feel safe, and having patience. Letting him progress at his own set speed and actively listening to him, considering the content, and responding from your heart, will work wonders.

Learning to Listen and the Art of Intimacy

Countless studies have been conducted on the healing power of love and intimacy. In fact, having a confidante to talk to and care about you reduces your risk of serious illness or, if you are already sick, raises your odds of survival. Forgive the cliché; the power of love has not only been the subject of prose and verse, it has also been tested, documented, and proved to help a human remain, or become, well. So, how does this talk of love relate to your partner's abuse issues? Perfectly. The power of human connection is exactly the sort of "medicine" your mate might need to put his abuse behind him and begin a life free from the psychological burdens of abuse (i.e., secrecy, isolation, self-loathing, guilt, and shame).

Although the transcendent power of emotional connection to a loved one might seem obvious to you, it probably isn't as immediately apparent to your partner. Results from studies on abuse survivors and their relationships tell us that many feel unable to confide personal information to their mates and feel less satisfied in their relationships. What does one do when he can't tell his secrets, concerns, and fears to his partner in life? Well, you—the partner—can take certain steps to encourage him to modify his behavior so he can share his feelings and bare his soul to you. First, you must acquire the art of couples' communication, or "reflective listening."

This section explores the methods that facilitate listening and give you the verbal and nonverbal language that will help you and your mate connect and stay connected. After you learn to identify and employ the kinds of phrases and gestures that promote communication (versus those that don't), you can hone your new communication skills for immediate use with your partner. Bear in mind that for two people to communicate effectively, both people have to be present, patient, and accommodating (don't even think about interrupting or arguing before the other person has had a chance to finish).

Here's what the experts say is required: The initiator "observes" the issue or event that will be the subject of his communication.

Next, he puts his view of the matter (i.e., his "perception") into verbal and nonverbal form (he "encodes" his thoughts and perceptions). Then the initiator speaks ("transmits") and the recipient listens (has "reception"). Upon receipt, the listener must interpret ("decode") according to her view (her "perceptions"), and voilà: A thought is conveyed from one person to another. But what about ensuring a two-person exchange?

Harville Hendrix (recall his imago theory from Chapter 8) coined the term *couples dialogue* to describe the three-step process of communication he encourages. Hendrix distills his method to three steps, a variation on the communication tool commonly called *reflective listening*. They are:

1. Mirroring ("I think I hear you saying that my being late without calling you makes you upset.")
2. Validation ("It is upsetting to not get a phone call when I said I'd be home.")
3. Empathy ("I understand why you're upset, and I would be too if I were in your place.")

According to Hendrix, taking these three steps forces you to actively listen to your partner's point of view. "Mirroring" forces you to confirm that what you heard your partner say is, in fact, what he said. If you didn't get it right, or if your partner misspoke, "mirroring" what you heard allows him to rephrase his words so they convey his intended meaning. Then, once you can agree that you heard what he meant to express, "validating" affirms that you grasp the gist of the issue. Finally, "empathizing" shows that—while not necessarily agreeing—you appreciate the other person's point of view. Having heard your partner clearly communicate his thoughts or feelings about the matter, you both can resolve the point in a mutually respectful, nondefensive way. Certainly, Hendrix's tri-part formula has helped hundreds of thousands of couples communicate with each other, but you needn't worry if the system doesn't feel comfortable to you. The purpose of his formula is to make you focus on the speaker. Implementing the three steps compels you to listen, recognize, and identify with another's viewpoint.

Remember, people of intelligence and goodwill often differ in opinion and can, in good faith, agree to disagree on issues or arguments. However, if your partner is trying to tell you about his feelings, listen. Besides, he's never wrong with his feelings (and neither are you with yours). Emotions are what they are, and people are entitled to them. Your mate's feelings are valid and real (whether or not they are based on mistaken beliefs, misperceptions, or unreasonable fears) and worthy of your attention.

Sharing Starts the Healing

"People who have been abused as children are uncomfortable talking about their experiences, but that is exactly what they should start doing. . . . If people share their emotionally painful past with a partner or sibling or someone they trust, it can start the healing process."— Vincent J. Felitti, M.D., Kaiser Permanente Medical Care Program

Variations on the Hendrix Triumvirate

While Hendrix's model for communication is very good, here are more therapeutic examples from my practice, along with a brief explanation and examples to guide you:

Silence: This is an effective tool for both the listener (it shows the speaker that you are weighing what's just been said, before thoughtfully responding) and the speaker (it allows him to collect his thoughts, expand on them, or emphasize a point). The problem with a speaker's silence (a long or "pregnant" pause) generally arises when the listener, faced with a silent gap, rushes in to fill the empty space. If you feel more comfortable, instead of speaking just to avoid the silence, try instead to simply nod to indicate that you heard, or say, "uh-huh" or "go on."

Giving recognition: When you show respect for your partner's point of view, even if you don't agree, you validate his feelings. Example: "I understand how you could see it that way."

Offering of self: When you verbalize—generally at the beginning of the discussion—that you will listen to your partner and not interrupt him (or allow other interruptions to interfere with your discussion, such as answering your phone), it is another form of validation. Sometimes it is useful to set a time frame for this commitment so that you don't have to break the trust that you are trying to establish. Example: "I have thirty minutes that I would like to spend with you and I would like to hear your thoughts."

Using expansive statements: "Tell me more," "Go on," and "What else?" are wonderful phrases to use when you want your partner to know that you want to hear the whole story.

Placing the event in the appropriate time sequence: This technique guides the speaker to tell you something the way it occurred, to help focus on what happened and when. Examples: "About what age do you think you were at the time?" "Tell me when this occurred." "What happened next?"

Observing and stating observations: If you note some behavior change that occurs with the same subject or involving the same person, you may want to note this to your partner. He will most likely be unaware of this behavior. Don't insist or even suggest he should comment. Example: "I notice when you speak of your older brother you become quiet and your face flushes." (It is important not to make a judgment on this; just make the observation.)

Restating (also "reflecting" or "mirroring"): This is when you play back (like a tape recorder) what the other person said, as you heard it, but without any interpretation on your part. Example: "You said that you never knew happiness as a child?"

Pondering: This technique (sometimes accompanied by "hmmm" or "that's interesting") lets your partner know that you need to mull over what he's just said, or that he's just made a provocative statement. Pondering can follow a pause. (This is one of those times when the listener invokes silence before speaking.) Example: "I have to give this more thought" or "I need time to process this."

Focusing on specifics: This is a technique that may be used when you don't understand what the speaker is saying, when you question the veracity of the statement, or when what you are hearing just doesn't seem plausible to you. (Note: It does not mean that what the person is saying is not valid. Rather, it is possible that you just could not conceive of these matters being discussed.) Example: "You're telling me you have childhood memories at three months old?"

Just the Opposite
Some statements hinder or oppose communication. We call them *stalls*. We all use them socially. If, however, if you are

making a good effort to get the most out of your communication skills, avoid them. The following is a list of "don'ts," or to put it more formally, nontherapeutic or unhelpful communication techniques.

False reassuring: Resist this kind of response even though you think it might make your partner feel better at first (examples: "You will feel better tomorrow"; "Everything will work out fine"). While factual assurance is fine (you can back up what you're saying because it's true), false reassurance is actually another way of lying. It is also unfair and unhelpful, especially as your partner has probably been lied to in the past. In order to establish trust, avoid giving any reassurance unless you can guarantee your statement.

Giving unwanted approval: This is another device to avoid (examples: "I like how you are handling our talks"; "You're doing much better"). Such statements are demeaning and give the impression that your partner needs your approval.

Rejecting: A refusal or nonacceptance of a situation is not productive. An example is saying something like, "I will not be part of this" or "This is your problem, not mine; you work it out." (Need I say more about why this approach is not helpful?)

Disapproval: Voicing your disapproval is a way of making judgment, when the idea is to be nonjudgmental. Example: "I don't think therapy is a good idea. Why do you have to expose the whole messy thing?"

Agreeing against better judgment: This shows poor judgment on your part and is typically not constructive. While it may seem like the path of least resistance, and it might prevent confrontation, it's fundamentally dishonest. (And remember, you're trying to establish trust.) Example: "I think it's a good idea for you to go to Las Vegas for the weekend" (when his travel companions will be his bachelor friends who drink too much and have no sense of propriety).

Disagreeing unnecessarily: This is a device usually performed in anger, and it is really an act of aggression. The last thing a person who has been abused needs is more abuse. Example: "You couldn't have been 'abused' as a child; if you had, you would have fought back!"

Advising: Telling someone what you think should be done or giving your solution to his problem is not productive. While advising someone if fine, if you're asked and if you have some expertise on the topic, it's not helpful if neither apply. Example: "I think you should confront your abuser." You have no idea if that would be appropriate in his case. If you'd like to advise your partner, ask him if he'd like to hear it—but remember, advising is not communicating, it's directing.

Probing: Though typically performed out of curiosity, when you probe you are really going where you don't belong, just to satisfy your own interest. It shows disregard for the person you're probing. Example: "Tell me what kind of hotels you were taken to when you were abused."

Challenging: Challenging another person is not usually helpful, even in social situations. People find it aggressive and distasteful. Example: "I dare you to confront your abuser."

Testing: This device places you in a position of superiority in which you question the other person in such a way that it indicates you don't really believe him. No one likes this. Example: "Exactly what year was it that all this happened to you? And who was president? And what grade were you in?"

Putting the speaker on the defensive: Much of the communication with your partner will involve feelings and expression of those feelings. They should never have to be defended. Example: "How could you feel that way?"

Changing subjects: This shows a lack of respect for the speaker and lets him know that you have grown weary or bored with the topic and want to change it to something that better suits you. This will not help your partner's self-esteem. Example: "You were speaking of your mother and your childhood, but what is going on now that you are an adult?"

Interpreting for him: Telling him what you think his issues are, which may really be your own projections of the situation, is not helpful. Example: "I don't think you have gotten angry enough to be well."

Ignoring context: This response does not show respect or caring for what the speaker is going through. Example: As your partner is sharing painful and intimate material, you ask if he noticed that it was snowing outside and then mention that it's time to unpack the ski clothes.

Don't Take Away His Power

Be aware that the following phrases will promote the feeling of "victim" and therefore are not helpful in restoring your partner's power:

"That is so sad": It is important to know the difference between empathy and pity. Empathy is fine in this case, while making a judgment about him (sad, wretched, etc.) is not helpful. Example of empathy: "That sounds difficult. I don't know if I would have managed as well under the same circumstances." Example of judgment: "How could you possibly function when your family was so wretched?"

"I can't believe that could happen to you": Disbelief is another way of saying it's not true. A better thing to say: "How did you handle all that you describe?"

"You poor thing": Unlike empathy, which is showing that you understand his point of view, pitying him casts him once more as a victim and takes away his power as a person.

No matter how you wish to conduct your dialogue, try to have an open heart and be nonjudgmental, accepting, and congruent (making sure your body language and tone of voice match what you say), and, as always, warmth and humor (not at your partner's expense) are usually welcome. By the way, bear in mind that your posture, appearance, hand gestures, facial expressions, timing, touch, tone, and stance (distance between speakers) communicate just as much, if not more, than your words. So if you're trying to be open to what your mate has to say, don't cross your arms. If you're trying to exhibit patience, don't tap your fingers or check your watch. (You get the idea.)

Adapting to His Needs

The victim, who's in recovery of his manhood and life, wants to be in control—not told again what to do or what not to do. He was controlled as a victim and doesn't want to be controlled by you, his mate. He needs to go at his own speed. He needs to make his own decisions about his recovery and be encouraged to regain his power and self-esteem. (This process could leave you potentially less powerful than you were before, but you'll get a more authentic lover in return.) This can be a slippery slope, because it is a fine line between offering this kind of altruistic help to your partner and losing your identity in the process. It can be done, but with care.

Although he might feel inferior and inadequate on many levels due to the abuse and his subsequent maladaptive ways of coping with the psychological, and perhaps physical pain of his experience, emphasize his resilience to have come this far, and make sure he knows that you will see him through it as long as he sticks with it. As the song goes, accentuate the positive.

Facilitate, but don't mandate. Give him encouragement and, when requested, feedback; but make sure the feedback is based on his behavior, not on your wishes, hopes, or projections. Don't direct your partner's healing process and don't demand a timetable from him or his therapist. Remember, it's his life and it's his recovery. You're the helper, the guardian, but he's subject and object of the cure. Let him be. For now, your role as partner is to provide emotional support, accept who he is now, and be patient with him until his external behavior matches the transformation going on inside him. Your patience will affirm your love and trust, which will fortify as well as encourage him to explore further. Hopefully, with you at his side, he'll obtain a greater degree of emotional fortitude. Think of yourself as a welcome guest on his emotional roller coaster ride. Hang on!

Chapter Ten

Sustaining a Union in Recovery

Now that you have the basic tools to foster communication between you and your partner as you work your way as a couple through his recovery as an abuse victim, it's time to examine how to maintain your union during this time. This chapter will focus on the most intimate acts between two people, as well as what to do when things seem out of control and you need to respond in a way that supports your relationship—yet respects your rights as an individual. Finally, there is another section on intimacy and forgiveness that might come in helpful in the days ahead.

Sexual Healing

Back in Part I we examined the symptoms and traits common to male abuse survivors. Some men face sexual orientation and gender confusion issues after having been abused as boys, particularly if the perpetrator was male and if the abuse occurred while the youngster was an adolescent—that is, old enough to understand something about sex, but too young to process the trauma experience in a more helpful, mature way. We also explored, in a general manner, some of the sexual problems associated with having been abused. In this section, we'll examine what happens when it's just the two of you and love is on your mind.

As we consider this topic, remember that not every man who's been abused psychologically, physically, or sexually has difficulty expressing his love for a partner in a physical, intimate way. Many men who've suffered abuse in the past have no problem performing, or to put it less clinically, giving and receiving pleasure in a healthy, loving, life-affirming manner. If, however, your man is having trouble when it's time for sharing a physical relationship, this section could shed light on what might be happening and why, and what you can do about it. First (and this should not surprise you), studies confirm that victims of sexual abuse are more profoundly affected by adulthood sexual dysfunction than any other kind of abuse victim (i.e., psychological or physical). What's more, of the sexual abuse victims concerned, research reveals that the higher the frequency of their abuse experiences and the more closely the abuser was related to them—and the more forceful, shaming, or manipulative the abuser was—the more likely the victim will experience sexual problems in his adult life. The reasons for this predicament are easy to comprehend when you consider that the physical and psychological circumstances under which their abuse took place and under which most consensual adult sexual relations occur are remarkably similar. Both involve the victim, another person, exposure, genitals, and contact of some kind. There might even be more common characteristics: a bed, a couch, a floor (most child victims are abused in the home—theirs, or their abuser's), and, often, isolation—with just the victim and his abuser present in the space. Think about it for a moment: When you are with your partner, ready to make love, aren't you alone, on a bed, a couch, or a floor? Aren't you both exposed—physically and emotionally—and making, or expecting, genital contact?

The literature on sexual abuse survivors details why and how such similar physical, visual, olfactory, or auditory circumstances or "triggers" (such as a phrase, a sexual position, a place, a gesture, a taste, a scent, a sound) can cause a victim to suffer "flashbacks" (also known as *re-experiencing*). It also details other common post-traumatic stress disorder symptoms, such as avoidance and hyperarousal. (in this case, hyperarousal is not a good thing but rather the psychological term for severe psychic stress, often accompanied by the fight-or-flight physiological response). Unfortunately, for the victim, his psychological and physiological responses to your sexual encounter can be as overwhelming as the ones he had while he was being abused. For instance, touching the back of your mate's neck, though performed with loving intent, could cause him to "re-experience" the trauma of his abuse if that's the way his abuser approached him before having forced sex with him. Similarly, kissing your mate after using a certain toothpaste or mouthwash, if it's similar to the one his abuser used, could trigger a "flashback," causing him to return, psychologically, to the place where he was when he was abused all those years ago.

Commonly, to avoid these horrifying effects, abuse victims will simply try to avoid sex altogether, or they will "dissociate" (emotionally "check out"), whereby their minds—or hearts—leave their bodies during the sexual encounter in an effort to live through it, as painlessly as possible, separated from the physical experience. In the same vein, other victims will resort to "numbing" by getting drunk or high to avoid being emotionally present and re-experiencing the pain or feeling the intense discomfort of psychological "hyperarousal" during the physical act of sex and all that precedes and follows it. Although they might have helped him survive the devastation accompanying his abuse, none of these coping mechanisms makes for a satisfying love life or reinforces a couple's intimate connection.

But there is hope. Over the last twenty or so years, counselors have borrowed techniques used by cognitive-behavioral therapists to explore the thoughts and actions of the patient (the victim) to clarify to the patient that the situation in the present, though superficially similar, is not the same as the one in which the abuse took place. Once the patient understands this (this is not so much of a challenge), then work begins to separate the pathological behaviors (his troubling emotional and physical responses) from the stimulation, or "triggers." To succeed in breaking the bad associations with sex (and the related touching), some therapists give patients "exercises" to perform at home, allowing them to engage in safe touching with their partners, at their speed, in the comfort of their own environment. A good book to read on this topic is *The Sexual Healing Journey: A Guide for Survivors of Sexual Abuse* by Wendy Maltz, a licensed social worker and author on the topic of sexual therapy for abuse survivors. Eventually, with therapy, effort, and determination, a person can learn to enjoy the feeling of his lover's affectionate physical contact in the present, without re-experiencing the degrading, shaming, guilt-producing sensations they felt from the abusive sex of their past. When the treatment is successful, the victim replaces his trauma responses with healthy, loving associations gained from respectful, joyous, emotionally and physically safe sex with his mate.

Sometimes the maladaptive yet simple physical responses to sexual contact are easier to address and adjust than the deep-seated psychological harm that can accompany the trauma of CSA. There are victims who, due to their abusive sexual experiences, prefer impersonal promiscuous sex or masturbation—often accompanied by pornography—to any shared physical intimacy. Others, though able to withstand sexual touching by an intimate partner, are unable to climax or become aroused without violent or humiliating fantasies (many times mimicking, or growing from, their sexual abuse).

Consider Tim's story. He was eight years old when he became an altar boy. Tim loved the whole thing, particularly the positive attention from the adults in his life for getting up early, going to church, and fulfilling his duties at mass. He was never late, always kind, and quickly became part of the small clique of boys who were given special responsibilities to serve the priests of the parish. Tim particularly enjoyed the warm, close relationship that developed with his mentor, Father John. Soon Father John was giving Tim all the time and attention that he never received from his own dad. Basking in the glory of Father John's special treatment,

Tim felt honored and privileged. Tim would do anything for Father John.

Not long after Father John took an interest in Tim, he invited Tim and some of the other altar boys on an overnight trip to his mountain home—an event that would lead to a life-altering situation for Tim. After the other boys went to bed, Father John summoned Tim to his room and asked him to climb into bed with him. Father John told him stories and even some jokes. All was fine. Father John was treating Tim as if he were special. Father John asked that Tim not tell the other boys about their secret because they would be jealous and then he would have to share his nighttime stories with them as well.

When he returned home, Tim never told anyone about being invited into Father John's bed. The trips continued, and after several more similar episodes, things changed. One night, Tim remembered, instead of just talking, Father John's storytelling became interactive. He asked Tim to perform acts that he didn't understand but innately knew were not right. Still, Tim loved Father John, and if he wanted Tim to do some things, he figured, they couldn't be that bad. Father John swore Tim to secrecy, explaining that what they did was so special that no could ever know, or Father John would never see Tim again. Tim was confused by this threat and kept the secret—a classic "trauma bond."

The trips continued and the acts that Father John requested became more physical and more frightening. Tim had to watch movies of people doing sexual things, and then Father John directed him to imitate these acts. Sometimes Father John would film them and would make Tim watch the home movies. By the age of nine, Tim was engaged in a sexual relationship far beyond anything he could consent to or cope with at that young age. It didn't take long before Tim faltered in his studies and his grades plummeted. His parents noticed that Tim had lost weight and was not sleeping well. They took him to the family physician, who gave him some vitamins, told him to get to bed earlier, and cut down on the TV.

Meanwhile, the trips with Father John continued until Tim was thirteen years old, when his family moved to another town and he changed schools. After the move, Tim was no longer an altar boy and his interaction with Father John stopped. Although Tim was relieved that he did not have to do those terrible things Father had requested, he was disappointed that Father John never tried to get in touch with him again. Now he was really confused. Tim hated what he had to do in that bedroom in the mountains, yet he loved Father John. These conflicted feelings were too much for a young mind to sort out. Tim dealt with the dilemma by deciding to forget the whole thing and get on with his life, which he did.

Tim enjoyed high school and went on to college, but he never became involved in a physical relationship with a girl—or boy. He liked girls and would date and go to all the socials, but was not interested in a relationship—that is, until he met Nora. She was lovely and lively and beautiful. Nora also had a religious upbringing and attended services regularly. Tim was in love and wanted to marry Nora. They courted for a year. Since Nora was religious, she thought it wonderful that Tim made no sexual demands on her before the marriage. He made it easy for her to save herself for him.

They married, and the problem, from Nora's perspective, began. Tim made no demands, or even attempts, to approach Nora on a physical level after their wedding. Nora came from an Irish-Catholic family in which even communication was easy and humorous and the house was filled with laughter, warmth, and kids. And even though she was religious, Nora was not a prude. She had looked forward to the day when she was married and could enjoy the pleasures of a married woman. Nora knew from the twinkle in her parents' eyes when they went to bed together and from how they treated each other that she, too, would have lots of joy from a marriage partner. This was not the case at all for her and Tim. Nora became, by turns, worried, angry, and frustrated.

The more she tried to address the problem, the worse it got. Nora would climb into bed with Tim and try to talk to him softly and kindly. Unconsciously, Tim found Nora's efforts eerily reminiscent of his childhood experiences in that mountain bedroom with Father John. (Tim was not consciously aware of this; all he knew was that he just reacted in a horrible rage.) Nora was confused by his reaction and at a loss as to what to do next. She confided in her mother, who suggested that she and Tim talk to their priest. When Nora relayed this, Tim responded with an angry scene. Nora read books that suggested watching pornography together and talking dirty to interest her husband in sex, but everything she suggested enraged Tim. Finally, having reached her limit, Nora told Tim he would have to seek help or she would leave him. Although she loved him, she was not going to be a celibate wife.

Tim agreed to therapy, and soon we were working on personal history. When we got back to his childhood, Tim was overwhelmed by an outpouring of shame, guilt, and rage, followed by self-hate and revulsion. Tim understood how Nora's actions and the suppressed (not repressed) memories of his youth were intertwined in a pathological way. Tim became open in his treatment sessions and was able to finally separate the memories from the past and the reality of the present as different aspects of his life. Once we reached this point, Tim was on his way to a joyful life with Nora, with a baby soon due. Interestingly, in an effort not to affect his wife's strong affiliation with the Catholic Church, Tim never revealed that his abuser was a priest, but he won't allow his child to be alone with anyone he doesn't know well and trust.

When, despite your protests and distress, your partner persists in having promiscuous encounters, insists that you perform some kind of abuse on him, needs to degrade or abuse you, continues to depend upon violent or humiliating fantasies for sexual release, or prefers masturbation and pornography to sexual intimacy with you, it's time for professional help from a therapist and, perhaps, a twelve-step sexual dysfunction group. Ultimately, however, no matter how many shrinks he sees or groups he attends, your man's sexual healing will depend on his desire (as opposed to your need) for emotional change and physical intimacy. Your role in this matter is limited. Punishment, reprisal, or rejection from you will not cure your mate of his sexual problems. Generally, wanting to please or placate a partner is not enough of a motivation to bring about a change in deeply rooted sexual behavior. For true transformation to occur, a man must gather the courage to delve into the demons that underlie his unhealthy fantasies, obsessions, and compulsions. So unless your mate recognizes that he has a problem and is resolved to do the internal work required to alter his conduct, there is little hope of change. Instead, he'll probably try not to disturb you with his familiar (yet destructive—and for you, upsetting) sexual habits by finding other outlets (read: other people, places, things) for his release. The problem is your mate's natural resistance to modifying sexual practices that—though unhealthy—have successfully relieved his tension most of his adult life.

Clinical experience tells us that once a person matures, some behaviors are so durably wired into mental patterns of sexual response that only continuous, conscious commitment and motivation—helped by therapy and often a twelve-step support program—will overcome the problem over time. Fortunately, many victims succeed when they acknowledge their problem, make their minds up to help themselves, and accept help from others (family, friends, professionals, fellow survivors) and, often, a higher power (whatever that means to the person).

Addressing Unacceptable Behavior

What do you do when your mate refuses to address his sexual compulsions or addictions, or—outside the range of sexual activity—engages in other behaviors that you just can't tolerate (such as exploding in rages or becoming hostile or physically or psychologically abusive with you or your family members)? The first fact to acknowledge is that you can't control other people's behavior—at

The Twelve Steps as Adapted by Sexaholics Anonymous, Inc.

1. We admitted that we were powerless over lust—that our lives had become unmanageable.
2. Came to believe that a Power greater than ourselves could restore us to sanity.
3. Made a decision to turn our will and our lives over to the care of God as we understood Him.
4. Made a searching and fearless moral inventory of ourselves.
5. Admitted to God, to ourselves, and to another human being the exact nature of our wrongs.
6. Were entirely ready to have God remove all these defects of character.
7. Humbly asked Him to remove our shortcomings.
8. Made a list of all persons we had harmed, and became willing to make amends to them all.
9. Made direct amends to such people wherever possible, except when to do so would injure them or others.
10. Continued to take personal inventory and when we were wrong, promptly admitted it.
11. Sought through prayer and meditation to improve our conscious contact with God as we understood Him, praying only for knowledge of His will for us and the power to carry that out.
12. Having had a spiritual awakening as the result of these Steps, we tried to carry this message to sexaholics, and to practice these principles in all our affairs.

least not after age five. If your partner does things that bother you, or worse, make you upset or put your emotional, spiritual, or physical safety in jeopardy, you must do the only thing you can: act on your behalf. While we'll address setting limits and boundaries in the next section, this segment underscores the importance of your actions in the face of unacceptable behaviors.

Let's take the example of a partner who bursts out in fury at the slightest provocation or frustration, upsetting you or anyone else unlucky enough to be present. While you might understand why he behaves that way (it's the anger and frustration remaining from the unresolved issues from his abuse as described in Part I), you are not obliged to be abused just because he was. You can be supportive, you can suggest he see a therapist or attend support groups or even write about his feelings in a journal or diary, but being an emotional punching bag isn't healthy for you, your family, or him. That's fine advice, you might be thinking, but how do I respond when he's in the throes of a fit? Well, if you're in the middle of it, you can tell him that you're not the source of his anger and that you're not going to be the object of his rage. You can ask him to leave until he cools down, or you can leave the immediate area or even go out for while.

When you feel he's calmed down, it's best to attempt a dialogue using the communication techniques set forth in the last chapter to address your concerns. While the last chapter focused on facilitating your listening, this instance requires you to be the initiator and for him to listen. So instead of railing back at him

In An Emergency

If your partner has more than lost his temper, and has begun a violent rage in which you believe that you or those around you are in imminent physical danger, call 911. In matters of domestic violence, safety is paramount. Get yourself out of danger immediately and follow through with a protective order. Better safe than dead.

for being insensitive or out of control, try using the proverbial "I" statements to tell him how his raging makes you feel. (You'll note that "I" statements focus on your feelings, whereas "you" statements tend to be critical—for example, "You are such an ass when you rage at me over nothing.") What's more, using "I" statements (for example, "I become upset and feel attacked and unable to function well when you rage at me") focuses on how you feel and lets him know why you think it's inappropriate to express his anger or frustration in ways that violate your boundaries and right to peaceful living. On the other hand, "you" statements tend to accuse or recriminate and can create even more conflict and distance between you than before the incident occurred. Remember, you're trying to bridge the gap and begin a constructive dialogue, not build a stone wall between you.

While your mate's perfectly entitled to his feelings, he's not entitled to batter you with them—even if he's angry or frustrated as a result of something you said or did. There are healthy ways to express differences or anger, and there are unhealthy ways. Exploding in a rage at others is neither healthy nor acceptable. If his fury is directed at you, suggest that he calmly tell you what you did or said to upset him. Listen to him and, if he's right, apologize and try to come to a mutual solution to the problem. If, on the other hand, his wrath comes from another source, allowing him to talk about what set him off might help him realize that he's displacing his feelings from the real person or object of his anger onto you—because he can. The point is, peacefully discussing the matter (not yelling at or criticizing each other) should help him to identify what is causing his overreaction and help him to understand that you will not consent to his verbal—or any other kind—of abuse.

If your partner's objectionable conduct involves carnal activity that makes you uncomfortable (such as a fetish, a compulsion, or an addiction), you are always responsible for making the choice to accept or reject his sexual requests or conduct, whatever the intolerable behavior entails. While he might have completely understandable reasons for having these behaviors (in view of how he was abused), your partner has no right to subject you to activities that you find loathsome or inappropriate. As always, the way to address any disagreement or dispute is through communication or, more specifically, through dialogue: understanding, validation, and a mutual desire to address the needs of the other, while respecting oneself. Of course, it might not be so comfortable to begin the big conversation about your sexual differences while you're in bed. However, you always retain the right to say no. While you might choose to explain yourself then and there (again, being mindful of the most effective communication techniques—i.e., actively listening, being open to what your partner has to say, and not being judgmental or defensive), you might prefer to discuss the matter later, in a neutral setting, when you can tell your mate how his sexual conduct makes you feel and why you choose not to participate, submit, or tolerate what he's been doing (or asking you to do) in bed or otherwise.

Consider Debbie's story. An attractive twenty-six-year old, she was working on a master's degree in social work when her physician referred her to me. He felt she needed psychological help because he thought she was depressed and believed that her level of functioning on a daily basis was declining. He also noticed multiple and various topical injuries that Debbie could not, or would not, explain during her last checkup.

When she arrived at my office she was appropriately dressed for the unusually cold day in May. She was cooperative and answered questions when asked, but she did not offer anything on her own. During the next session, I noted that although it was spring, she wore a jacket with long sleeves to her appointment. Each time she saw me, her arms and legs were covered. After a few sessions, I addressed this with her, and she replied that she figured that I would eventually notice. I requested that she remove her jacket and show me her arms, which she did. I was suspicious of some kind of abuse, but not ready for what I observed. Debbie had injuries from her shoulders to her wrists—not just bruises, but cigarette burns and other assorted mutilations.

When questioned about the cause, she didn't hesitate to say that her husband, Kevin, did it, but she also defended him by saying, "He only does this if I make him angry." She also confided that Kevin sexually abused her and that she believed he was addicted to this behavior. I informed her that his actions were violent, illegal, and amounted to domestic violence. I gave her relevant information so she could protect herself. I told her nothing could justify his behavior. Debbie said that it did not happen all the time and that there were weeks—sometimes months—when she never got hurt at all. She said that those were the times in which she became more immersed in the relationship, with the hope that it would all work out.

I asked her to tell me about Kevin, her husband. She started out with a long pause and stated that his was quite a story, a horror story. She related how Kevin, now a journalist for a national magazine, was one of three children born out of wedlock to a woman whom he referred to as "the bitch." Kevin's mother worked as a waitress to support her children and never let them forget how lucky they were not to be in an orphanage. When the kids did not obey her commands instantly, she would physically abuse them, hitting them with anything on hand. Kevin and his siblings were hospitalized on a number of occasions for injuries, but no one ever figured out that the mother caused them. Kevin's mother told them never to report her, saying that they would be taken away and put in juvenile detention hall if they did. Debbie related that as much as Kevin hated his mother, he also loved her; after all, she was his mother and she did sacrifice for him and his family. I asked if Kevin would come in to see me, and Debbie said that she thought he might if he thought it was for her, because he believed that Debbie had major problems. The next week, Kevin made an appointment.

Kevin was a small man. He walked with his shoulders down, making him appear even smaller. He began by letting me know that he was there for Debbie and not for himself. When I questioned him about his family history, he gave me pretty much the same information that Debbie had given. He then shared his personal history. When I said that it sounded as if he had a difficult child-hood, it was like a floodgate opened. He said, "You want to hear the rest of it?" I told him to go on. And he did. Kevin explained how as a boy he was sent out to babysit to earn some extra money, but it was not a baby he had to sit. It was his mother's older sister, Aunt Lorraine.

Aunt Lorraine was an alcoholic with a bad temper who needed to have sex all the time. At age ten, Kevin was meeting his aunt's sexual needs with the approval and consent of his mother. His mother told Kevin that he should consider himself a lucky kid and to learn all he could from Aunt Lorraine because she was a pro. Kevin said he thought it was at that point that he lost all respect for women, and he'd never changed his mind. When ques-tioned about marriage, he told me that every man needs a wife for cooking, for chores, and for something to kick around. I told him that this was dysfunctional thinking and criminal behavior. I suggested he come to treatment and told him that perhaps we could work together to make some sense of what had happened to him and could make his life better for him and his family. He agreed and began treatment. Kevin realized that he loved his wife and did not want her to leave him or have him arrested, and both were likely to happen if his behaviors continued. His first goal was to stop abusing, and the next step was to learn why he abused. I referred him to a self-help group in his community, which he declined. He did agree, however, to join a twelve-step program so he could be anonymous.

After three years of therapy, with new insight and new cop-ing mechanisms in place, Kevin is doing better. He is open about the pain and suffering caused by abuse, whether one is abused or abusing, and attends a support group for men who were abused and are abusing. His marriage is intact, and Debbie has become assertive and feels she would never let herself become involved in a situation where she is a scapegoat. She is in treatment, gaining self-esteem and learning what caused her behavior. Kevin and Debbie are trying to get funding to open a center for battered women. It is important to note that both of them knew how to communicate; however, they needed to have their problems addressed by a professional. Debbie was wise enough to give nonverbal cues to her physician to get him to inaugurate therapy for her.

The principle to bear in mind is that while you might cherish your role as your mate's life partner, profoundly concerned with his state of mind and state of heart, you are not obliged to endure abuse or abasement in the process of his healing and recovery. To do otherwise shows a lack of self-respect and merely continues the cycle of abuse on you and your family. But whatever you do (how you act or react), it's ultimately his choice to deal with his past and how it affects his life in the present—or not. In reality, exercising the choice to overcome his childhood trauma is a significant step in regaining the control and prerogative he lacked when he was abused as a boy. By helping your mate in his recovery, you empower him; enabling his bad behavior (despite the fact that you understand its cause) serves only to prolong the pathology and continues his victimhood.

Setting Your Limits and Boundaries

Knowing that you're not impeding his progress if you "just say no" to the things that are unacceptable to you, how do you implement your boundaries? Many couples decide to discuss in advance how to handle a dispute about sex, long before they are in the act. For instance, couples can agree that "no" really does mean no and, once uttered, it's a "safe word" telling the other to back off. No pleading, no cajoling, no berating. Just "no." When it comes to setting limits on nonsexual behaviors, here too many couples find it helpful to set aside times when they are relaxed and have privacy (or, perhaps, in a joint therapy session) to discuss the parameter of what's acceptable and what's not in everyday life. The topics can be as broad as picking up after oneself to a promise to talk to the other partner when the urge to drink, get high, or log on to an Internet porn site hits. (The idea is to address what's prompting the urge—e.g., stress, boredom, tension—and deal with the impulse in a more productive, couple-enhancing way using communication skills and loving understanding.)

By the way, boundaries aren't just for you. Your mate also has the right to tell you what his limits are. For instance, some victims in the process of sexual healing require a period of abstinence or a "sex vacation" as they try to do the internal work necessary to reassociate pleasure with physical intimacy. During that time, your mate has every right to tell you that he's not in the mood. In this case, what's good for the goose is helpful for the gander. In fact, for an abuse survivor, setting boundaries is beneficial on several fronts. It allows him to decide what he'll tolerate and define what he finds objectionable and, in the long run, it can restore his sense of mastery and security. Remember, when he was abused, his boundaries were not respected. Setting limits allows him control, while helping you to understand his needs in relation to your behavior. For him, knowing your boundaries eliminates the guesswork about what you like and what you don't—what makes for a happy mate and what doesn't. Ultimately, your relationship should grow from the trust and safety engendered by the communication of, and respect for, mutual boundaries.

"T"—Therapy—for Two

In Part I we examined how healing from abuse occurs and how your man could benefit from a therapist, counselor, or a support group. In this section we explore how having a couple's counselor could help your relationship during the time of his recovery and, perhaps, beyond. It's important to make the distinction between the individual therapist that your man might be seeing—to help him recover in a general way from his abuse—and what we're talking about now: a counselor devoted to helping you both function better as a couple, a unit of two. In fact, these therapeutic roles are so different that some analysts refuse to wear two hats simultaneously. They will either treat the man (for the problems associated with his childhood abuse), or they will treat the man and his wife (or partner) for "couples counseling," but generally they will not do both. Here's why: When your man sees his individual therapist, together they concentrate on your partner's problems, goals, dreams, aspirations, fears, setbacks, and anything else that interferes with or affects his daily functioning. For instance, although your mate's communication abilities or sexual problems might be explored during an individual therapy session, reviewing how those issues affect your relationship might not be on the agenda. Moreover, even if his flawed interpersonal skills are the chief subject of his individual analysis, the focus of the treatment is not you, or even your relationship. Rather, the therapist is primarily concerned with his patient (your mate) and his overall mental health and functioning. You simply can't assume that once your partner is undergoing individual psychotherapy that your relationship concerns will be addressed, much less solved.

Couples therapy (or "marital therapy"), on the other hand, exists to help the individuals concentrate on their interpersonal issues with a goal of achieving a more satisfying, enriching, intimate relationship with each other. While your mate's individual symptoms (e.g. depression or anger or hostility) will undoubtedly be addressed in couples therapy, the counselor will deal with them in an effort to help the two of you function better as a unit. Moreover, unlike individual therapy, where the person undergoing treatment is the center of therapeutic attention, in couples therapy, you, the committed partner, will be just as significant to the process as your abused partner. As the song says, it really does take two, and marriage and family therapists know this and analyze accordingly.

Therefore, be prepared for the marital therapist to ask each of you to discuss what's happening in the present, in addition to asking questions about your respective pasts: your family histories, your personal experiences, your prior relationships, if apropos, and what led the two of you to become a couple in the first place. For instance, during the session, the therapist will learn about your family of origin. If you disclose that you are the daughter of alcoholic or authoritarian parents, the counselor will explore whether you have associated issues: Are you a persistent people-pleaser, always putting others first, while unable to get your own needs met? If so, are you seething with hostility and repressed anger that poison your present interpersonal relationships? (See the next chapter for more information on you and your relationships.) But don't expect to dump all the relationship problems on your mate's abusive past and engage in the so-called benevolent blame game (i.e., you understand why your mate has problems—after all, he was abused as a kid—but he is, nonetheless, the cause of most, if not all, of the relationship's problems). This brand of "it's him, not me" attitude won't cut it in most couples therapy sessions. Whatever your background, whether wretched or trouble-free, you too will be held accountable for your actions and reactions and how they influence your effectiveness as a mate in the couple dynamic. But don't worry. Analysis can be useful, and insight is power. Besides, as Socrates said, "The unexamined life is not worth living;" so give it a go and see for yourself whether gaining a professional's objective input on what makes you tick and why helps you deal with life—and your mate—in a more sensible way.

Ironically, couples therapy enables you and your mate to concentrate on your individual strengths and work on your respective weaknesses, while accepting who each of you are with an eye toward enjoying a more intimate, satisfying, functional future as a dyad. For more information about marriage and family therapy, check out the American Association for Marriage and Family Therapy (AAMFT) Web site: *www.aamft.org*.

Committing Yourself to a Shared Future

We discussed the art of intimacy in the previous chapter about communication. While communication is essential for nourishing continued emotional intimacy, sharing a future requires even more than that. Living by the "golden rule" can help you get along in any circumstances but is remarkably effective in facilitating a nurturing environment in your day-to-day life with your mate. "Doing unto him as you would have done unto you" means that whenever you say something or do something, you should think about how your words or actions would affect your partner. Are they life-affirming or negative? Do they hurt or do they help? If you and your partner are committed to a shared future, both of you must act with the highest regard and respect for each other. And, foremost, follow the Hippocratic oath as a model: First, do no harm to your partner. But if you do hurt him, learn how to say you're sorry, mean it, and try to make amends.

Moreover, just as knowing when to apologize goes a long way toward healing any hurt feelings and healing the relationship, being able to accept a heartfelt, sincere apology with forgiveness makes living with another imperfect human possible and rewarding. By communicating your feelings and fears and accepting responsibility for your actions (with your mate doing the same), you establish a special bond, characterized by closeness and satisfaction, with room to grow and prosper in every sense.

Chapter Eleven

Taking Care of You

While most of this book is devoted to your partner and how his abuse might have affected him, you, and your relationship and family, in this chapter we examine how to keep your own life on track as your mate does whatever he must to make life less painful and ultimately more rewarding for you both. Being present and fully functional as a person, fulfilling all the roles in your life—wife, partner, mother, daughter, sister, friend, employee (or employer)—requires you to sustain the necessary emotional, physical, and spiritual reserves (i.e., those beliefs, activities, thoughts, and feelings that keep you motivated, interested, hopeful, and able to get the job done). In the following sections we'll expand on several themes: pursuing (or maintaining) your Delphic quest (i.e., to know thyself) and fulfilling your Shakespearian mission (i.e., "to thine own self be true") while attaining the support and coping skills to maintain a dynamic relationship with a partner in flux. Much as a flight attendant instructs you to don your oxygen mask first in case of an unexpected drop in cabin pressure (allowing you to breathe while tending to others), throughout this chapter you'll receive an underlying analogous, self-preserving message: Take care of yourself.

In the meantime, keeping with the flight instruction theme, I ask that you sit back, relax, and enjoy this chapter written to help you stay the course (or to find it, if it's not already apparent) in the midst of your man's healing and renewal. With the information that follows, you are sure to gain insight, serenity, and confidence in your actions and decisions.

Identify Your Life Desires

When you are emotionally, spiritually, physically, and even materially (i.e., you jointly own "stuff") involved with a man who was abused, it's easy to get lost in his problems, his deficits, his needs, and, yes, even his excuses. Part I of this book explained why abuse takes such a toll, for such a long time, on a man in this society. Hopefully, armed with the latest information, you and your partner will be able to address what remains from the past, make the best of the present, and prepare for a better, rewarding future. Yet as you direct your energies to his recovery and well-being, you too have a life that needs living and tending to. It's possible and even likely—particularly if times with your mate have been rocky—that your efforts have been exclusively directed at making sure he could function and your relationship endured the damage from the detritus of his abusive past. While your devotion to your partner's well-being is understandable and perhaps even laudable (more about your loyalty in the next chapter), for maximum couple happiness, your needs also require attention. Before we continue, let's take a good look at how people identify their needs and what makes them happy. Also, now's a good time to revisit those mental mechanisms we discussed earlier in relationship to your mate's behavior, especially introjection. Remember, you too will be using mental (or "defense") mechanisms to allow your psyche to deal with all this life turmoil.

Researchers have found that people seem most satisfied with life (have good health, are resilient to setbacks, and are optimistic about the future) when their desires are articulated and their natural or acquired strengths dovetail with their occupations or avocations. The first step is to identify your desires or, put another way, to determine your goals and values. Take a few minutes to reflect on what makes you happy (not focusing on your man or his difficulties), and see what emerges. For instance, do your thoughts focus on external and material objectives, like wealth, power, recognition, and status? Or do abstract ideals like peace, serenity, or the four Rockwellian aspirations (i.e., freedom from fear, from want, of speech, and of worship) come to mind?

Are you stuck trying to identify your desires, goals, or values? Consider the work of Eduard Spranger. He believed that humans fell into types, depending on the values that they held. According to Spranger, there were six kinds of ideals. Although a person could embrace more than one, Spranger's categories might help you think about what's important to you as you share your life and time with your partner.

> **Theoretical:** You are an intellectual, a thinker. You are rational and logical and interested in learning and truth.
> **Economic:** You are driven by work, wealth, practicality, and all things related to commerce and survival.
> **Aesthetic:** You value beauty, harmony, and the arts.
> **Social:** You are altruistic and value service to your fellow man.
> **Political:** You value influence, power, and authority.
> **Religious:** You are philosophical, mystical, and transcendent, interested in the big questions in life.

Reviewing these values should give you a clue about what makes you tick. (There's no judgment here, just assessment of the facts.) Now, having thought about your desires (whether for personal wealth or world peace), think about whether your values have changed recently or have remained the same throughout your life. Consider the actions you've taken toward attaining your goals. If you haven't done either (i.e., taken action or accomplished your aims), ponder why you chose the course you did, realizing that perhaps your values have shifted over time, particularly as you've developed and matured. You are sure to desire things as an adult that you did not as a teenager, and vice versa. For instance, if your goal on leaving school was to attain great wealth (but instead you're living a secure—but not lavish—life with your man, being a supportive, loving, intimate partner), your present circumstances might not reflect a deficiency on your part; rather, it may be an indication that your desires have changed from the acquisition and accumulation of riches to the nurturing and intimacy found in a relationship. On the other hand, if you still find that affluence and, say, traveling the world are your primary desires, and your present life does not lend itself to achieving either, try re-examining your decisions and choices to consider what you did, and why, to end up where you are, and, naturally, with whom.

While you might settle for less than the things you want from life, generally, someone (you or someone close to you) will pay for your frustration in not being able to go after what's dear to you. Disappointment and dissatisfaction do not make for a contented human. So, if the desire-identifying exercise leads you to a dead end or unsettling questions, it's time to rethink the entire matter of what makes for a meaningful life.

Finding Meaning in Your Life

Whether you've pursued your desires (to be a teacher, to volunteer at a hospital, to become a concert pianist) or have been frustrated due to your own inertia or the things that have happened (such as an illness or accident involving you or a loved one, the birth of children, restricted financial opportunity), there is something to be said for finding contentment or happiness in the physical and emotional place where you find yourself now, knowing that you have an inner compass that can lead you to change whatever you

A Question as old as Antiquity

What is a good life? Aristotle answered this question by using the word *eudaimonia* (εδαιμονα), translated as "human flourishing" or "living with meaning and purpose."

must, when time and circumstances present the opportunity. But until then, being centered and focused can alleviate the pangs of remorse and regret for not having attained what you set out to or for having lost some things along the road of life. Viktor Frankl (the doctor we talked about earlier, who lost his wife, his parents, and his grandparents in the Holocaust and was interred in Nazi concentration camps) wisely concluded that it didn't matter what a person expected from life, but rather how a person managed what life expected from her.

Since we're taking about a sense of well-being in the present—wherever you find yourself (i.e., perhaps struggling to maintain a relationship with a man who's been abused, and all that that status might bring or take from you as an individual)—let's consider what others have written on the topics of contentment and happiness. While some experts believe that happiness happens when a person's life desires, temperament, character, strengths, and interests are integrated into a lifestyle, others have distilled happiness into one word: *meaning*. Although some of the greatest psychological

The Essence of Meaning

Here is the distilled version of what having a meaningful life entails, per the best minds who thought about such things:

Assimilation and Integration of Opposites Within Self (Jung)
Ego Integrity (Erikson)
Engagement (Sartre)
Faith and Redemption Through Christ (Tillich)
Fulfillment and Self-Actualization (Maslow)
Integration (Buehler)
Living by a Value System (May and Yalom)
Order and Coherence in the Face of Chaos (Wong)
Sense of Coherence (Antonovsky)
Sense of Wholeness and Belonging (Weisskopf-Joelson)
Shared Beliefs Causing Purposeful Behavior (Baumeister)
Tenacity and Self-Transcendence (Frankl)

theorists have differed on how one experiences meaning, they agree that happiness derives from meaning *in* (not *of*) life and the positive feelings (significance, triumph, strength) that flow from meeting and mastering life's constant challenges.

Someone in your position might find Frankl's view particularly interesting. He believed that a person could find meaning from, among other actions, encountering and caring for a beloved. This concept can provide a certain solace to the intimate partner of a man suffering from the remnants of his childhood trauma, knowing that your efforts are not only helping him but also might be exactly what you are meant to do at this point in your life. Frankl famously put it like this: "A [person] who becomes conscious of the responsibility [s]he bears toward a human being who affectionately waits for [her], or to an unfinished work, will never be able to throw away [her] life. [She] knows the 'why' for [her] existence, and will be able to bear almost any 'how.'" (From Frankl's *Man's Search for Meaning*.)

Now that you have a feel for meaning and, perhaps, a purpose in life that leads to contentment, let's look at how you measure up.

Taking Your "Purpose in Life" Pulse

In 1964, researchers James Crumbaugh and Leonard Maholick created the Purpose in Life Test (PIL) in an effort to measure the occurrence of meaning and motivation in a person's life (or, as they put it, "the ontological significance of life from the point of view of the experiencing individual").

Curious as to how you'd stack up? Take the following Purpose In Life Test. For each, circle the number that best expresses your reality. Note that the numbers reflect a continuum of responses, with 1 and 7 expressing opposite feelings. Circling the number 4 means you are "neutral" and have no opinion. Note: Before calculating the total score of circled answers, notice that there are nine items for which the scoring is reversed—that is, a 7 is at the left margin and a 1 is at the right. Total scores range from 20 (low purpose) to 140 (high purpose).

I am usually:

1	2	3	4	5	6	7
completely bored			(neutral)			exuberant, enthusiastic

Life to me seems:

7	6	5	4	3	2	1
always exciting			(neutral)			completely routine

Reverse scoring

In life I have:

1	2	3	4	5	6	7
no goals or aims at all			(neutral)			very clear goals and aims

My personal existence is:

1	2	3	4	5	6	7
utterly meaningless, without purpose			(neutral)			very purposeful and meaningful

Every day is:

7	6	5	4	3	2	1
constantly new and different			(neutral)			exactly the same

Reverse scoring

If I could choose, I would:

1	2	3	4	5	6	7
prefer never to have been born			(neutral)			like nine more lives just like this one

After retiring, I would:

7	6	5	4	3	2	1
do things I've always wanted to do			(neutral)			loaf the rest of my life

Reverse scoring

In achieving life goals I have:

1	2	3	4	5	6	7
made no progress whatsoever			(neutral)			progressed to complete fulfillment

My life is:

1	2	3	4	5	6	7
empty, filled with despair			(neutral)			full of exciting good things

If I should die today, I would feel that my life has been:

7	6	5	4	3	2	1
very worthwhile			(neutral)			completely worthless

Reverse scoring

In thinking of my life, I:

1	2	3	4	5	6	7
often wonder why I exist			(neutral)			see a reason for my being here

As I view the world in relation to my life, the world:

1	2	3	4	5	6	7
completely confuses me			(neutral)			fits meaningfully with my life

I am a:

1	2	3	4	5	6	7
very irresponsible person			(neutral)			very responsible person

Concerning man's freedom to make his own choices, I believe man is:

7	6	5	4	3	2	1
free to make all life choices			(neutral)			limited by heredity and situation

Reverse scoring

With regard to death, I am:

7	6	5	4	3	2	1
prepared and unafraid			(neutral)			unprepared and fearful

Reverse scoring

With regard to suicide, I have:

1	2	3	4	5	6	7
thought of it seriously as a way out			(neutral)			never given it a second thought

I regard my ability to find a meaning, purpose, or mission in life as:

7	6	5	4	3	2	1
very great			(neutral)			practically none

Reverse scoring

My life is:

7	6	5	4	3	2	1
under my control			(neutral)			controlled by external factors

Reverse scoring

Facing my daily tasks is:

7	6	5	4	3	2	1
a source of pleasure and satisfaction			(neutral)			a painful and boring experience

Reverse scoring

I have discovered:

1	2	3	4	5	6	7
no mission or purpose in life			(neutral)			goals and a satisfying life purpose

No matter how fulfilled you feel, don't expect to rate a perfect score of 140 (college kids average about 110, while successful businessmen average just under 120). This test has been criticized for not measuring the allusive "purpose" or "meaning" in life, but rather serving only as an indicator of depression. Other critics say the test detects one's satisfaction in life more than purpose or meaning. Still, it's interesting to see how you do and to think about the areas touched by the statements.

Life Regard Test
Another interesting test to take is the Life Regard Index (LRI) created by medical doctors John Battista and Richard Almond in 1973. Below you'll find twenty-eight statements (called the Orientation to Life Questionnaire) for you to agree or disagree with based on a three-point scale. These statements were constructed to measure life meaning through "framework" (i.e., the structure forming a person's beliefs) and "fulfillment" (i.e., working toward, or accomplishing, one's goals). Use the numbers from 1 to 3 to express the range of your answer as follows:

1 = strongly disagree
2 = neutral
3 = strongly agree

Framework Items (*scoring from 7 to 21, higher is positive*)
___ I feel like I have found a significant meaning for leading my life.
___ I have come to terms with what's important for me in my life.
___ I have a system or framework that allows me to truly understand my being alive.
___ I have a very clear idea of what I'd like to do with my life.
___ There are things that I devote all my life's energy to.
___ I have a philosophy of life that gives my living significance.
___ I have some aims and goals that would personally give me a great deal of satisfaction if I could accomplish them.
___ **Total**

Framework Items (*scoring from 7 to 21, higher is positive*)

___ I just don't know what I really want to do with my life.

___ I really don't have much of a purpose for living, even for myself.

___ I need to find something that I can really be committed to.

___ I get completely confused when I try to understand my life.

___ There honestly isn't anything that I totally want to do.

___ I really don't believe in anything about my life very deeply.

___ Other people seem to have a much better idea of what they want to do with their lives than I do.

___ **Total**

Fulfillment Items (*scoring from 7 to 21, higher is positive*)

___ I have real passion in my life.

___ I really feel good about my life.

___ Living is deeply fulfilling.

___ I feel that I am living fully.

___ I feel that I'm really going to attain what I want in life.

___ I get so excited by what I'm doing that I find new stores of energy I didn't know that I had.

___ When I look at my life I feel the satisfaction of having worked to accomplish something.

___ **Total**

Fulfillment Items (*scoring from 7 to 21, higher is positive*)

___ I don't seem to be able to accomplish those things that are really important to me.

___ Other people seem to feel better about their lives than I do.

___ I have a lot of potential that I don't normally use.

___ I spend most of my time doing things that really aren't very important to me.

___ Something seems to stop me from doing what I really want to do.

___ Nothing very outstanding ever seems to happen to me.

___ I don't really value what I'm doing.

___ **Total**

Reaffirming Your Needs with Compassion

Let's assume you have read the chapter so far, have taken the tests and scored them, and are feeling miserable, or not too great. Naturally, unless you are emotionally or physically disabled, you are, at the core, responsible for making your life what you want it to be. Perhaps picking up this book and learning about your mate's special needs and means of recovery was the first step toward a more fulfilling relationship, if not life. But no matter what your partner accomplishes in his recovery, you are responsible for making the most of your talents and desires. Identifying what you want is the first step toward getting it. The next step is to be clear with others about what you need and want and expect from them. This, as you'd guess, brings us back to the concept of communication. As you hone your listening skills, you want to make sure your verbal and nonverbal interactions are just as clear and focused. So while you are mirroring, empathizing, and validating your man's vocalizations, make sure that you in turn assert whatever it is that you need from him. For more information on how to make sure your message gets through in a mutually supportive, compassionate way, pick up a copy of *Emotional Literacy: Intelligence with a Heart*, by transactional therapist Claude Steiner, Ph.D.

Support for You

Before moving on to the last chapter in this part, you should know that studies show that people who lack meaning or purpose in their lives are not only unhappy as a whole, but they are more likely to suffer from psychological illnesses as well. On the other hand, those with a strong sense of life purpose, or meaning, enjoy better health and are able to withstand stress and cope more effectively in the face of life's inevitable setbacks and disappointments.

While I hope you are able to manage the stresses of life in general (and having a mate with a traumatic past in particular), it's important that you feel comfortable about your right to seek out support and knowledge to sustain you as your partner undergoes his recovery journey. As touched upon in previous chapters, there are plenty of self-help books, therapists, and support groups just for the partners of men who are afflicted with a problem, from depression to substance abuse. For instance, if your mate suffers from alcoholism (or any addiction), you might want to review more of Dr. Steiner's work. He claims that alcoholism results from a person's faulty "life script" (as opposed to a disease) and unless he changes the script, the alcoholic will merely repeat his patterns. To learn more about transactional analysis (TA) and the theory of "life scripts" and other methods of dealing with an addiction like alcoholism, consider reading Dr. Steiner's books *Scripts People Live: Transactional Analysis of Life Scripts, Games Alcoholics Play,* and *Healing Alcoholism.*

If you are inclined to a more traditional approach, you might avail yourself of the benefits of Al-Anon, an AA-related support group. Joining Al-Anon could help you deal with issues that are unique to a mate with an addiction affliction. By reaching out for your own support, Al-Anon will teach you to detach from your partner's problems and focus on your needs (and perhaps your distress), as well as understanding your role in the complex problem of addiction or alcoholism. With the help of those who have been—or who are—in your shoes, you will learn to cope, reclaim your life, and hopefully, be whole and healthy as your man gains insight into his behaviors and the reasons for them.

Chapter Twelve

Coping Skills and Common Obstacles

Before we leave this part of the book, focused on your needs as the partner of a man who has been abused, we'll explore several concepts that will help to see you through until your man heals, or if that's not looking likely, we'll discuss your options. Also, we'll cover some of the common obstacles that are present when a couple begins a journey of recovery together, noting that one partner's healing can and will change the nature of the relationship. In most cases this change is good (e.g., as your man deals with the pain of his childhood trauma, he eliminates numbing or other negative behavior); however, sometimes a mate's healing so changes the balance of power (e.g., he's no longer the "lost boy" who depends on you for everything) that the relationship is entirely transformed and sometimes not to the other partner's (that could be you) liking. Thus, we'll be covering a lot a ground as we sum up your place as a partner in your mate's healing.

General Coping Strategies

We begin this last chapter with a section on coping. With all that you've read so far about the causes and consequences of abuse and the ways to deal with their fallout, you'd be well served by having some knowledge of how to cope, not only with the problems that might have existed due to your man's abusive past but also with the changes that are sure to accompany his effort to overcome his traumatic experience and become healthy and whole. Before we examine some of the stressors that you, as a partner of an abused man, are likely to encounter, let's first review the general concept of coping.

So what is coping? In lay terms, it's what we do (or don't do) as well as what we feel and what we think in response to social, physiological, or psychological stressors that are seemingly beyond our present ability to handle. Technically speaking, the experts have defined coping as a dynamic function: "constantly changing cognitive and behavioral efforts to manage specific external and/or internal demands that are appraised as taxing or exceeding the resources of the person" (from *Stress, Appraisal and Coping*, the 1984 book by noted "coping" researchers Richard S. Lazarus and Susan Folkman). When we face a dilemma that we can't immediately manage, we cope with the situation as best we can to find a solution to the problem or alleviate our stress or anxiety about it. First, we cope by conducting an analytical triage, evaluating the situation's threat to our personal or psychological well-being; then we assess these results against our own personal resources (e.g., creativity, intellect, adaptability, patience, poise, time, money, connections, versatility, tenacity) to handle the problem.

Researchers have grouped our coping strategies into three primary categories: problem-solving (or "task-focused"), in which one actively addresses the dilemma with the goal of working it out; emotion-focused, in which one dwells on how one feels as a result of the problem (e.g., concentrating on his one's irritation or frustration or anger or feelings of inadequacy); and avoidant-focused, in which one ignores or dodges the problem, generally with a distraction (by turning one's attention elsewhere) or social or psychological diversion (turning one's attention to more pleasant matters, e.g., dating or daydreaming).

Studies show us that we tend to employ all the different coping strategies, depending on the nature of the stressor. When dealing with a work-related problem, we tend to problem-solve. When dealing with a health-related problem, we often focus on our emotions. On the other hand, we tend to avoid it or distract ourselves in which the stressor is chronic and beyond our perceived ability to tackle it. Still, research teaches that the most effective and beneficial coping strategy, from a psychological point of view, is the problem-solving method, while the psychological effects of avoidance (not dealing with the problem) appear to be the most potentially damaging to the psyche.

Coping with Special Challenges

Now that you have a primer on the basics of coping, let's take a look at the special circumstances that commonly affect couples (or families) when one member seeks emotional mending from abuse or trauma. Even if your mate is not fighting an abuse-induced addiction (as many abuse victims are), throughout your partner's recovery, you can expect changes on every level, not only in his behavior but also in yours, as you react and act in response to your partner's therapeutic evolution. Furthermore, you can expect the essentials of family life to be in flux, or at least affected, as your mate undergoes his abuse-healing metamorphosis. If your spouse is one of the many abuse victims who developed an addiction, you know all too well how your relationship (and probably your entire family) was affected by his actions or inactions. In fact, researchers have studied the effects of alcoholism and addiction on wives, partners, and other family members ("concerned and affected others," a.k.a. CAOs). Their work can give someone in your position insight into how your coping skills can help or hurt you as well as your mate, as he works through this childhood trauma.

First, let me provide a backdrop to the more recent studies on the matter of CAO stress and coping mechanisms. Much of what we know today stems from the work of academics and social scientists working under the "stress-strain-coping-support model," which grew from work with those whose family members were problem drinkers or drug users. Yet your partner doesn't have to be a substance abuser for you to benefit from the collective wisdom obtained from these studies. After all, you now know the effects of childhood abuse; as a partner of an abused man, you are likely to experience some, if not all, of the challenges that the loved ones of alcoholics and drug users have endured. For instance, researchers found that they were often stressed, which was caused by not knowing when their mates (or relatives) would go on a bender, what he would do with his paycheck (pay household bills or blow it on drugs), whether he would become violent, and similar concerns. This stress led to strain, the physical and psychological symptoms caused by stress (weight loss, illness, compromised immune function, anxiety, sleeplessness, social isolation, depression, fatigue, loss of vitality, and the like). What's more, studies on the concerned and affected others demonstrated that strain is influenced by the types of coping strategies used and whether the individuals had social support.

Studies suggest there are three types of coping responses that are unique to individuals dealing with addicted loved ones: "engaged," in which the partner of the addict actively tries to limit the offending behavior by controlling him or the environment; "tolerant," in which the partner takes up the slack, or "covers for," or makes excuses to others for the addict's bad behavior or lapses (also known as *tolerant-sacrificing*), or when the loved one simply

Measuring the Stress-Strain-Coping

The tests that researchers use to quantify the effects of a person's addictive behavior on his family are:

1. Family Member Impact Scale (FMI)—measures stress
2. Symptom Rating Test (SRT)—measures strain
3. Coping Questionnaire (CQ)—measures coping styles: engaged, tolerant, withdrawal
4. Hopefulness-Hopelessness Scale (HOPE)—measures hope
5. Family Environment Scale (FES)—measures home atmosphere, i.e., whether positive or in conflict.

does nothing, allowing the bad behavior to continue (also known as *tolerant-accepting*), due to a sense of hopelessness; and "withdrawal," when the partner detaches from the addict's problem and focuses on her life, allowing the substance abuser to look after himself and letting the chips fall where they may (not protecting the addict or controlling him, but rather letting him suffer the consequences of his actions).

Of these strategies, studies suggest that the best for you—the partner of the substance abuser—to employ is withdrawal. Engagement (actively trying to control your mate's behavior) and toleration (actively or passively fostering the status quo) are the worst strategies to use. Withdrawal, in contrast, allows the addict's partner to focus on the things she can control—herself—and to give up the illusory idea that she can "rescue" or restrain her mate. In general, people can't be "rescued" from their own behavior and, under ordinary circumstances (lacking coercion or duress), no one can control another's thoughts, desires, and actions. What's more, some research reveals that a highly engaged partner who's trying to actively supervise her mate's behavior can instead create a negative effect, causing the mate to behave even worse. (Does anyone like being controlled?) A tolerant mate, while not aggravating the situation, normally does nothing to resolve it, either. So it seems that detaching, or having a withdrawn coping mechanism (i.e., placing your energy and focus on meeting your needs rather than your mate's), is the most effective way for everyone involved to deal with the problem. Finally, we know from numerous studies that when the loved ones of addicts receive social support, their own psychological health improves, regardless of the status of their mate's substance abuse. Lesson: Be helpful but be self-preserving. The only person who can change your mate is, at last, your mate.

Your Stress Reduction
Now that you have information on the best ways to cope with stress, let's look at things you can do to reduce the stress in the first place—or, at least lessen its grip on your body, mind, and soul.

Before we delve into specifics, it bears repeating what you've probably heard your doctor say at least fifty times: eat right, exercise, get enough sleep, manage your time efficiently, and set limits on what you'll do for others (gasp!), if it means you'll be frazzled by the end of the day. Moreover, the advice that's good for your mate is good for you: Don't take solace in alcohol. If you have problems that seem insoluble, avoidance is not the answer. If you've developed (or already had) a substance abuse problem of your own, now (while your mate is trying to overhaul his life habits) would be the time for you to address it. Think about it: If your mate is coming clean, your using won't help him a bit; in the end, it will present a problem to his sobriety and your own good health. Failing to address your own problems often leads to sabotage, which means that you will unconsciously do things that will hinder your partner's progress or make him regress. For example, when he stops drinking, you might begin to order wine at dinner, or use alcohol for cooking, which had never been your practice before. Behaviors like this could make it more difficult for your mate and also give him an indication of your lack of support. In the meantime, working on your communication skills, as set forth in earlier chapters, learning to take care of yourself, and, critically, getting support from others will help you manage whatever stress you have more effectively and with less strain.

And there's more. Relaxation techniques can be a literal lifesaver to anyone going through a tough spell or whose resources are taxed by an unusual amount of stress. From formal yoga and hypnosis to simple deep-breathing exercises, the goal of most stress-reduction techniques is to quiet your mind and calm your body's stress reaction (i.e., the flight-or-fight response) caused by the release of catecholamines in your body (for more information on catecholamines, refer to the glossary). You can even learn the art of self-hypnosis and use it as a tool as needed or as doctors would advise. You know from Part I that stress hormones can cause organ damage and disease (so-called *allostatic load*). Fortunately, studies over the last three decades demonstrate that a person can minimize this harm by employing proven relaxation techniques. Whether structured like yoga, guided imagery, hypnosis, relaxation exercises, or biofeedback (learning how to lower one's own pulse and decrease one's own respirations, functions that are normally outside our control) or unstructured like deep breathing, meditation, or just plain old quiet time, these activities (or intentions) promote relaxation and calmness while enhancing overall health. For more information on how to make the best use of these techniques (and to gain some Eastern wisdom about life), check out the book *The Relaxation Response* by Herbert Benson, M.D., president and founder of Harvard's Mind-Body Medical Institute (*www.mbmi .org*), another good resource.

When something stressful ultimately happens, don't react immediately. Instead, take a breath and realize that few things are irreparable except death, incurable disease, and permanent disability (and you even have the power to cope with these tragedies with the passage of time and adequate social support). So, by contrast, when you are confronting a mere setback (like your mate's bad behavior—however that manifests itself) or any other normal stressor, review the following list for helpful hints on approaching life's inevitable trials and tribulations. Inspired by the "10 faulty thought patterns"—or "cognitive distortions"—listed in the popular self-help book *Feeling Good: The New Mood Therapy* by cognitive-behavioral therapist David D. Burns, M.D., these items can remind you to view your day-to-day situation more realistically and with less personal psychic pain (and besides, they can't hurt).

- Consider all the options. Rarely does life present a yes or no, good or bad, all or nothing circumstance.
- One bad thing does not a trend (a life without luck) make. It's just one bad thing, no more, no less.
- Take off your black-colored glasses. Don't see the world as mainly negative.
- Show the world—or remind yourself of—the good stuff you've achieved or strived to achieve. (e.g., Is the loser of a national

election a loser? Of course not.) Take pride in your strengths; give yourself a break on your weaknesses. (You know what they are; you don't have to beat yourself up with them).

- Don't prejudge a situation.
- Don't assume the worst from people without a good reason.
- Don't automatically assume the worst outcomes.
- Don't overreact, don't underreact. Try to see things as they are and realize that in most cases, this too shall pass.
- Base your conclusion on rational thoughts, not emotions, which are notoriously irrational. Feeling like an idiot does not make you one.
- Lay off the hypercriticism of self and others. (Dr. Burns calls the propensity to criticize oneself and others as "masturbatory thinking" and "shoulding all over yourself").
- Call a spade a spade—making a mistake is human; it doesn't make you a loser.
- You are not the center of everyone's universe. Don't take things personally that are not personal. On the other hand, you are not to blame for things over which you had no (or not exclusive) control.

Finally, though not on the preceding practical list of what to do and not do when faced with stress, spirituality (or, if you prefer, religion), can offer solace and a special source of coping for a person when the world otherwise makes no sense.

In the Shadows of His Healing

Having the concepts of coping and stress reduction firmly under your belt, what do you do with the reality of living a life in which you may feel like a supporting character as opposed to the leading lady? Put less dramatically, even if you're destressing and coping as best you can, how do you deal with the fact that your mate will be preoccupied, at least for a while, meeting his own needs as he undergoes his therapy (or does whatever he must do to overcome his abuse and the emotional marks that remain)? Generally, the answer is to live with it for a while, using the detachment method (or withdrawal style of coping) that allows you to meet your own needs while he tends to his business of rebuilding a life apart from the shame and self-loathing with which he's been living. It won't be this way forever; a relationship, like most human endeavors, is a give-and-take enterprise in which at some point one of the partners is doing all the giving and the other all the taking. With all that you know about your partner's abuse and the common psychological scars it leaves, you can—with assurance that he's working in good faith to help himself and your relationship—wait it out for a time. Live your life, of course. Under the circumstances, it's not unusual for a person in your partner's position to devote most of his emotional resources to himself as he's healing from a lifetime full of shame and perhaps depression and trying to unlearn bad habits (his maladaptive but lifesaving coping methods) he acquired along the way.

If at this time you find that the changes your spouse is trying to make disturb you, don't be alarmed. The roles in your relationship may be changing, and change is usually difficult to adjust to at first. Harder to handle is the control (over him, the relationship, the family, etc.) that you will lose as he becomes more effective. Frankly, as he progresses in his journey of emotional health, you may find yourself involved in an emotional power struggle in which you are reluctant to abdicate your role as the competent

Getting Fed Up?

During this time you may have feel resentment and anger. The fact that your mate is now getting positive reinforcement and attention for behaviors that he should have been displaying all along can make you livid. Also, the attention you were getting for your support has dwindled while everyone focuses on your mate. This is where your soul searching comes into play. What were you getting from the relationship? Only you can say.

one. Expect this reaction for a number of reasons. First, you might harbor doubts about his ability to be a full partner so soon, and second, why should you give up control just because he wants it now? The answer to both questions is you give up all the power because you ultimately want a functional family, which gives power to both partners. When this occurs, you will find a pleasant release from the burden of having what you perceived as the responsibility for everything and everyone. In a healthy relationship, both partners share responsibilities. Trusting in his ability to carry his share of the load will be worth your effort.

Your Man's Occasional Regression

In addition to feeling like you're playing second fiddle in the dyad, if your man is deep into therapy or self-work (through journaling or participation in support groups), be prepared for some acting out as he re-engages with the feelings from his past. Bouts of anger, frustration, guilt, or shame are common as old wounds are reopened for proper cleansing and healing. Remember, you, as his partner, are an easy target for him during this time. (Recall the ego defense mechanisms we discussed in Part I?) While I don't suggest condoning any kind of abuse, I do want you to be aware of the normal cathartic emotions that a person has and that are often expressed in the safety of a home environment (the one he shares with you) during the course of psychotherapy, introspection, and reflection.

This is the time that you have to learn to set firm limits on behavior. For instance, let him know that he can tell you his feelings but that you will not be the recipient of the emotionally troubling aftermath of his innerwork. You will not be a scapegoat for all the emotional baggage he's yet to shed. You are there as support for him, but not at the expense of your own emotional well-being. You must tell him your limitations and give him guidelines. Remember, he is swimming in unfamiliar and deep waters and will need a chart to safely navigate the journey. Define your role (e.g., lifeline or lifeguard) in his recovery as you see it, and tell him about it. Be prepared for your role to change as he progresses and his own role in the relationship is redefined.

When Is It Too Much?

After all the coping and relaxing and understanding and putting up with a mate who's deeply involved with his own life, are there times when you should walk away? Of course. But the decision to stay or go is no less serious, or in some cases lifesaving, than in situations that don't involve a partner who suffers from the consequences of childhood abuse. For instance, feeling trapped or bored is generally not a reason to leave a marriage, a loving relationship, or even a friend in need. If you are having those feelings, you have your own work to do. Perhaps you need to discover your meaning or your purpose while your mate is doing what he must to regain his vitality.

However, as stated throughout this book, no one should be subject to abuse. If your mate has become abusive (or has continued abusing you, despite his promises to confront his abusive past and seek help), you should end all contact between you. No good comes from your taking and his doling out psychological, physical, or sexual abuse. Such behaviors might bring you to the conclusion that enough is enough and it's time to part ways. How do you know when you've reached that point? When you are feeling that you can no longer regroup, when the pain is too great,

Should You Stay or Should You Go Now?

The ancients had two concepts that might interest you at this point. The first is *chronos*, the objective passing of time, the thing that marches forward, regardless, waiting for no man or woman. The second is *kairos*, a revelation or critical event that seems divinely ordained. In other words, *kairos* is the presenting of an opportunity. In this context, the *kairos* might be just the right time—an opportunity—for you to start anew. Ultimately, you will know if it's right to stay or go.

and when your own well-being is at stake, the relationship should cease. It is always a good idea to approach a professional for guidance when you reach this point.

Remember, there is a difference between loyal support of a mate (think back to the self-in-relation theory) and dysfunctional codependency. The former is admirable, the latter futile, even damaging. If, in addition to assuming responsibility for your mate's behavior, you have difficulty communicating your needs and feelings, you're forever putting yourself last, and all the while you're denying who and what you are, you might be locked to your partner in a codependent vice grip. Your best bet for a life of contentment and fulfillment is to seek help for your issues, regardless of what your mate is doing. Remaining in a damaging, codependent relationship will leave you ultimately angry and unsatisfied. Besides, if this description fits you, beware of the hazards ahead. If your mate is changing, he might not want a partner who clings to him. No matter what else you do (e.g., maintain the status quo or not), you have the right to a healthy, mutual, loving relationship with a partner who is worthy of you and vice versa. And you never know, you and your mate—once whole, healed, and healthy—could fit that bill together.

Part Three

The Legacy of Abuse

Chapter Thirteen

Fatherhood and Children

Before we dive into the pros and cons of conceiving (or adopting or fostering) children with your partner, let's begin this chapter with a few words on fatherhood in general. (We'll deal with motherhood as well when we examine infant attachment, but for now the focus is on your guy.) Being a father means different things to different people, depending on their own experience of being fathered. Naturally, that experience is colored by a person's age, culture, ethnicity, socioeconomic context, and even gender (e.g., daughters sees dads differently than sons do). For some, fatherhood means being a nurturer or caretaker; for others, it means being a financial provider. For others still, being a father means taking total responsibility for the well-being of a new life on earth; while for a few, fatherhood simply means impregnating as many women as they can to show power and fertility. Probably the most esteemed view of "father" in twenty-first century Western culture is the one where dad invests his time and effort into ensuring the physical, emotional, spiritual, and financial well-being of a child in his care. If you read Father's Day cards, you know that these are the things that we are usually thanking our fathers for providing, noting the many sacrifices made for us along the way.

Generally, when humans become parents, many will naturally (read: unconsciously) do much that was done unto them by their parents. If one's experience with his or her folks was warm and good, drawing upon the past is fine. If, however, one's experiences in childhood or adolescence weren't so wonderful, then it's important to guard against automatically internalizing the bad parenting experience in an effort to re-enact what one never got, or got too much of (more on parenting styles later). Some interpreters tell us that the famous biblical phrase about the sons suffering for the sins of their fathers is not meant to be taken literally; rather, it is a figurative term referring to the conscious effort required by children to avoid repeating the mistakes of their parents and then suffering the same consequences. By the way, this warning goes for all humans, male and female, abused or not, regardless of whether you decide to remain childless or make a family of your own with biological, adopted, or foster kids.

The important concept here is that your past—or your partner's—is not necessarily a prelude to your future as parents. There are plenty of people who, as kids, endured awful parenting yet grew up to be wonderful parents themselves because they made an effort not to repeat the mistakes (or worse, misdeeds) that their parents committed. On the other hand, we all know kids who had loving, warm parents but who grew up into narcissistic, self-absorbed adults who couldn't be bothered caring for their own kids—what, and spend less time, money, energy on themselves? So, the key to good parenting is being aware of what our children need from us (security, love, engagement, and consistency); what our own issues were as kids (this often requires recognizing the shortcomings and the strengths of our own parents); and trying to do the best we can at any given moment. So before examining your man's suitability for fatherhood, step back and contemplate your own childhood experiences and consider your own role in the parenting experience (if you chose to have one) with your partner.

What Not to Fear

Here is the meat of the matter—the two-ton elephant-like question that, so far, no one's addressed: If your man was sexually abused as a boy, will he sexually abuse your kids? No one can tell you with certainty what will happen in any particular case, but the general answer is the paradoxical truth that while most sexual abusers were themselves abused as kids, most victims don't sexually abuse their kids. This statement is not nearly as counterintuitive as you might think, if you consider it for a minute. Just as any college freshman who's taken a course in Logic 101 is familiar with the adage "While most elephants are gray, most things that are gray are not elephants," the same premise holds true for abusers. While many abusers were abused (research tells us about 30 percent), most abuse victims never abuse others.

Moreover, research suggests that while there is no perfect profile to predict which victims will become perpetrators, we do have some facts about the life experiences of those who do and those who do not become sexual abusers:

1. Those victims who do not become perpetrators of abuse had a confidante or parent to whom they could report their own abuse, and were supported and helped in their lives.
2. Those victims who do become abusers tend to select kids outside their own family (e.g., they prey on kids in the neighborhood or at school) to abuse.
3. Those victims who do become abusers experienced physical violence within their family.
4. Those victims who do become abusers were more likely to have been abused by a female.
5. Those victims who do become abusers had little supervision and lax parenting during childhood.
6. Those victims who do become abusers do so in adolescence, most beginning by age fourteen. Yet even they can learn not to abuse as adults if they receive helping intervention when they start acting inappropriately.
7. One-third of boys who went on to become abusers had a history, when younger, of being cruel to animals (based on a 2003 *Lancet* study by David Salter and colleagues).

What does this list mean to you? It should tell you that if your partner is over the age of fourteen and has no history of abusing children, he will probably not begin abusing his kids. Also, if you know the circumstances under which your mate was abused, it can give you insight into whether the issue of "will he or won't he abuse your children" even applies. For instance, if your partner was abused by a babysitter or a parental acquaintance, the abuse was of short duration, and he was able to tell his parents and receive support, it's basically a nonissue. The alarms are not present in his personal history. The more dangerous situations arise when your mate was abused by his mother; was unable to get help, or worse, was rebuffed when he attempted to seek help; was steeped in family violence, learning no other way of addressing anger or frustration; or was isolated and unable to relate to peers on a social or sexual level. You will, however, generally have a sense of your partner's early life experiences before you decide to cohabit and have children together. And, even assuming your partner has the worst-case personal history, with the proper support, the odds are that he will be with the majority of men (seven out of eight, per Salter et al.) who suffered sexual abuse, yet do not become abusers themselves.

All the research reassures us that to be abused does not automatically make one an abuser. In fact, one's life circumstances,

Most Victims Don't Abuse Others

"It is vitally important that people understand that there is no direct link. This is crucial for parents who have been abused and may secretly fear that they will abuse their own children. . . . Abuse can happen to a person, but at some point an abuser will make a decision to offend in the knowledge that what he is doing is wrong. It is not an excuse. It is a crime."—Ian Hancock, director of Psychological Services at NHS Dumfries and Galloway (Scotland). See Stephen Mcginty, "Paedophile Plans to Sue Church over Priest Abuse Allegations," *The Scotsman*, August 20, 2005.

above and beyond the fact of sexual abuse, may have more to do with whether one "repeats the cycle of violence" than previously believed. According to everything we've learned so far, your man's temperament, social support, and personal resilience will be more an indicator of his propensity for future violence than whether he was sexually assaulted as a youngster.

A Personal Choice

Now that the big question has been answered—that your partner is probably safe father material—let's look at whether you should be parents. It's a profoundly life-changing, personal question that any couple should ask themselves—whether or not one of them has been abused—before taking the major leap of bringing a life into the world or under its roof. Ideally, all those who become parents would welcome that status, but that's not always the case. Unfortunately, for want of prevention during sex, education on pregnancy prevention, or just plain apathy, there are many couples with children they did not plan for and do not want.

Similarly, there are many couples who desire children but lack an understanding of the responsibility and duties that accompany the birth of a child. In this case, the unexpected and seemingly unending demands of a totally dependent infant are more than some individuals can tolerate. These parents' poor coping skills, regardless of an abusive or traumatic childhood, do not make for happy childrearing. In fact, the inability to handle, say, a colicky baby, causes these parents to hit or otherwise harm their infants. They strike not out of any sexual impulse but rather in an effort to

It Really Does Take a Village

Regardless of the person's abuse history, both the baby and the primary caregiver benefit from communal assistance—and respite—whether from family, friends, community, or church.

relieve what becomes unbearable tension (the relentless wails of a baby in distress) because they don't know another way of dealing with the disturbance. This kind of frustration, or "end of the rope" abuse, occurs most frequently when the caregiver is overtaxed and emotionally, socially, and often financially undersupported. Arising from situational stresses and often ignorance (as opposed to deep, abused-caused emotional baggage) of what parenting entails, this kind of abuse is often treated successfully by teaching the caregiver parenting skills and the basics of child development.

Not every person has the desire to procreate. Some people are self-directed and feel they have other ways of contributing to the universe and are perfectly happy not to become parents. Some of these very same adults can be great babysitters who fully enjoy the company of children—other people's children, kids that they can legally leave when their time is up. Not wanting children is a perfectly legitimate choice and should not be considered a negative decision if a couple is in agreement. If you and your partner don't feel that having children is the right choice for you, so be it. On the other hand, if you and your partner feel that a child will add to your happiness, terrific. If you are undecided about becoming parents, your mate has the advantage. Time is on his side. He can afford to wait, physiologically speaking, until the time is right. For you, after age thirty-five, the experts tell us that the biological clock ticks quickly. So know your options as you decide what's right, or nature could make your choice for you.

A final thought on parenting, to be or not to be: A child who is wanted will have parents with a better attitude toward all the life changes—sleep deprivation and physical exhaustion, not to mention mom's understandable baby-centered focus for a year or two or three—that accompany an infant's arrival in the household. If you know what you and your partner are in for, the joys of bringing a new life into the world in general and into your life, in particular, can be the most rewarding you've ever known. Besides, eventually the baby's patterns change and, like all the parents before you, you adapt and mature and you do your best for your kids. Remember, they belong to the world and are entrusted to your good care for a relatively short time.

Possible Parenting Styles

Assuming that you and your mate decide to have kids, now what? Psychologists tell us that parents' behaviors and their parenting styles directly influence the growth and development of their children. A "parenting style" refers to how a caregiver manages a child's behavior. When successful, parents fulfill their role as teachers, role models, and good socializing agents, helping their children become productive, socially adept citizens, able to adjust to independent adult life. While every parent has a unique relationship with his or her child, experts recognize several basic kinds of parenting styles. Let's explore them and see what looks familiar and what works best.

Authoritarian Parenting Style

The authoritarian parenting style is characterized by setting the bar high for kids (expecting straight As at school or excellence on the athletic front) but being tone deaf to the kids' own needs and desires. Typically, authoritarian parents are rigid and controlling, emphasizing punishment—or the threat of punishment—to make their children behave in a certain way. Authoritarian parents demand unquestioned obedience and respect from their kids. This style is common in households with a rigid hierarchy—dad is the head of the family and the major decision-maker, mom is next in line, and the children follow, seen and not heard, speaking only when spoken to. Authoritarian parents are strict on matters concerning chores and achievement and their children usually obey— or else. (Think retired naval captain Georg von Trapp in *The Sound of Music*—before Maria arrived.) These parents are generally quick to discipline, relying on external controls (hitting, grounding, no TV, etc.) as opposed to internal controls (discipline, a time-out) to teach the child right from wrong.

The authoritarian style can work, as long as parents show their love and try to attend to the needs of the child as they impose their own strict demands. Being a strict—but fair and consistent—disciplinarian does not mean that you do not love your child. Children often feel more comfortable when they have parental controls. It usually gives the child a feeling of security. But remember that warmth and affection are just as important as laying down the law.

Authoritative Parenting Style

This parenting style is characterized by high expectations and firm enforcement of rules and standards; yet it also features open communication with children. In other words, authoritative parents do not rely solely on punishment to achieve results with their children. Instead, while setting firm limits, they will also try to listen to their kids and understand what is going on in their lives. This style of engaged parenting is associated with healthy psychological development and lower levels of delinquent behavior than the authoritarian style.

Permissive or Indulgent Parenting Style

This style reflects a hands-off attitude toward children, in which rules are either nonexistent or inconsistently enforced. Permissive or indulgent parents are passive, making few if any demands on their kids. Most experts agree that this kind of approach gives children too much freedom and that they don't learn what's expected of them from society at large when reared in this manner. Permissive parents don't discipline their kids or make demands on them. Some indulgent parents adopt this style as a reaction to their own strict upbringing. These parents think that by being easy on their kids they are showing their love. They give the children freedom that they cannot handle. These parents also try to reason with their children when they should be giving them directives. Children of permissive parents quickly learn that they have as much—if not more—control as the parents do and can become selfish and manipulative. In some instances, the child takes over the role of adult and makes his own rules. Eventually, the permissive parents become angry at their children's lack of respect, and problems can develop. If you employ an indulgent parenting style, and it is not working for you or your kids, try setting firm limits on your children and get some help from your pediatrician (or a referral to a family therapist) to learn basic behavior modification—yours and your kids.

Disengaged or Indifferent Parenting Style

The indifferent parent is not permissive. (The permissive parent is aware of his or her lax attitude toward discipline and often adopts an indulgent approach as a way of showing the child love and respect, even though it's often counterproductive.) The indifferent or disengaged parent simply can't be bothered. These parents ignore their kids except when their demands interfere with the parent's agenda. When that happens, the parent becomes hostile and angry. This is a thoroughly bad way of parenting. In fact, it's not really parenting at all, it's an abdication of parenting.

Balanced Parenting Style

This style employs the democratic method of parenting. Parents and children are equals in the need for dignity and self-worth. This is the classic picture of a functional family unit when used properly. In this style, parents serve as role models and are consistent in their values. They present clear images for the children to internalize regarding appropriate, expected behaviors for our society. Children are taught good problem-solving methods and respect for others. If the child needs discipline (e.g., he may be punished for unacceptable behaviors), it is meted out fairly and consistently, with the goal of teaching the child right from wrong. Under this approach, discipline is dispensed with respect for the child, with the punishment fitting the behavior. The child is never scapegoated (blamed for things that are not his fault), and he has an opportunity to redeem himself without ridicule. In this kind of atmosphere, the child realizes that there are consequences to his actions. He knows his parents love him but that they expect him to act appropriately.

Positive Coparenting

Whether or not you are able to identify your parenting style, the goal is to help each other be good parents. How is this possible? You may be aware of the real estate mantra: location, location, location. With coparenting the mantra is respect, respect, respect; and consistency, consistency, consistency. Coparenting is the shared responsibility for the welfare and needs of your children, including their emotional, financial, and overall well-being. Children need—and thrive on—an emotional environment in which parents treat each other with respect and can come to an agreement on most major issues. Consistency and caring from each partner gives the children a sense of security and allows them to flourish and grow in a nontoxic arena. Children learn positive conflict management from you when you and your partner are supportive of each other and use effective problem-solving methods to work out issues on which you may disagree. Effective coparenting (even if your union should dissolve by divorce or separation) is extremely important for a child to feel comfortable in his environment and to become a secure adult. Whatever your kid sees you and your mate doing is what he'll have as a model to guide him as he navigates his way through his life relationships. If the child is reared in a nonsupportive, angry, oppositional household, embroiled in his parents' disagreements more than his own world of schoolwork, friends, and sports, he'll need a lot of couch time to undo the damage (assuming he's able to gain insight into his behavior, and how it was modeled on his parents' dysfunction in the first place). For more information on supportive coparenting and what's best for kids, check out the Web site of James McHale, Ph.D., at Clark University: *www.clarku.edu/faculty/jmchale.*

Fostering Secure Attachments

Now that you know about parenting styles, here we hit the place where motherhood is on the line, though perhaps not in the way you suspect. It's just that it seems Freud was correct. Our infantile behavior sets up a lifelong system of beliefs and expectations about relationships that will endure unless brought to our attention and consciously changed. Why bring this matter up in a chapter about having kids (or deciding not to have kids) with your partner? If you are to be the primary caregiver, you—mom—will be the one who exerts more influence over your new baby than your mate or anyone else. In a nutshell, researchers John Bowlby and Mary Ainsworth taught us that infants are programmed to behave in ways (cry, smile, and coo) that make their primary caretakers pay attention and meet their needs. If that primary caretaker (we'll call her "Mom") is loving and consistent, the baby feels secure and will go off and confidently explore the world, knowing that Mom is his safe base. If Mom is inconsistent, or worse, abusive or disengaged and unreliable, the baby won't be secure and will have difficulty doing what he must developmentally—such as explore the world and learn to trust in others.

In fact, further studies by Mary Main teach us that attachment styles, whether secure or insecure (broken down further as insecure-ambivalent, unsure if mom will be good or bad; or insecure-avoidant, where mom is avoided because she's not a source of comfort, a breeding ground for borderline personality disorder) remain with us to adulthood and affect how we act in our adult romantic relationships. Moreover, parents tend to pass on the same level of attachment to their kids that they had to their own parents (this is the so-called *transgenerational transmission of attachment patterns*). So if you and your partner want to check out your respective attachment patterns to your parents, call a therapist and ask her to administer Main's Adult Attachment Interview (AAI). Then see how your results compare to how you view your romantic relationship (with your partner) by taking the Current Relationship Interview (CRI), developed by Judith Crowell and

Everett Waters. If you were confidently and securely attached to your mom, chances are good you'll be confidently and securely attached to your mate and will pass on this secure attachment style to your kids. If not, it's never too late to learn and change for everyone's sake. Still, there's no avoiding that fact that Freud was, unfortunately, onto something when he blamed future relationship troubles on mom. (On the other hand, if you are well adjusted and happy in your adult romantic relationship, you have mom to thank.) For details on attachment that go beyond the scope of this book, see Theodore Waters' article, "Learning to Love: From Your Mother's Arms to Your Lover's Arms."

Feedback from Your Child

If psychological tests (psychometrics) aren't your thing, sometimes feedback from the mouths of babes can be all you need to let you know how you are doing as parents; sometimes, though, it's the nonverbal communication that will expose what is going on in your child's mind. His silence can be deafening, or he might act out some of the behaviors that he cannot verbalize. For instance, if your child begins to do things that seem strange to you, or perhaps just different from his normal behavior, it's time for a sit-down conversation with the child. Let him know that you notice the differences in his behavior and give him the freedom and comfort to speak to you, if he can, about his issues. Some children are verbal and, given the chance, will gladly tell you of their concerns. Too often, children are dismissed with little attention given to their problems or perceived problems. Listen and you will learn how to best parent your child.

Here's a great example of how kids can communicate just what they must to you. A patient arrived at my office with her adolescent daughter for their joint weekly session. Only this time, the babysitter canceled and the mother had to bring her three-year-old as well, whom she sat on the sofa outside my inner office with some toys. The mom asked the little girl to sit quietly in the waiting area with her while her sister talked to the doctor. The little girl agreed. After the session ended, the older sister rose from her chair and left, as usual. Then, quite unexpectedly, the little girl knocked on the door and asked if she could have a turn in the office. I said she could and questioned the reason for her request. She answered, "I want to tell you my problems, too." Remember, this was a three-year-old child. I asked what her problems were and she responded, "Same as my sister. My parents fight and my daddy drinks too much." (Neither her mother nor her sister ever discussed the father's drinking in the little girl's presence. They were astounded at her statement.) This little three-year-old went on to describe events that her family had no idea she was aware of. All this little one needed was the opportunity to have someone listen so she could communicate her distress. When she finished, she asked if she could come back when she was in junior high school, like her older sister. I said she could, and I have a feeling her mom will now be listening and attuned to the little one's concerns. That was literally from the mouth of a babe.

Chapter Fourteen

All in the Family—or Not

Having a mate who's been abused can be challenging in many ways. Yet it can also provide you with the unique opportunity to make a profound difference in the life of one you love. As you have read, being with a man who's brave enough to face his past and share the healing journey with you can make all the difference for him and, naturally, for you and your relationship. In this chapter, however, we'll turn the lens away from you and your partner and focus primarily on the other people in your lives. After exploring whether it is ever appropriate to disclose—either individually or as a couple—the facts of your partner's past to your friends, family, or children, we'll consider how your man's abusive past might affect your relationship with *his* family—and why.

John Donne famously wrote, in *Devotions upon Emergent Occasions*, "No man is an island," and it's true. Ideally, humans do not live in isolation. We live in communities; we have ties to friends and family members. We seek out the camaraderie and companionship of those who are dear to us, be they buddies or kin. Consequently, it's certainly feasible that a pal from your inner sanctum could sense or see signs of emotional, physical, or psychological distress in your household and then be concerned enough to make an inquiry in an effort to help you. (After all, that's what friends are for.) Assuming this happens, what do you—should you—say when your girlfriends or relatives ask what's wrong and want to know what's going on with you or your partner?

It's Not Your Story

Recognize that it's his story. You might be the leading lady, but it's his script and he should have the final word over who reads it. Unless your partner has given you license to tell others about his circumstances, you, as his confidante (from the Latin words meaning "in great trust"), have no right to disclose what you were told in private. You are an intimate. Your pals are just that, pals. In the hierarchy of human relations, your partner—with whom you share, presumably, a bed, a home, and perhaps kids and pets— ranks far above your girlfriends, or even your sister or mother, on the intimacy-relationship scale. If your mate has trusted you with a secret that he's been keeping for decades, it's probably because you gave him good reason. (Remember, abuse victims were betrayed as kids by the very people they trusted. Don't repeat that pattern.)

You know from the first part of this book how difficult it is for most men to admit to having been abused, particularly sexually abused. Your devoted compassion, patience, and trustworthiness were probably the very keys that unlocked your partner's secret in the first place, allowing him to shed the mislaid shame of his past and embark upon the future with renewed hope and a healthier sense of himself. Putting yourself in his shoes, and seeing you as he does, you'd probably understand why you should not reveal his private business. (After all, would you show your pals your income tax returns if they expressed concern about your finances?)

Try this: As his intimate partner, think of yourself as occupying the same position as a counselor or therapist. As such (much like a doctor, lawyer, or priest), you'd be violating your ethical canons of conduct, not to mention most states' statutes, if you voluntarily divulged the contents of any communications made to you in confidence. These privileged communications are protected under law from disclosure unless the person who is claiming the privilege (the patient, the client, or the penitent) reveals that he is about to commit a crime, or hurt himself or someone else. (Then, one has a duty to disclose the information to prevent the crime or the harm from occurring.) So, using this standard as your guide, spilling the beans to your best friend (i.e., betraying your partner's confidence, even in response to a well-meaning inquiry) is unacceptable. Your partner deemed you trustworthy enough to share his secrets; keeping his confidence should be high on your list of priorities. Telling friends or your family on your own, without your mate's consent, is a no-no under most circumstances.

On the other hand, if you need a professional to help you deal with some of the problems (e.g., lack of boundaries, sexual issues, depression, anger, substance abuse, or lack of intimacy) that can arise in an intimate relationship with an adult survivor of abuse, telling your therapist your secrets—his secrets, anyone's secrets—is fine. You are entitled to your own confidential support system. Similarly, if you are attending a support group, you have a right to fully participate as a member, secure in the knowledge that what is said—often anonymously—in the group stays in the group. (This mandate holds true whether or not the group actually meets in Vegas.) Finally, if you fear for your safety or for someone else's (e.g., his abuser's), you have a right—in fact, a duty—to disclose whatever information would be appropriate to protect you or another from harm. There is no confidence worth keeping when your life, or someone else's, is at stake. Short of this dire situation, his story is his—and not yours—to tell.

Silence Is Common

Speaking about disclosing his sexual abuse, former Boston Bruin Sheldon Kennedy, said: "It's difficult to discuss with anybody. . . . It was difficult to discuss with my mom, dad, sister and brother. I went 13 years without discussing it with anybody." (Source: *www.silentedge.org/kennedy.html,* attributed to Knight-Ridder, January 9, 1997.)

His Decision to Disclose

Apart from confronting his abuser, which we'll deal with last, there are many reasons that your mate might want to inform others—adult family and friends (kids are excluded from this discussion; they are covered next)—about his abuse experience. For instance, your partner could be reaching a point in his recovery where, in order to complete his empowerment, he needs to be able to discuss his abuse with those now in his life. Or your mate might feel the need to make amends, believing that the people in his life (and yours, too) deserve an explanation, and perhaps an apology, for his former behavior toward them. Or maybe your mate has come to a place (a rightful place) where there's no more shame attached to the abuse he suffered and he feels that sharing his story might help someone else within your social circle. If you, however, are reticent to reveal your mate's abuse history to third parties, discuss your concerns with him. You might find you have your own embarrassment (or other emotions) connected to your partner's abuse—or its disclosure—that need attention. As you'd expect, any shame-based beliefs you hold (though unconsciously) about what your mate experienced could negatively affect him as he works through his own feelings about the abuse he endured, let alone his present desire to disclose his past. Communication is the key to understanding. Use the opportunity to considerately "air and share" your thoughts and feelings with the goal of resolution, or at least, mutual respect (employing the dialogue tools you've mastered from Part II).

Once your mate has decided, or you both have agreed, to venture into the unknown emotional terrain of family and friends by divulging sensitive details to them, consider talking to a professional for feedback and guidance. For instance, before you actually sit down and disclose the particulars of your partner's abuse (be it psychological, physical, or sexual), a therapist could help your mate uncover (or review and reflect upon) the reasons that he wants to reveal information that is intensely personal and potentially embarrassing (for the listener), and that could cause lasting and unintended consequences for all involved (if, for instance, your husband's abuser is still within the family or circle of friends and acquaintances that are on the "to tell" list). Also, a therapist (or support group) could help your mate mine his expectations from the disclosure by asking about the kind of response your mate anticipates from his audience: sympathy, pity, revenge, support, discomfort, praise, shock and awe—or all or none of the above.

Once you do make the arrangements to tell other adults, expect the unexpected from them. Child abuse is a delicate subject for most people to think about, much less discuss with someone that they know and love and had no idea was abused. Do not be surprised if your friends or family reject initial attempts to discuss the topic or don't know how to respond to this information. A seemingly unenthusiastic response does not mean that they don't care about your partner or are not willing to continue their relationship with him.

Rather, it might reflect their general unease with or lack of insight about (and yes, even interest in) the subject matter. Although they may be friends and relations, as individuals they might not have the same emotional investment that you do in learning about (or dealing with) the consequences of childhood trauma. Moreover, some of these potential listeners might have their own abuse experiences but have not reached a point in their lives where they can deal with the issue—theirs or your mate's. These people may be unable to tell you of their dilemma but will become distressed and agitated upon hearing about the trauma. So as you begin the revelation (as a couple or your mate by himself), be alert for listeners' nonverbal clues (e.g., looking away, excessive body movements, or withdrawal—a subtle recoil or the more obvious, making an excuse to leave the room) and be prepared to respond in a way that allows everyone comfort and an acceptable exit strategy. (Of course, if the disclosure is meant as a confrontation and a means of inflicting pain, be prepared for hostility in return.) On the other hand, you might have the good fortune to have family or friends who can tolerate their own discomfort on hearing of your partner's suffering and be supportive of you and him through the journey of healing.

Whether and What to Tell Your Kids

Unlike the choice to tell friends and family, where your mate has the last word, the decision to tell—or not tell—your kids about his abuse experience should be a mutual one. While it remains true that the trauma belongs to your partner, your kids belong to you as much as they do to him. Naturally, if your mate is not the biological father or legal co-parent of your children, you alone will decide what they are told and when. First, let's review the reasons that dealing with children is so different from dealing with adults. Aside from the obvious reason—that kids are not equipped to deal with complex and threatening issues that mature adults find difficult—developmentally, kids need to be kids, free from the worry and concerns of adult life. Above all, kids need competent caregivers who can provide protection, consistency, warmth, and an interest in their well-being. Under usual circumstances, there is nothing to be gained by burdening children with the emotional turmoil that would accompany the knowledge that their daddy (or mommy's partner) was hurt when he was a little boy or young man. Let's look at how kids process trauma to learn why it's important that you minimize their stress and keep your cool.

Researchers have conducted studies on children and trauma in relation to natural disasters (e.g., floods), criminal events (sniper shootings at school), and terrorist attacks (concerning 9/11). Here's what they learned. On the whole, most children are resilient after tragedy. Only approximately two out of ten will exhibit long-term symptoms of the trauma. However, whether a child is resilient or vulnerable depends on her ability to regulate her emotions (calm herself down), her personal history of violence (its presence predicts vulnerability to trauma), her self-esteem (the higher, the better), her feeling of security (having a stable home with supportive, warm, reassuring caretakers is best), her coping style (active is better than avoidant), social support from community or religious organization (the more, the better), and her mental health and the mental health of her family of origin, particularly her mother or primary caretaker.

How does this trauma-processing information apply to your child in the context of whether you should tell her (or him) about your partner's experience of abuse? On the whole, it tells you that kids take their coping cues from their caregivers—particularly the primary caregiver—and the emotional tone of their home environments. If the child sees you actively coping with life's challenges, the child is more likely to emulate your behavior and become resilient. For instance, if you tell the child about your partner's abuse and appear to be very agitated or upset, the child will notice and likely become upset as well.

In many cases, even calmly telling a child that daddy was abused or hurt when he was a little boy will only make her scared and perhaps feel that it is inevitable that she, too, will be harmed. (Or she might want to make daddy feel better and become his

How Not to Do It

In the award-winning 2005 documentary film *Twist of Faith*, directed by Kirby Dick, you can see an example of how not to tell your child about daddy's abuse. In the movie, Tony Comes, a firefighter living in Toledo, Ohio, with his wife and young children, deals with the aftermath of being abused by a priest almost two decades before. Tony tells his eight-year-old daughter how a priest (who, ironically, lives five doors down from the home Tony has just purchased) hurt her daddy very much when he was young. (In fairness, he feels he must tell her about the abuse before she learns about it from the press.) Unfortunately, Tony overwhelms his young daughter with his anger, anxiety, depression, shame, fear, and self-loathing. The scene where he's in bed with his daughter, telling her how frightened he is, is almost unbearable to watch. This movie is worth viewing for many reasons, one of which is the poor example of how disclosure is handled.

caretaker—definitely not an appropriate role for a youngster.) If the reason you want to reveal to the child what happened to dad (or your partner) is to prevent your child from suffering the same fate, it can be accomplished without frightening the child or subjecting her to her dad's distress. Instead of bringing the subject up in relation to dad's painful experience of being abused, keep the issue in the present tense, in the child's time and place. In real time, the child has the opportunity to protect herself; in the past, dad did not, and that's frightening to a youngster. Keeping dad's abuse at bay, teach your child how to prevent abuse by working with her pediatrician and school professionals. Find out when her class will be dealing with child abuse prevention and reinforce the message at home in ways that are child-clear and nonthreatening. Of course, if your child hasn't yet begun school, you might, depending on her age and development, begin to teach her about the body: what the private parts are; the difference between good and bad touching; how to tell someone "no" when that person wants to touch her or have her touch (or see) a private part; and how she can and should tell you anything, ever, that concerns her.

Finally, as you know, in spite of the sensational cable news stories, "stranger danger" is much less a risk to your child's welfare than the babysitter, teacher, priest, or coach that you and your child trust. Yet if there is a clear and present danger in the neighborhood (a registered sex offender living next door), work with your neighbors and law enforcement to manage that risk and protect your child in the present, but don't frighten her about dad's past. If you need more information on how to empower your child to make the right choices and stay safe, ask your child's school psychologist, pediatrician, or the local police department for help. Also, log on to *www.stopitnow.org*. For information on Megan's law in your state, log onto *www.fbi.gov/hq/cid/cac/states.htm*.

Confronting a Family Abuser

In Part I we addressed the possibility of your mate's confronting his abuser (psychologically speaking) in connection with his recovery and healing. In this section we explore what can happen when the abuser is a family member who still lives and breathes and attends family functions and the confrontation your partner seeks is person to person, on his terms. This scenario usually arises when a victim's repressed memories of incest surface as a result of a trigger event and he realizes that he was abused when he was younger, but repressed the event so deeply that he was unable to recover the memory until something forced it into his consciousness. Now that he recalls the abuse, he wants to confront the abuser about it. A personal confrontation can brew over a course of many years, when a victim carries the memory of his abuse in his consciousness, from the time it happens through maturity; but instead of dealing with the abuser by either cutting him (or her) out of his life or confronting the abuser and forgiving him, he says and does nothing, letting his anger simmer till it can no longer be contained. And here we are.

When confronting an abuser, your mate has to be prepared for a showdown (denial or defense dripping with hostility and self-righteous anger, often ending in rejection of the victim); rationalization (you liked it; you made me do it; I was so lonely; I was so drunk); or utter denial and dismissal (I don't remember; it never happened). (Recall the characteristics of many pedophiles: denial and rationalization.) So if your partner is looking for an apology or a mea culpa, he might be sorely disappointed. As always, it's best to know your audience beforehand and be ready for the likely range of responses. In this case, I urge your mate to discuss the pros and cons of confrontation with his therapist or counselor (or support group, with its collective experience and wisdom). Ultimately, he must be prepared for the worst: His entire family will disbelieve him, disown him, and side with the abuser (remember, he—or she—might be a "central attachment" figure upon whom the family relies for its existence, no matter how dysfunctional). If your man has weighed his options and likely outcomes—including estrangement from siblings and rejection from not only the abuser but also the other "nonabusing" (but potentially enabling) parent—and decides it is worth the consequences, then it's his right to act. What do you do after your mate confronts his mother, father, sister, brother, uncle, cousin, whomever? Well, you take a great interest because you want to prevent that abuser from doing more harm to any more children, within or outside the family. If you learn that the abuser is no longer able or inclined to act in a sexual (or other harmful way) with children, the issue is less of a risk problem but not less emotionally complex. For example, if your mate's abuser was his older brother, who was an adolescent or young teen when it happened and has since grown up, settled down, and has well-adjusted, happy, functional kids and everyone seems content and joyous, you don't have to worry that he'll be a threat to your kids or his neighbors'.

Still, you are likely to harbor antagonistic feelings about the man who was the young brother who abused your mate. In this case, following your partner's lead is helpful. If he forgives his brother (who might have apologized, or not), then you should let it go, too. This laissez-faire tack is not possible when a family abuser continues to be a risk to children in his reach—yours and everyone else's. In that case, you must be vigilant and report any abuse you see or in good faith suspect. (There's more on reporting abuse in the next chapter.)

Relating to Your Man's Family

Regardless of whether your mate confronts his family abuser, you have to deal with the fact that his family allowed incest to occur. Or if your mate's abuser wasn't kin, you still have to deal with the fact that your partner was abused and that his family either didn't notice or couldn't be bothered to notice the signs that something was wrong with their son. Your feelings are completely understandable, but you weren't there and you were not privy to the family dynamics by which others were bound. In addition, times were different. Twenty years ago, child abuse was not the public issue that is it today. Plus, back when your man grew up, authority figures like parents, priests, and teachers were universally respected.

It was almost unthinkable that they would use their access and influence over children in their care to abuse them. Moreover, most adults never suspected that pedophiles sought jobs with kids just to be close to their quarry. Furthermore, even if your mate's abuse was incestuous and his nonoffending parent should have known, or did know, about the abuse, consider his or her position and circumstances. Was the nonoffending parent being abused as well? Was she stuck in a marriage due to financial hardship or because of other children that were young and still needed tending and a roof over their heads? Was she coerced or threatened in any way while the abuse occurred? Were there other psychological reasons that the nonoffending parent could not see what was probably going on beneath her nose? Does the term *denial* mean anything here? These are not excuses, because what happens in an incestuous household is inexcusable; but from a human point of view, not many people seek a home where their partner is abusing their child. People often do the best they can under the circumstances in which they find themselves. Just remember, you were not in those circumstances and you don't know what was happening to other family members, and, in many instances, neither does your partner.

Meanwhile, of course you have the right to make sure your kids are not in the nonoffending parent's presence without supervision—if she (or he) didn't protect your husband when he was growing up, why would expect she (or he) would be able to protect your children now? Or if kids aren't the issue, you can choose to avoid his or her company. If your mate's view of his nonoffending parent tends toward reconciliation and forgiveness, you have to respect that, as long as no one is imperiled by his decision. Remember, he has only one family of origin. He ultimately has the right and the power to decide what type of contact he'll allow between him and his family. If his decision is a problem for you, then the two you of you should be able to discuss it and come to an acceptable compromise. You'll see that dealing with your partner's family is a fluid situation (true in almost any in-law relationship, regardless of the abuse issue) requiring your constant assessment and judgment. Try treating his family members as individuals and resist the urge to judge them by their relationship to other family members with whom they share complex psychological and probably biological bonds. Make your own assessment of how they affect your life and the life of your children—if you have them. If there's some good there, weigh it; if it's all bad, you can move on. Your partner might even follow suit.

I will give you an example of what not to do and of the fall-out that can result from disclosing a loved one's abuse against his wishes. Barbara was finding it intolerable to deal with her husband's drinking. She threatened to leave if he didn't get help. He told her that he would seek psychological counseling and asked her to stay with him as he fought his battle with alcohol. Not long after seeing a psychologist, Jim, Barbara's husband, confided to her that he was abused as a child and that he thought this abuse was involved with his alcoholism. Furthermore, he told her that the abuse he suffered as a child was at the hands of a family member. He was not ready or willing to say more than that. Upon hearing this news, Barbara agreed to stay and vowed to be supportive while he was trying to deal with his problem. She did not realize what this new revelation was going to do to her emotional state. Barbara was convinced her husband's drinking was due to stress at work, maybe financial worries, and a myriad of other reasons, none of which involved any kind of childhood abuse. Barbara considered herself quite sophisticated and worldly, yet she was not prepared for her own reaction to this news. She felt inadequate to deal with her own feelings, much less be supportive to her husband. Barbara was not, however, willing to seek help for her discomfort. In Barbara's mind, her husband was the one who needed therapy, not her.

Barbara found herself probing for information that Jim would not share. A holiday was approaching that Jim and Barbara traditionally spent with Jim's family. They were married ten years, and every Thanksgiving was celebrated with Jim's family at their home. Barbara always enjoyed this tradition and looked forward to the event with all the generations getting together, telling family stories, sharing laughter, and enjoying the wonderful food.

This year was different. Barbara didn't think she could bear being in the company of someone who had hurt her husband to such an extent that he became an alcoholic to cope with the pain. She wondered what her life would be like if Jim had not been abused as a child and had not turned to drinking. It was not only about Jim; now it also concerned her and the kids. She pleaded with Jim to at least divulge the identity of the abuser, so that she could have some degree of comfort with the other members of her extended family, for the sake of her children's safety, and to satisfy her own curiosity. In spite of her earnest request, Jim was unwilling to tell her. Barbara finally agreed to the visit anyway and packed up the children for the annual trek. When she arrived at her in-laws' home, she felt paranoid, wondering who among this joyful group could have betrayed her husband so. When seated for dinner, Barbara began conversations about Jim's childhood and was in obvious pursuit of some answers. The fact that Barbara is an investigative reporter for a national paper only made her interrogation more intense. Jim called her to another room and asked that she stop the interrogation of his family, telling her that he was feeling very uncomfortable with her conduct. Barbara was not even aware she was doing this.

At one point, Jim's mother asked Barbara what she was "getting at with her questions" and the references to child abuse. Jim's mother told her that it was not appropriate conversation for the dinner table, particularly not at Thanksgiving. That was the straw that broke the camel's back! Barbara asked her mother-in-law when it would be a good time to discuss the abuse that was allowed in the family. That ended the celebration. Jim packed up and left with the kids, and so did other family members. Barbara had to call a car service to get home. When she arrived home, the kids were asleep and Jim was drunk. He later told her that her conduct that evening felt very similar to the betrayal that he suffered as a child. He asked her if she would leave the house and said if she did not, he would. He felt he could not trust her and, at that juncture, was afraid of his rage toward her.

They separated for six months and then began counseling with the intent of examining their marriage to see if it could be repaired. Barbara was now willing to accept the fact that she too had suffered major trauma upon learning of Jim's abuse, and was willing to address it in therapy. They continued treatment along with attending twelve-step programs (AA for Jim and Al-Anon for Barbara). They have progressed to the point of thinking about renewing their wedding vows for their next anniversary. The relationship, however, with Jim's family is still estranged and uncomfortable—which may never change. Jim still has not disclosed the abuser (his mother) to his wife and continues to have difficulty dealing with his trauma.

Chapter Fifteen

If He Should Fall

W e've devoted most of this book to talking about the challenges your partner faces as a victim of abuse. Now we'll
look at the problems your family might encounter on account of
his past. But before we do that, let's review the most important
message so far in this book. Your partner was traumatized at a
time when he lacked power and control over his life. He does not,
by virtue of that traumatic experience, become an automatic men-
ace to you, your children (if any), or anyone else. Both clinical
and anecdotal data show us that the person most likely to be hurt
as a result of childhood abuse is the childhood victim himself.
The primary way that you (and your kids, if you have them) will
be affected is by witnessing him suffer the consequences from a
life of self-doubt, low self-esteem, and shame; or by watching him
engage in maladaptive or self-destructive behaviors that make
relationships difficult and contentment and peace elusive. (Recall
the lessons of Parts I and II.)

The crucial message to convey is that no matter how challenging it's been for you to be with your man on account of his
post-abuse symptoms, it's been far worse for him He is the one
living with the pain of abuse—or trying to bury it every day. So
it is critical that you understand (as we discussed in great detail
in Chapter 13) that most men who were abused do not—I repeat,

do not—go on to abuse others. In fact, one of the many reasons that male victims fail to disclose their abuse is their fear that they will be seen as potential abusers themselves. (Recall the "myths" in Chapter 1?)

After all the research on the "cycle of abuse," we've learned that while many sexual predators (male and female) were abused one way or another as youngsters, most victims do not abuse others. In fact, some victims form a reaction formation (remember Freud's defense mechanisms?) to the circumstances or behaviors that gave rise to their own abuse and, as a result, will gravitate toward the opposite—situations that don't allow for abuse—to reduce the possibility of trauma reappearing in their lives, in any form (e.g., having their children abused). With these facts in mind, let us now address what to do if your partner does cross that line and abuses you, your kids, or anyone else.

Defining Abuse Yet Again

At the beginning of this book, we defined the most common types of violence that your mate could have endured: psychological (ranging from the emotional aloofness of a caregiver, to insults and raging verbal attacks); physical (from beatings to neglect, abandonment, and isolation); and, generally most damaging from the victim's point of view, sexual abuse. I bring these topics up to remind you that all sources of maltreatment cause harm to the individual who experiences them, and in this chapter we are

Remember the Adverse Childhood Experiences

Remember from Chapter 1, there are many circumstances (i.e., ACEs) besides the more straight-forward, easily identified categories of abuse—psychological, physical, and sexual—that can invoke fear in a kid and cause him or her emotional harm and even sow the seeds for future disease. Keep this in mind as we explore the ramifications of a mate behaving badly.

addressing all types of abuse, not just sexual abuse. So when we are examining the possibility of your mate abusing you, your kids, or anyone outside your family, we are not limiting the discussion to sexual contact.

A final fact to note before we begin this most dreaded chapter: While all forms of abuse are odious, some of the research tells us that the victims of physical abuse are the ones most likely to grow up and be physically violent with their children. Moreover, other academics have found that sexual abuse survivors are slightly more likely than those who were never abused to become physical (but not sexual) with their kids. Parental substance abuse, domestic violence, and depression are also identified as known risk factors for physical child abuse. So the "cycle of abuse" (or, to use the researchers' jargon, "intergenerational transmission of violence") seems to predict physical violence (as well as the psychological abuse that nearly always accompanies it) but not necessarily sexual abuse. Furthermore, one study revealed that a child's experience of maternal (as opposed to paternal) violence is a far greater predictor of whether someone will perpetrate violence in his future intimate relationships than previously thought. (So all you moms out there: Watch how you act around the kids, too.) This same study also suggests that if one member of a couple lacks a violent family of origin, then the likelihood of intimate partner violence occurring in that relationship is drastically reduced. Finally, several studies expose the not-much-discussed-fact that intimate partner violence is often a "bidirectional" phenomenon, wherein both partners, male and female, are emotionally and physically aggressive to each other. So with these findings in mind, let's tackle the worst that could happen.

If He Abuses You

If your partner engages in abusive conduct—running the gamut from psychological abuse (controlling your access to money or isolating you by limiting your human contact by phone, computer, or other normal channels of communication; or making you frightened for your personal safety or the safety of a loved one) to physical abuse (beating you) to sexual abuse (forcing you to perform acts to which you don't consent or that humiliate you)—you have a personal and legal right to protect yourself and put an end to it. Just because your partner's boundaries were violated gives him no license to violate yours, or anyone else's, much less put you in mortal fear or harm a hair on your head. On the personal front, you have a right to refuse to be bullied. Putting up with bad or dangerous behavior doesn't help either one of you; rather, it's a form of enabling or "martyrdom," neither of which is healthy. On the legal side, if you feel unsafe, call 911 or the domestic violence national hotline: 1-800-799-SAFE (7233) or 1-800-787-3224 (TTY). Trained crisis counselors (who speak many languages besides English) answer these confidential, toll-free numbers 24-7, and can provide urgent help, as well as connect you with local domestic violence (DV) resources. Once you are in touch with the local domestic violence advocate, she can steer you through the process of obtaining a protective order, getting financial support through the courts, and, if need be, finding shelter (although it's more likely that your partner, not you or the kids, will be leaving home, on account of the restraining order).

If his conduct is just bad but not life-threatening, your relationship might be helped by the intervention of a therapist or counselor. Using clinical tools like interviews, diagnosis, specialized treatment plans, and follow-up visits, a specially trained expert in the dynamics of domestic violence, or intimate partner violence (IPV), can help you both understand what's happening in his head when he loses his temper. The therapist will normally begin by helping the perpetrator to dissect the external stressors and internal cues that set him off and teaching him to cope with them in a healthier way. For instance, we know that there's a general pattern to domestic violence. It goes something like this: First there's a buildup of stress or pressure. During this time the perpetrator's temper begins to escalate. Whatever is happening between the couple is not communicated, and resentments turn into hostility

Warning Signs of Real Danger

1. He has already threatened to kill you, the kids, relatives, or himself.
2. He's told you that he'd rather see you dead than to see you with another man, or anyone else.
3. He has access to weapons (guns, knives, explosives, toxic chemicals, etc.).
4. He has assaulted or battered you in the past.
5. He sexually abused you or seriously degraded you (made you beg for mercy or perform a debasing act) in the past, and this conduct persists.
6. He has seriously injured you, the kids, or a family pet before.
7. He has kidnapped you or your kids, taken you hostage, or threatened to do so.
8. He has a history of violence or a criminal record.
9. He uses or abuses drugs or alcohol.
10. He seems to feel hopeless or to be suffering from acute depression.
11. You've recently separated from him and he's enraged that he can't (or won't) live without you.
12. He has attempted suicide in the past.
13. He has told you exactly how he'd kill you or himself. (This may mean he's worked out a plan.)
14. He has no one but you for social support, and your living apart means the loss of all comfort to him.
15. He has no fear of authority or legal intervention. In the past, he's even dared you to call the police.
16. He has an explosive temper and has a propensity for aggressive or violent behavior.
17. He has an obsessive, controlling view of you as his property that he will not tolerate losing.

(Source: Adapted from lists at *groups.msn.com/INTIMATEMURDERAREYOUNEXT/ indicatorsthatanabusermaybelethal.msnw* and *www.cobar.org/group/display.cfm? GenID=292.*)

that in turn seethes and turns to anger. The longer this period goes on, the more anger is accumulated and the less likely it is that the perpetrator can keep a lid on his temper or take an adult time-out. The classic second phase is the explosion that releases the pent-up tension and stress and results in the violent behavior (whatever it is). Then, finally, and perhaps ironically, the final phase is the make-up or "I'm sorry" phase, during which the perpetrator, now relieved of the stress, feels sorry for what's happened and tries to woo the victim back to him by offering affection, gifts, apologies, or promises not to do it again.

Although these phases are common, they are not present in every case. Furthermore, the longer the abuse continues, the shorter the cycle becomes between the apology and the next abusive incident. Finally, in addition to analyzing the underpinning of the violence in your relationship (and this analysis will include you as well as him), a professional probably will assist you with couples' communication (sound familiar?), role-playing, and conflict management skills.

Role-playing is a therapeutic technique in which you will act out particular behaviors and roles in order to expand your awareness and become enlightened to different points of view. The idea is to reduce social conflict. In role-playing you have the freedom to exhibit some of the behaviors that you have difficulty dealing with or displaying to your partner. Each of you gets the chance to live in the other's skin, under the guidance of your therapist, who will help you unravel the material you present to each other. It can become your own personal psychodrama—in a good, cathartic, edifying way. Conflict management, another technique used when people disagree, involves taking steps to define the conflict, find points of agreement, and explore various methods (needs-based, as opposed to position-based, negotiation, mediation, arbitration, collective bargaining, and the like) to resolve the issues. I personally find this technique to be less effective with couples and more useful when dealing with organizations, but it's all about what you and your mate feel comfortable with.

If He Abuses Your Children

When dealing with children, there's a specific federal statute you should know about. The Child Abuse Prevention and Treatment Act (CAPTA), amended and reauthorized by the Keeping Children and Families Safe Act of 2003, defines the term *child abuse and neglect* as "at a minimum, any recent act or failure to act on the part of a parent or caretaker, which results in death, serious physical or emotional harm, sexual abuse or exploitation, or an act or failure to act which presents an imminent risk of serious harm." CAPTA goes on to define the term *sexual abuse* to include "the employment, use, persuasion, inducement, enticement, or coercion of any child to engage in, or assist any other person to engage in, any sexually explicit conduct or simulation of such conduct for the purpose of producing a visual depiction of such conduct; or the rape, and in cases of caretaker or inter-familial relationships, statutory rape, molestation, prostitution, or other form of sexual exploitation of children, or incest with children."

Although the wording of the statute might not be the model of clarity, when it comes to whether your child has been abused, much as Potter Stewart, former justice of the Supreme Court, said of pornography, you'll probably know it when you see it. While

Blood Is Thicker Than Water

Statistics show a much higher probability of physical child abuse leading to death (so-called *fatal inflicted injuries*) to children under age five when an unrelated adult lives in the household than when no unrelated adult is present—that is, a romantic partner of the biological parent, particularly a male with little child care knowledge and a weak commitment to a child's well-being. This isn't to say that your live-in partner who is not kin to your kids will kill them. Yet you should have the facts to make your own judgments about who takes care of your youngsters when you're not home. (Source: Schnitzer and Ewigman, 2005.)

physical abuse is easy to spot by the marks that are often left, sexual contact can be much more difficult to discern. Allow me a digression here. You know that as humans, we need affection and touch not only to bond and form attachments but also to develop emotionally and even physically. (You've heard about failure to thrive [FTT] disease, wherein otherwise healthy babies fail to grow and develop, because of neglect and the lack of human touch and attention.)

Knowing that not all touch is bad, just what is appropriate and healthy touching between an adult and a child? Generally, touching that is done in public, or out in the open (not in secret, or behind closed doors) is fine—i.e., affectionate touches that include hugs and kisses on nonprivate body parts; pats on the head; hand-holding, embraces, or strokes on a child's arm or back. In contrast, child sexual abuse is secretive, concealed, and furtive. If the contact is happening in the open, then there is nothing to hide and there can be no secret. So don't worry about public displays of affection between your partner and your child. Such displays are decent, safe, and suitable loving expressions between humans who care for each other. If, on the other hand, you get a sense that unusual incidents occur while you are absent, or when the child and your partner are isolated or in private, you have every right and reason to inquire further. Don't assume something's wrong. Rather, you have a right and duty to check out what's going on when you're away.

Warning Signs of Child Sexual Abuse

There are a variety of possible physical and behavioral indicators of child sexual abuse. Look for these signs and listen to your child:

- Masturbating at an early age, or excessively, or engaging in inappropriate sexual play with others, toys, even pets
- Hurting (cutting, etc.) themselves or others
- Sleep disturbances, perhaps including fear of the dark, being left alone in the bedroom, and nightmares about being chased, held down, abducted, or attacked

- Showing unusually aggressive behavior with others
- Having pain when eliminating or having symptoms of infection (discharge, order, sores) in genital area
- Losing interest in school, social activities, or playmates that once brought pleasure
- Showing symptoms of depression, stress, and anxiety (from having to keep a secret?) or having drastic mood swings
- Having an irrational fear of certain places, situations, or people
- Eating disturbances, including a loss of appetite or a problem swallowing, gagging or choking on food
- Regression to an earlier age or stage of development—this may be accompanied by encopresis (defecation or "soiling" in inappropriate places, in clothing or bed), enuresis (wetting oneself or bedwetting), or thumb-sucking.

For more information on how to spot warning signs of child sexual abuse, log onto the National Clearinghouse on Child Abuse and Neglect Information (NCCANCH) Web site at: *http://nccanch.acf.hhs.gov/topics/prevention/childabuse_neglect/recognize.cfm*, or if you need confidential assistance about the problem, call the Stop It Now! helpline, 1-888-PREVENT (1-888-773-8368), or visit its Web site: *www.stopitnow.org.*

There is no sure way to tell exactly what is happening when you are not with your child, but the items in the previous checklist should give you enough information to alert you to a potential problem. Talk to your child, and if you sense something is wrong, it's best to trust your instinct and take him or her to a physician. The physician, a "mandatory" reporter in every state (we'll cover this subject in the next section), will discuss the subject with you and, after conducting an examination of the child, will tell you what he or she thinks is going on. If findings are positive for sexual abuse, the primary focus shifts to the welfare and protection of the child victim. Depending on the circumstances and the child's age, temperament, and intelligence, he or she might undergo psychological testing and individual therapy. Family or group therapy might be an option as well. Meanwhile, the matter will be reported to your state's child protection agency and fully investigated. If there is probable cause that your partner perpetrated the abuse, he will be prosecuted consistent with your state's child abuse statutes.

If He Abuses Outside the Family

Some men still plagued by their own abuse issues will try to deal with them outside the family unit. Instead of abusing or mistreating you or your kids, your mate will deal with his impulses by taking an interest in an unrelated child or will do something such as make obscene phone calls, or become a voyeur (i.e., "peeping tom"), or expose himself in inappropriate ways to inappropriate subjects. Due to the nature of the law, you will be one of the last people to find out if your partner is being investigated for abusing a child. Yet the following sections will give you an idea of what to expect if he's suspected of the crime.

Mandatory Reporting

Remember the federal statute defining child abuse and neglect? Well, it also requires mandatory reporting by certain people who have reason to suspect (or can confirm) that a crime has been committed, that a child has been harmed. Here's how the law works. The Child Abuse Prevention and Treatment Act (CAPTA)—as amended and reauthorized by the Keeping Children and Families Safe Act of 2003—conditions states' receipt of federal funds on their having enacted mandatory child abuse reporting laws and establishing child protective agencies. Although the federal law allows each state to define child abuse in its law, CAPTA establishes the bare essentials. (The definitions are set forth in the preceding section.) As a consequence, state laws differ across the country, both in defining what constitutes abuse and who must report it. Some states require only "professionals" (e.g., health or child care providers, educators, law enforcement personnel) to report suspected abuse; others widen the net to include clergy and film developers as mandatory reporters. (Notice that when it comes to child abuse, normal legal protections—like the doctor-patient or priest-penitent privilege—against disclosing the contents of certain kinds of communications don't apply.) In some states media reporters are mandatory reporters. Other jurisdictions have breathtakingly broad reporting laws that require anyone who suspects child abuse (or neglect), in good faith, to report it. If a mandatory reporter under the law intentionally fails to alert the proper state authority of a suspected case of abuse, he or she can be fined or imprisoned.

What's more, under CAPTA, the states must enact laws to protect (in other words, "provide legal immunity") for those mandatory reporters who, in good faith, notify authorities of suspected child abuse or neglect, even if their suspicions turn out to be wrong. Note that in your state, a "discretionary reporter" might not be entitled to immunity even if his or her account was based upon a good faith belief that abuse occurred—or was ongoing. (Those who report child abuse in bad faith—to cause the "suspect" a legal problem—can, in most states, be prosecuted themselves for false reporting and, depending on the facts and jurisdiction, perhaps be sued in civil court for malicious prosecution and abuse of process.) For the mandatory requirements in your jurisdiction, log on to *http://nccanch.acf.hhs.gov/general/legal/statutes/resources.pdf* and scroll through until you find your specific state and subject.

If your partner becomes embroiled in a child abuse investigation as a result of reporting (mandatory or otherwise), the next practical matter to address is the legal ramifications. (Your own repercussions are equally dire and depend on how much you are willing to endure and accept concerning your mate's role in the suspected abuse case.)

Legal Issues

In this day and age, no book on abuse with a chapter like this one would be complete without giving you a short primer on the legal process unleashed once a loved one is accused of abusing an adult or a child. If your partner has abused you, he will be subject to the domestic violence laws of your state (which, though quasi-criminal, are still in many states part of the civil courts). Depending, however, on the nature of his conduct, your states' prosecutor could step in and charge him with the underlying counts of assault, battery, stalking, kidnapping, attempted murder—whatever crime fits his conduct. Once the matter is in the prosecutor's hands, it's the people's case (not your case) against your partner. Although you might refuse to testify, the case can go forward with other evidence (like photographs of your injuries, medical reports, police reports, including their descriptions of what they saw on the scene or on you). If convicted of these crimes, your partner will be sentenced pursuant to the law of the jurisdiction. Moreover, depending on your motivation and your mate's assets, you could choose to sue him in civil court for the very same injuries. In this way, you can recover monetary damages for the injuries he caused you, much as you'd sue a person who hit you on the highway and hurt you.

If your partner harms your child, the same process occurs in the criminal court; that is, if the underlying conduct violated state criminal statutes, he can be charged. Meanwhile, domestic violence protective orders are also available when a child is hurt in a domestic setting. If you have any questions, call your local police or the national domestic violence hotline. Additionally, in many states, children have their own right to sue the person who hurt them. Most states allow such a child to file a civil suit (even against his own parent) within two to five years after he attains majority, which, in most jurisdictions, is eighteen years of age. This way, the child doesn't have to sue the abuser during minority, when the child is neither legally capable of making adult decisions nor properly burdened by the pressures of a lawsuit.

While the preceding paragraphs describe the legal possibilities your partner could face if he abuses you or your children (whether his, or from another union), the material that follows differs in that it addresses the legal ramifications of your partner's perpetration of abuse outside the house. As frightening as that prospect might sound, it's even worse when you take a closer look at what can happen—to you. You see, in addition to having to deal with your mate's involvement in the criminal legal process, the person who your partner abused can sue him—and possibly you, too—in civil court for monetary damages. That means if a civil court or jury finds that your partner did the things his victim said (and, due to the lesser burden of proof in civil courts, this will be a foregone conclusion if your man's already been tried and convicted of the underlying conduct in criminal court), his property, and possibly yours, could be used to satisfy any monetary judgment that arises from the suit.

This is what happens: Your mate is sued in civil court for his conduct (e.g., abusing a neighborhood child). That child, his parents, or both, depending on the facts, can sue you and your partner in civil court. If the plaintiff (the one who sues in civil court) obtains a favorable verdict, reduced to judgment (a dollar sum), against you or your partner, that plaintiff (or his lawyer) will try to collect the money by executing these judgments against any assets you and your partner have (after going for your homeowner's insurance—but that will work only if the conduct was unintentional, a pretty unlikely finding when abuse is involved). These assets could

How You—Wife or Partner—Become a Defendant in His Suit

One much-cited state supreme court case ruled that a wife could be held accountable for the sexual abuse her husband perpetrated on two young girls, ages twelve and fifteen, who spent time at the couple's home, lured by their barn and their horses. The court held that the wife in this case could be held responsible by the girls because she, as the spouse, had actual knowledge or a special reason to know that her spouse was likely to engage in sexually abusive behavior against them. (See *J.S. v. R.T.H.*, 155 N.J. 330 [1998]. Available at *lawlibrary.rutgers.edu/courts/supreme/a-98-97.opn.html*.)

include the house you live in, the savings you rely upon, the cars you use, the boats you enjoy—you get the idea.

By the way, in the horse barn case mentioned in the prior sidebar, the girls won a money judgment against the husband/abuser, with each receiving $100,000 in compensatory damages, $25,000 in punitive damages, and $12,439.72 in prejudgment interest. Their prospects for full recovery (i.e., collection) of that money were unlikely, however, as the husband/abuser and his wife declared bankruptcy and the sexual abuse (intentional conduct) was not covered by their homeowners' policy.

Property Protection, Proactive Conduct

So, even after all that you know about the unlikelihood of your mate abusing others just because he suffered abuse, what do you do if you think that your partner has, after all, a proclivity to abuse children? You get him help and you make sure that he's never alone with a person (child, teen, young or disabled adult) to abuse. In fact, under the common law that has developed across the country, if you, as the wife or partner, have a reason to believe your mate will harm a particular person, you have a duty not only to warn, but also to prevent and protect that person.

Now, for the practical side of protecting yourself from a possible money judgment, there are many legal things you can do to take your assets outside the hands of future creditors. (Notice I said *future*. If there's already an action—lawsuit—pending, it's too late. Anything you do at this point will be set aside as a fraudulent conveyance.) Planning is just that, and must occur years before trouble arises. Although obtaining asset protection will cost you something, it might be worth it to you. You'll see by conducting a simple Google search, using the terms *asset protection* and *judgment proof*, that there are thousands of people who provide this kind of service (most are attorneys or CPAs who know the loopholes in the laws of judgment and tax collection). Without espousing any particular method, you'll see for yourself that most "asset protectors" (some would say, "asset hiders") suggest using special Nevada corporations to shield assets, or using "friendly" liens to eat up all the available equity on real property. Some suggest establishing insured offshore accounts in island nations like Bermuda, the Bahamas, or Grand Cayman Island. Still others advise using estate-planning trusts and other devices to protect your assets from a third party's levy (a legal term for attachment and collection).

To sum up this most unpropitious chapter, if you and your hard-earned assets could be at stake, you should be aware of your options and have time to take whatever actions you think appropriate. Of course, the best is to make sure that no one is harmed and that you and your man live happily together ever after—the most likely prospect of all, given all that we know so far.

Chapter Sixteen

Long-Term Prospects for Couples

After all that you have read about your partner, his likely experiences as a result of his abuse, and the multiple effects on his functioning—with you, his family, your kids, and the world in general—this final chapter will provide useful, direct information for the realistic and laudable goal of giving your relationship an infusion of life, warmth, interest, and mutual support and satisfaction. Offering insights into what successful, well-adjusted families look like on paper (i.e., their attributes and characteristics) versus what we've learned does not work so well, you can consider your own family's style and work toward any necessary and salutary adjustments. Moreover, we will review easy to implement guidelines that summarize behaviors that maximize mutual trust and intimacy between a couple and those that bring about the opposite results.

Bear in mind, as you read the words of this final chapter and begin the work of putting your mate's abuse experience into perspective, you'll both be learning things about each other that perhaps you had not bargained for when you first committed to a relationship. While divulging or receiving new information might seem daunting, be brave about it. Intimacy means having the courage to learn and reveal more about each other every day. Take this moment in your life as an opportunity to know each other well and grow stronger as a result. But don't, as a result of this new information, assume roles in your lives where one of you is "sick" (or damaged or otherwise unhealthy) and the other is "fine" (i.e., unacquainted directly with abuse or childhood trauma). Instead, see yourselves as a couple that is infinitely greater than the sum of its parts—its individuals. With this shared view, you can help each other as your partner releases his abuse-induced pain and your relationship heals from the wounds of the past. Shared triumph after enduring a withering ordeal will give you unique confidence as a couple. You'll see.

What We Know Works

Before you close this chapter, you should be aware of what works, as far as family function is concerned. The "Circumplex Model of Marital and Family Systems" tells us that family units have two fundamental dimensions, cohesion and adaptability. Whether the family unit is "functional" or "dysfunctional" can be determined (or predicted) by how each family rates on the cohesion and adaptability scales. By *cohesion*, researchers mean the attachment between family members, specifically assessing emotional bonding and involvement among all members; the parents' own relationship as a couple; their parenting style; and the internal and external boundaries among members and between family and nonfamily members. After rating them, families fall into one of four degrees of cohesion: disengaged (members lack loyalty, dependence, or sense of intimacy); separated (more engaged, but still independent of each other); connected (this family is close, loyal, and healthily bonded); and finally, enmeshed (this family unit is too dependent on each other, with members lacking autonomy and freedom). As you could guess, those families who score in the middle, as either separated or connected on the cohesion scale, are deemed most functional.

Meanwhile, when experts test a family's adaptability, they look for members' ability to vary family and social roles and relationships as a consequence of changing circumstances. As with cohesiveness, in gauging adaptability, researchers look to different elements: who has power to direct the family; who handles punishment; how the members cooperate; how positions within the family change; and how the family sets (and changes) its rules and conventions. Once evaluated, families again fall into four degrees of adaptability: rigid (authoritarian households with set roles, strict discipline, and little to no change in response to varying circumstances); structured (having set rules, but with the ability to change in some degree to stressors); flexible (able to adjust family roles and rules without difficulty as required by circumstances); and chaotic (lacks direction and control, roles shift randomly, and the family unit experiences unpredictable or excessive changes). Once again, falling into either extreme on the adaptability scale (i.e., rigid or chaotic) is considered dysfunctional, whereas being more balanced (i.e., structured or flexible) is deemed functional and healthy for the family and its members.

Finally, studies reveal that communication is the lubricant of family function. More is good; less is bad. When assessing a family's ability to communicate, researchers look to different aspects of the art: listening and speaking skills, willingness to self-disclose, the presence of "clarity-continuity-tracking" (i.e., being clear and consistent with messages), having admiration and respect for the people involved. They found a positive-feedback loop. The more a family is balanced in terms of cohesiveness and adaptability, the more positively they communicate, and vice versa. In addition to being less-skilled communicators, dysfunctional family members are less supportive than their functional counterparts, and chaotic families—surprise, surprise—are the most difficult for children to endure. So, here's to talking it out, having healthy connections, and being versatile.

If the Circumplex Model is the macroview, the microview of family functioning is just as compelling. Family members do best when the kids have secure attachments to well-adjusted, engaged, fair, consistent parents who provide a warm, supportive, positive environment; when the home is free from conflict and hostility;

and when the parents set limits and high but reasonable expectations of what children can and should accomplish (giving them high self-esteem, thinking they are capable of what you think they can do). It's also helpful to recognize a child's need to explore and develop outside the family, certain that his parents are there for him should he need their sanctuary or assistance. Finally, sharing caregiving with relatives or nurturing, committed adults who are role models to kids doesn't hurt, either. (But make sure that you can trust any caregiver who goes near your child. As they say, if an adult wants to spend more time alone with your kid than you do, watch out!)

Overcoming the Trauma

Knowing how functional families operate is useful, but understand that personally overcoming the trauma of a loved one's abuse can take time. For some families (whether that means you and your partner or includes kids and in-laws, too) it can be a matter of weeks or months: for others, years. While the road is different for each individual—and as a consequence, each couple or family unit—it is possible to overcome trauma. In fact, 80 percent of all adult survivors function very well. Those that don't generally failed to get help, or they had unrelated psychiatric problems that prevented them from leading a normal, healthy life.

In any case, the prognosis for each couple is unique and will depend on the level of investment, the amount of emotional energy, and the love the couple shares.

Tom Paciorek, the major-league baseball player (and chronic sexual abuse victim) mentioned in Chapter 7, told the media that his relationship with his wife failed because he lacked the ability to trust and could not reveal his pain or emotions. He stated, "I was never able to share any type of intimacy with her." Paciorek explained how he tried to bury the pain caused by his sexual abuse, but that "irrational behavior took its place." ("Stories of Broken Victims Lie Behind Catholic Summit," *Detroit Free Press*, April 23, 2002.) Paciorek recalled how he would have affairs on the road and that he marveled at how some of the ballplayers had fulfilling marriages. He just didn't understand how that was possible. Paciorek, however, said that he was repairing the damage he'd done to the people in his life and that telling others about his experience has helped him deal with his past.

In a similar vein, if you and your mate are willing to address your abuse-based relationship issues (e.g., lack of trust, inability to be intimate and share feelings, or irrational behavior) with compassion and conviction, your chance for a successful outcome is excellent. On the way to this place of learning and shared growth, you and your partner will have learned new and improved communication methods, providing a strong basis not only for future conflict resolution but also for the present expression of needs, beliefs, emotions, and desires—the prerequisites for intimacy and couple satisfaction. With good support, in whatever form is right for you and your partner (be it private counseling, couples' therapy, a group, writing, or reading), healing is possible. Both of you will emerge from this process with a transformed sense of self. Both of you will gain a clearer perspective on your own past, understanding how it has influenced how you relate to, talk with, and touch each other. Gaining this insight is the first step to making conscious changes to improve your lives and your relationship.

In the meantime, give you and your partner time to process all the changes that are likely to occur when confronting pain from the past. Another sports figure, former Boston Bruin Sheldon Kennedy, sexually abused as a teen for years by his hockey coach, put it like this: "I feel like I am 10 months old inside a 27-year-old body. You are learning to live again. You are learning to have friends. You have to learn to love and relax. . . . I can't remember the last time I relaxed totally." (Source: Attributed to the *Tampa Tribune*, January 7, 1997, on the Silent Edge Web site, *www.silent-edge.org/kennedy.html*.) Knowing that others have come through this ordeal to live happier, peaceful lives should give you encouragement as you embark upon your own healing journey as a couple.

Here's an example that might sustain you. After ten years of marriage, Donna was ready to pack up and leave. She felt alone, isolated, and abandoned in her marriage. They had one child whom they both adored, but even this was not enough for Donna to continue her married life of despair. She felt that her husband was not emotionally available to her or the child. He refused to go to therapy but did agree to talk to their minister. After weeks of meetings, the minister asked Jake to get an evaluation from a therapist. The minister felt that Jake had major issues that he was not willing to deal with, and he believed the marriage was in jeopardy.

Jake and Donna arrived for the first meeting, and if they had not identified themselves as a married couple, you would have thought they were polite strangers. When I was taking their history, Donna seemed unaware of some of the very basic background material. When questioned about this, both partners agreed that they did not speak to each other much and, in fact, never did. When asked how this worked out during their courtship, they stated that it was basically a physical relationship and needed very few words. Donna stated that she thought Jake was just shy and that he would become verbal and more attentive once they married. Jake responded that she should not have expected more than what she got. He did not deceive her; he just could not invest in another human—even his wife. At this point I suggested separate sessions for a while to get to know what was happening emotionally with each person individually.

Jake's first session was one of many very quiet meetings and left little room for a therapeutic relationship. Jake let me know he was going through the motions and had no positive expectations. He felt his future was doomed and had been since he was a child. (This was my first opening as a therapist to explore what he meant.) He then began to relate how he was the scapegoat in his family. Whatever went wrong, he was the cause. He began to believe this after a while and took responsibility for any disturbing or disruptive events in the family.

He was five years old when his father brought home one of his golfing buddies to stay for a while and had him share Jake's room. Jake was asked to sleep on the floor (Jake was quick to add it was in a sleeping bag, in defense of his parents), and his dad's friend took his bed. Jake had no problem with this, and even thought it was fun to share his father's friend. After a few nights this man allowed Jake to sleep with him and "tucked him in." By the fourth night this fifty-plus man was masturbating Jake and asking him to do things that Jake was not at all comfortable with. Jake first approached his father to tell him that his friend was a "bad" man. Jake's father rebuked him and told him not to ruin a thirty-year friendship. Jake had to return to his room, and the abuse continued. Jake then approached his mother with what was happening and was told not to get his father upset.

No one heard or addressed the issue. Jake was alone and at that point adopted the attitude of silence. He vowed never to humiliate himself again by trying to get himself heard. He trusted no one, and that mantra continued throughout his life. He met and married Donna because it was time to marry and he didn't want to be alone. Back then, she expected nothing of him emotionally and the sex was good.

When questioned at what point he realized that he came from a dysfunctional family, he asked what I meant. He had no insight into this dysfunction. I gave him some material to read before his next visit. He was astounded by what he read. He stated that his family was textbook dysfunctional and he never realized there was a definition for this kind of behavior. He was able to give examples of the behaviors he now recognized as maladaptive. He went on about the lack of "togetherness," the "blaming," "the scapegoating," the "every man for himself," "the lack of problem-solving," and "the lack of taking care of the children." And he said the only "loyalty" was to his father.

This new awareness gave Jake the freedom to save himself. He felt that he could, with help and support from Donna, learn to be functional. Jake was a physician and knew about "cures." He wanted now to be a member of a functional family unit. He set goals and began by inviting Donna to his session. He confided in her and told her some of the abuses he suffered from his parents, but he could not yet tell her of the sexual abuse. He did tell her that he had much more to say that he needed her to know, but it would take time for him to disclose it and for her to process it.

Donna was thrilled that he even considered that she might need time for "processing." This was the first time that she could remember Jake identifying her needs, much less addressing them. He told her he thought he might also have to confront his parents, but he would make that decision at a later time. He asked her to be his partner and give him feedback when she could. He also requested that she not take offense if he did not take her advice. They were talking to each other, making plans, listening to each other, and the anger was gone.

They are now a functional family and have since had another child. Jake has started a support group for children with a psychiatrist friend. Jake wants to make kids aware that if you try enough people, someone will listen, and, hopefully, long before you are nearly forty and married with your own dysfunctional family.

Having Confidence

Having confidence as a couple is a learning process. To make things as easy as possible to refer to, here's a list of activities that promote intimacy, commitment, and connectedness between partners. You'll see that most of the items involve attention, caring, and communication—no surprise there. Expect a time of trial and error until the new behaviors become second nature. Then, when sincerity, simplicity, and directness guide your actions, see how your mate responds and your relationship deepens and becomes more satisfying.

- Consistently give your mate, yourself, and the relationship your attention, empathy, and respect.
- Express caring and encouragement toward your partner, yourself, and the relationship.
- Engage in consistent, healthy verbal communication.
- Use conflict resolution skills when differences occur.
- Express and resolve anger and resentments constructively and without shaming or blaming your partner.
- Take responsibility for your part in the relationship and life problems.
- Understand how your upbringing and childhood experiences affect your conduct and your relationship.
- Communicate realistic expectations—of partner, self, and relationship—consistently and clearly.
- Ask for what you want in a forthright, respectful way with your partner.
- Express feelings in an honest and respectful manner.
- Be a "reflective listener," paying attention and giving consideration to your partner's thoughts and feelings. (Recall the Hendrix trio: mirror, reflect, empathize.)
- Seek eye contact with your partner.
- Have regular and mutually satisfying physical contact (according to partner's needs and touch tolerance in view of his abuse history).
- Promote physical and emotional safety at all times.
- Create regular time alone together, without distraction.
- Surprise your partner on occasion—sustaining passion, excitement, and fun together.
- Accept your partner's personality and characteristics (while helping him work on acquired bad habits or maladaptive coping mechanisms).
- Promote your partner's individual growth and development: Take pride in his accomplishments, support his goals, and don't compete.
- Live in the present and envision a positive future together.

- Emphasize solutions and positive emotions: joy, interest, pleasure, kindness, contentment, and gratitude.

Now the "don't" list. You'll find the behaviors that prevent, damage, or destroy intimacy between partners:

- Failing to give your time, attention, compassion, or respect to your partner and the relationship
- Failing to convey your needs, feelings, hope, goals, concerns, and even resentments in a nonhostile, respectful way
- Losing your physical expression of tenderness—that is, not being affectionate with your partner (according to shared needs and his touch tolerance, given abuse history)
- Averting eye contact
- Deficiency of passion, excitement, and fun together; losing your couple connection
- Engaging in psychological, physical and/or emotional abuse or neglect
- Failing to maintain interest in each other and the relationship (i.e., falling into a rut of predictable habits or routines)
- Rarely expressing caring and tenderness toward your partner
- Being inconsiderate, self-absorbed, or competitive (as opposed to supportive and nurturing toward your partner and the relationship)
- Avoiding conflict or avoiding resolution of conflict; allowing unspoken or unresolved anger and resentments to grow into contempt and disregard of your partner and the relationship
- Avoiding time alone together
- Holding unrealistic or unexpressed expectations and/or assumptions about your partner and the relationship
- Not asking for what you want and need
- Saying and/or doing only what you think your partner wants, ignoring your needs, feelings, beliefs, and desires
- Lying, deceiving, playing games, or being passively aggressive
- Trying to change your partner's basic character

- Stifling your partner's growth as an individual (i.e., interfering with his self-actualization and eventual transcendence)
- Blaming your partner for most or all of your relationship/life problems
- Ignoring the effect your upbringing and child experiences have had on your behavior and your relationship
- Assuming you know what your partner thinks and feels
- Living in the past and refusing to let go of old resentments
- Emphasizing problems, obstacles, and negative emotions: anger, resentment, bitterness, envy, and scorn

Source: Both lists adapted with permission from the Relationship Institute, Copyright © 2005. All rights reserved.

Making Your Bond Stronger

We know what works for couples: Mutual trust and intimacy are achieved and improved through communication. After you have traveled on this emotional journey together, you're likely to find that your bond is even stronger than it was before. Your mate will, with your support, know what security and trust feel like, perhaps for the first time in his life, giving both of you the

Take the Time to Ask How Your Mate Is Doing.

The following open-ended questions are ideal communication starters for you as your mate begins his abuse recovery:

- "How does this affect you now?"
- "How does this make you feel?"
- "How can I help you?"
- "What can I do to make this better for you?"

Not intrusive, yet showing that you care and are willing to listen and to help, these questions are usually well received. They allow your partner to respond as simply or as elaborately as makes him comfortable.

emotional fortitude to go into uncharted water. As a couple, you will go forward having the ability to face issues and knowing that you will emotionally support each other with hard-earned, carefully tended, mutual love.

During the process of healing, you will see that your partner might feel a need to share his experiences immediately; for others, it might take awhile. Still, there are some who might prefer to address and release the trauma of their abuse by themselves, or confidentially, with a therapist or within the safe confines of a group of fellow supporters. Do not judge his level of caring by whether your mate includes you in this endeavor. As the significant other of a man who has been abused, you have to realize that he owns the healing process. Although his abuse has caused a pain and hurt that often affects others (particularly a romantic mate), it's an experience that can be reconciled only by the person who was abused. When and if your partner is ready, your greatest gift to him will be your steady, nonintrusive supportive and care. Later, you'll reap the reward of your patience and emotional generosity through your deepening bond of commitment and a warm, fulfilling relationship.

Finally, always speak with your partner clearly, calmly, and from the heart. Strive for harmony when possible and de-escalate conflict when it arises. Always discuss differences respectfully and peacefully, allowing for differences of perception and possible options for resolution. As with all things precious, human relationships are complex, and maintaining them requires effort. A relationship with a man who has been abused is even more fragile, calling for even more emotional resources. As his mate, you will need patience and commitment to be steady, waiting, "[T]ill the bridge you will need, be form'd—till the ductile anchor hold; Till the gossamer thread you fling, catch somewhere" (Walt Whitman, "A Noiseless Patient Spider").

Glossary

adrenal hormones: hormones that control important functions such as blood pressure.

affect: the word used to describe a person's emotional state from an observer's perspective. It is a generalized feeling tone, an external, observable manifestation of emotion or feeling, such as *labile*, which means having rapid mood swings from happy to sad.

allostasis: maintaining homeostasis (stability) through change, referring to the adaptive output of stress hormones for a time in response to a perceived external threat. The system turns off when safety is restored, allowing the organism to return to balance and stability.

allostatic load: a lack of adaptation, when the body is no longer able to regulate the output of stress hormones, due to overload. Over time, this "load" can lead to organ destruction and other disease.

alexithymia: difficulty identifying, describing, and communicating one's feelings.

amygdala: the part of the brain that regulates emotions and triggers danger. This is important for conditional learning.

antidepressants: medications used in the treatment of depression.

attachment: the term generally used to describe the tie of an infant or a child to a parent or caregiver.

avoidance: the act of removing oneself physically or emotionally or the act of shunning another.

bonding: the term referring to the emotional tie from parent to infant or a mature person for another mature person.

BPD: see *borderline personality disorder*.

borderline personality disorder (BPD): a disorder characterized by extreme instability and impulsivity with fear of abandonment, which can be self-injurious.

cognitive-behavioral therapy (CBT): a form of therapy in which the therapist teaches the patient to reconstruct his cognitive beliefs (thought patterns) that will hopefully then alter behaviors.

CAOs: "concerned and affected others," referring to a spouse, parent, partner, child, or other family member of a problem drinker or substance abuser.

CAT: see *cognitive analytic therapy.*

catecholamines: chemicals that act as hormones or neurotransmitters, including adrenaline (epinephrine), noradrenaline (norepinephrine), and dopamine, that affect body and brain function through the sympathetic nervous system, particularly in response to stress.

child sexual abuse (CSA): sexual contact, in which one party (the victim) is a child (or at least five years younger than the other party) and the other party (the perpetrator) is in a position of power.

COAs: "children of alcoholics."

codependence: the state in which one exhibits overdependence on another person or thing. Often that person will attempt to influence the thoughts, actions, or behaviors of another.

cognitive analytic therapy (CAT): an eclectic form of therapy where the patient works along with the therapist as the patient learns how to change or moderate his behaviors. The goal is to show the patient how he can modify his behaviors and give the patient a sense of control and power over his life.

cognitive distortion: negative thinking that leads to negative emotions. The elimination of these negative thoughts is believed to help rid the person of, or lessen, depression and anxiety. The term used for this process is *cognitive restructuring.*

corticotropin-releasing factor (CRF): a hormone believed to have a role in the stress responses, which may play a role in affective disorders.

CSA: see *child sexual abuse.*

DBT: see *dialectical behavior therapy.*

defense mechanism: an automatic, mostly unconscious, psychological process that serves to protect the psyche from anxiety and internal or external stressors.

delusions: false beliefs that are obviously untrue but that cannot be reasoned away. For example, a person with schizophrenia may believe that he is the president of the United States when he is not.

dialectical behavior therapy (DBT): a form of therapy used in the treatment of borderline personality disorder. The therapist works to reduce behaviors impinging on the patient's life. DBT is used to teach the patient skills that will allow him to cope with the severe mood changes he experiences. This is done on a weekly basis and may also involve group therapy to teach interpersonal relations.

DID: see *dissociative identity disorder.*

dissociative behavior: an interruption of the person's usual functioning of memory, identity, or perceptions of his environment.

dissociative identity disorder (DID): a disorder characterized by the existence in an individual with two or more personalities with distinct thoughts and behaviors. The host personality may be completely unaware of the other personalities.

dopamine: a hormonelike substance or chemical (neurotransmitter) that transmits signals between nerve cells. It plays an important role in our mental and physical health. Drugs like Effexor (venlafaxine) affect dopamine levels.

DSM: *Diagnostic and Statistical Manual of Mental Disorders,* the American Psychological Association's classification system for mental disorders.

ego defense mechanism: an automatic psychological process that protects the person from anxiety or perceived stressors.

enabling: acting to protect a person from the consequences (usually harmful) of his (or her) behavior. Enablers typically "enable," or protect, the person by lying to others about his (or her) bad behavior, keeping secrets, making excuses, or providing shelter, jobs, or money. Unlike helping, enabling permits a person to act irresponsibly when he (or she) could, if he (or she) wanted to, act differently.

encopresis: defecation or "soiling" in inappropriate places, in clothing or bed.

enuresis: wetting oneself or bedwetting,

ephebophilia: a word literally derived from combining the Greek words *ephebos* (ε'φηβoς), meaning "adolescent," and *philia*, (φιλια) meaning "friendship" or "love." It is now used to describe those who are sexually attracted to postpubescent youngsters (ranging in age from twelve to seventeen years) of either sex. The term *ephebophile* is most commonly encountered in articles about priests, coaches, or teachers who sexually abuse the adolescents (but not technically "children") in their care.

exhibitionism: a paraphiliac behavior characterized by sexual arousal produced by exposure of the person's genitals, usually to strangers

externalizing: the state in which a person outwardly directs emotional symptoms, resulting in conduct that is angry, aggressive, antisocial, and undercontrolled.

family of origin: the family in which one was born or raised.

Federal Child Abuse Prevention and Treatment Act (CAPTA): a federal law setting forth standards for the states to protect children from abuse.

fetishism: a paraphiliac behavior in which one achieves sexual arousal from inanimate objects, such as shoes or clothing.

fight-or-flight response: an instinctual, automatic response to danger or perceived danger whereby the brain signals the release of stress hormones from adrenal glands that cause increased heartbeat and respirations; blood flows away from extremities to larger muscles, perspiration increases, pupils dilate, senses of hearing and smell are heightened, and digestion, growth, tissue repair, immune system functioning are interrupted, preparing the body to flee or fight.

free association: a psychoanalytic term that refers to uncensored material that the patient presents during therapy.

Freudian slip: a verbal misspeak (unconscious) that is thought to have some hidden meaning.

frotteurism: a paraphiliac behavior in which one's arousal is attained from rubbing or touching unsuspecting others without permission, often achieved in crowded public places like trains, buses, or elevators.

glucocorticoids: a chemical that helps convert proteins and fats (lipids) to carbohydrates to replenish the body's energy reserves after a time of activity. It also plays a role in increasing appetite and food-seeking behavior.

guilt: feeling regret or remorse over an action or deed that one has committed.

hallucinations: false sensory perceptions, often hearing voices or seeing visions that other people can't hear or see.

hippocampus: a small structure shaped like a seahorse, found deep in the forebrain. We have two, one in each brain hemisphere. The hippocampus is part of the limbic system, and its primary function is to encode memories so they can be stored in the brain. It is constantly forming new neurons throughout life.

hyperarousal: an extreme level of arousal marked by easy startle-response, intense reactions, and insomnia, often occurring when the nervous system is malfunctioning.

hypothalamic-pituitary-adrenal axis (HPA): the glands that release the substances such as cortisol that are known to be elevated in abused children. These substances are also suspected to cause possible abnormalities in behaviors such as sleep disturbances and anxiety.

incest: from the Latin word *incestum*, meaning "not chaste." Today it refers to sexual relations between people who are too closely related to marry, generally, parent-child and siblings.

interdependence: the dynamic of being mutually responsible to, and dependent on, others, recognizing the interrelatedness of individuals within family, community, and society.

internalizing: the state in which a person inwardly directs emotional symptoms, resulting in conduct that is anxious, fearful, inhibited, depressed, and overcontrolled.

iatrogenic: an ailment, an adverse condition, or a complication in a patient that is physician-induced or caused by medical treatment.

libido: the Latin word for "I desire"; now understood as sex drive or, per Freud, the life drive.

Likert scale: a range in which people indicate their level of agreement with statements that express a favorable or unfavorable attitude toward what is being measured, usually expressed on a number continuum from zero to five, with each end being the most extreme answers.

limbic system: a system of neural structures deep in the brain, about the size of peach pit, that regulates one's sense of smell, primary drives (sex, hunger, thirst, aggression, pleasure, pain, fear, greed), feelings (i.e., "affective states," including emotions like joy, amusement, sorrow, and contentment), memory, and motivation. It also controls the body's endocrine (hormonal) and autonomic (involuntary) nervous systems (governing muscle movement, like breathing, heartbeat, and digestion).

marriage and family therapist: a professional licensed to treat family and individuals and who treats many forms of mental illnesses. License requirements depend on the state.

masochism: a paraphiliac behavior in which the person's sexual urges and arousal are based on suffering, whether emotional—like being humiliated—or physical—like being whipped; but in whatever form, receiving or experiencing infliction of pain from another, is necessary for release.

Minnesota Multiphasic Personality Inventory-II (MMPI-II): a standardized test used to sort out behavior that will indicate the possibility of pathology. It is based on self-reported responses—true, false, or can not say—from a series of 567 questions that address a person's feelings, behaviors, and attitudes as well as overt symptoms of psychopathology. As a result of their trauma and resulting psychological distress—such as dissociation, social isolation, and depression—adult victims of child sexual abuse may have an elevated "F" scale score. (The "F" scale in the MMPI-II is generally a means to determine a person's "malingering" or overreporting—exaggeration or fabrication—of symptoms.)

National Child Protection Act (NCPA): also known as the Oprah Winfrey Act; established procedures for child care providers to perform national background checks on potential workers. The goal was to enable an employer or organization to check a person's fingerprints against this national registry and prevent criminals from obtaining jobs or volunteer positions with access to kids, the disabled, or the elderly. In 1998, the NCPA was amended and strengthened by passage of the Volunteers for Children Act (VCA).

neurotic: from the Latin word for "nervous," a term used for people who suffer from any mental disorder that may cause distress but that does not interfere with rational thoughts or the ability to function, unlike psychosis, which refers to severe disorders. Many psychology teachers explain the difference between the neurotic and psychotic by saying, "The neurotic builds sand castles in the sky; the psychotic lives in them; and the psychiatrist collects the rent."

neuroleptics: antipsychotic drugs sometimes used to treat borderline personality disorder. They can reduce hostility and irritability in some patients, though with possibly unpleasant side effects.

neurotransmitters: substances such as norepinephrine, dopamine, and serotonin, which are released in the brain.

noogenic neurosis: a term used in logotherapy; the belief that noogenic neurosis is not from the psychological but (from the Greek *noos*, meaning "mind") from human existence.

ontological: a branch of philosophy involved with the logical investigation of ways in which things exist, such as numbers or concepts.

paranoia: suspicions of others not based on facts.

paraphilia: sexual urges or sexual fantasies concerning items or actions that some would call "kinky" and involving humiliation or suffering. Paraphilia can interfere with a person's ability to engage in mutually satisfying sexual relationships.

PD: see *personality disorder.*

pederasty: a word literally derived from combining the Greek word *pais* (παις), meaning "boy" or "child," and *erastês*, meaning "lover." Today, the term is used to describe sexual relations between adult men and young men or boys to whom they are not biologically related.

pedophilia: a word literally derived from combining the Greek words *pais* (παις), meaning "boy" or "child," and *philia* (φιλια), meaning "friendship" or "love." It is now used to describe those who are sexually attracted to prepubescent children, which means children under age twelve or thirteen.

personality disorder (PD): a maladaptive set of characteristics, which when examined by a professional can be diagnosed as a known mental disorder.

post-traumatic stress disorder (PTSD): a disorder that includes heightened startle responses. The symptoms include re-experiencing the trauma through flashbacks or perhaps dreams. Some will use avoidance to cope.

privilege: See *privileged communications.*

privileged communications: the idea that a conversation between an individual and certain other classes of individuals or professionals are protected from disclosure, even against the power of a subpoena demanding their divulgence. The oldest—in this country—and most rigorously guarded privileged communication is the attorney-client privilege, which protects all confidential interactions between a client and his or her counsel, deeming them sacrosanct and beyond intrusion from third parties. An exception to this privilege exists, however, in the event that the client tells the lawyer of his or her intent (relating to future—not past—conduct) to commit a crime or perpetrate a fraud on the court; then the lawyer has a duty to alert the appropriate authorities. Other kinds of privileges exist, but are sometimes accorded less protection than that of the attorney-client privilege. They are the doctor-patient privilege; the psychiatrist- or psychologist-patient privilege; the husband-wife privilege; and the clergy-penitent privilege. The privilege is held by the one protected, not the one who must keep the secret, and can only be waived by that protected person, such as the client in the case of the attorney-client privilege. In the world of mandatory reporting of child abuse, privilege does not exempt someone from the duty to report.

psychasthenia: a disorder characterized by phobias, obsessive compulsion, or excessive anxiety. (This term is no longer in scientific use.)

psychotic: a term used for loss of contact with reality, whereby a person might experience hallucinations, delusions, and withdrawal.

psychiatrist: a medical doctor who specializes in mental illnesses.

psychologist: a licensed professional who treats all forms of mental illness. Licensure requirements depend on the state.

psychopathology: the research dealing with or study of diagnostic categories of clinical psychiatry.

psychotropic: medication used for treatment of mental illness.

PTSD: see *post-traumatic stress disorder.*

sadism: a paraphiliac behavior characterized by arousal or urges based on conduct that inflicts and causes humiliation—or some form of suffering—to another.

schizophrenia: a mental illness that often begins in adolescence or early childhood. Symptoms may include delusions, hallucinations, disorganized thoughts and speech, and inappropriate affect.

sequela (*pl.* **sequalae**): a condition or symptom following an illness, incident (e.g., sexual abuse), or disorder.

serotonin: a neurotransmitter involved in mood, sleep, appetite, and impulsive behavior.

shame: feeling bad about oneself.

SNRIs: "Selective Norepinephrine Reuptake Inhibitors"; antidepressants that affect serotonin and norepinephrine pathways in the brain. SNRIs may be effective in people who do not find relief with an SSRI. Venlafaxine (Effexor) is an example of an SNRI.

SSRIs: "Selective Serotonin Reuptake Inhibitors"; drugs that work by balancing the brain's serotonin levels. They reduce anxiety, aggression, depression, and impulsive behavior in some people. Here are the common generic and brand names: citalopram (Celexa); escitalopram (Lexapro); fluoxetine (Prozac); fluovoxamine (Luvox); paroxetine (Paxil); and sertraline (Zoloft).

somatic complaints: physical complaints not found, upon medical examination, to have a physical source.

sympathetic nervous system (SNS): a branch of the autonomic nervous system that is responsible for the body's energy during stress. This is part of the nervous system over which the person has no conscious control—that is, it regulates the heart, lungs, and blood vessels.

transvestitism: a paraphiliac activity characterized by enjoyment, and some arousal, from wearing the clothing of the opposite gender.

voyeurism: a paraphiliac activity in which a person has the urge to observe unsuspecting people, usually strangers, who are naked, or disrobing, or in the act of sex. This is proverbial "peeping tom" behavior.

References

Chapter One

Chandy, J., R. Blum, and M. Resnick, "Gender-Specific Outcomes and Sexually Abused Adolescents," *Child Abuse and Neglect*, Vol. 20, no. 12, 1996, pp. 1219–231.

Dallam, S. J., "Science or Propaganda? An Examination of Rind, Tromovitch and Bauserman (1998)," *Journal of Child Sexual Abuse*, Vol. 9, nos. 3/4, 2002, pp. 109–34. Also appearing as a chapter in: Whitfield, Charles L., Joyanna Silberg, and Paul Jay Fink, eds., *Misinformation Concerning Child Sexual Abuse and Adult Survivors* (Binghamton, NY: Haworth Press, 2002).

Dong, M., R. F. Anda, V. J. Felitti, S. R. Dube, D. F. Williamson, T. J. Thompson, C. M. Loo, and W. H. Giles, "The Interrelatedness of Multiple Forms of Childhood Abuse, Neglect, and Household Dysfunction," *Child Abuse and Neglect*, Vol. 28, no. 7, 2004, pp. 771–84.

Dube, S. R., R. F. Anda, C. L. Whitfield, D. W. Brown, V. J. Felitti, M. Dong, and W. H. Giles, "Long-Term Consequences of Childhood Sexual Abuse by Gender of Victim," *American Journal of Preventive Medicine*, Vol. 28, 2005, pp. 430–38.

Edwards, V. J., R. F. Anda, S. R. Dube, M. Dong, D. F. Chapman and V. J. Felitti, "The Wide-Ranging Health Consequences of Adverse Childhood Experiences," in Kathleen Kendall-Tackett and Sarah Giacomoni, eds., *Victimization of Children and Youth: Patterns of Abuse, Response Strategies* (Kingston, NJ: Civic Research Institute, 2005).

Finkelhor, D., and A. Browne, "The Traumatic Impact of Child Sexual Abuse: A Conceptualization," *American Journal Orthopsychiatry*, Vol. 55, 1985, pp. 530–41.

Finkelhor, D., G. Hotaling, I. A. Lewis, and C. Smith, "Sexual Abuse in a National Survey of Adult Men and Women: Prevalence, Characteristics, and Risk Factors," *Child Abuse and Neglect*, Vol. 14, 1990, pp. 19–28.

Garnefski, N., and E. Arends, "Sexual Abuse and Adolescent Maladjustment: Differences Between Male and Female Victims," *Journal of Adolescence*, Vol. 21, 1998, pp. 99–107.

Hunter, M., *Abused Boys: The Neglected Victims of Sexual Abuse* (New York: Fawcett Columbine/Ballantine, 1990).

Hunter, M., ed., *The Sexually Abused Male*. Volume I: *Prevalence, Impact, and Treatment* (New York: Lexington Books, 1990).

Roesler, T. A., and N. McKenzie, "Effects of Childhood Trauma on Psychological Functioning in Adults Sexually Abused as Children," *Journal of Nervous and Mental Disease*, Vol. 182, 1994, pp. 145–50.

Chapter Two

Araki, G. (Director). *Mysterious Skin* [Motion picture], (2005).

Berry, J. *Lead Us Not into Temptation: Catholic Priests and the Sexual Abuse of Children* (New York: Doubleday, 2000).

Boston Globe (Investigative Staff). *Betrayal: The Crisis in the Catholic Church* (Boston: Little, Brown, 2002).

Boyle, P. *Scout's Honor: Sexual Abuse in America's Most Trusted Institution* (Rocklin, CA: Prima Lifestyles, 1995).

Conroy, P. *Prince of Tides* (Boston: Houghton Mifflin, 1986).

De Milly, W. *In My Father's Arms: A True Story of Incest* (Madison, WI: University of Wisconsin Press, 1999).

Dick, K. (Director). *Twist of Faith* [Motion picture], (2005).

Elliott, M., K. Browne, and J. Kilcoyne, "Child Sexual Abuse Prevention: What Offenders Tell Us," *Child Abuse and Neglect*, Vol. 19, 1995, pp. 279–94.

Finkelhor, David. *Child Sexual Abuse* (New York: Free Press, 1984).

Gilgun, J. F. "Children and Adolescents with Problematic Sexual Behaviors: Lessons from Research on Resilience," in R. Longo and D. Prescott, eds., *Current Perspectives on Working with Sexually Aggressive Youth and Youth with Sexual Behavior Problems* (Holyoke, MA: Neari Press, in press).

Heim, S. *Mysterious Skin* (New York: HarperCollins, 1995).

John Jay College of Criminal Justice. "The Nature and Scope of Sexual Abuse of Minors by Catholic Priests and Deacons in the United States 1950–2002," 2004, *www.jjay.cuny.edu*.

Krug, R., "Adult Male Report of Childhood Sexual Abuse by Mothers," *Child Abuse & Neglect*, Vol. 13, no. 1, 1989, pp. 111–19.

Nelson, R. M., with R. M. Fitzgibbon, "Why I'm Every Mother's Worst Fear," *Redbook*, April 1992, pp. 85–87, 116.

Rossetti, S. J., "The Impact of Child Sexual Abuse on Attitudes Toward God and the Catholic Church," *Child Abuse and Neglect*, Vol. 19, 1995, pp. 1469–481.

Salter, A. C., *Predators: Pedophiles, Rapists and Other Sex Offenders: Who They Are, How They Operate, and How We Can Protect Ourselves and Our Children.* (New York: Basic Books, 2003).

Spandauer, T. *The Man Who Fell in Love with the Moon* (New York: HarperCollins, 1992).

Winn, M. E., "The Strategic and Systematic Management of Denial in the Cognitive/Behavioral Treatment of Sexual Offenders," *Sexual Abuse: A Journal of Research and Treatment*, Vol. 8, no. 1, 1996, pp. 25–36.

Chapter Three

Binder, R. L., D. E. McNiel, and R. L. Goldstone, "Is Adaptive Coping Possible for Adult Survivors of Childhood Sexual Abuse?" *Psychiatric Services*, Vol. 47, no. 2, 1996, pp. 186–88.

Friedrich, W. N., and P. N. Gorber, "Autoerotic Asphyxia: The Development of a Paraphilia," *Journal of the American Academy of Child and Adolescent Psychiatry*, Vol. 33, no. 7, 1994, pp. 970–74.

McEwen, B. S., "Allostasis and Allostatic Load: Implications for Neuropsychopharmacology," *Neuropsychopharmacology*, Vol. 22, no. 2, 2000, pp. 108–24.

McEwen, B. S., "Protective and Damaging Effects of Stress Mediators," *The New England Journal of Medicine*, Vol. 338, 1998, pp. 171–79.

Schaaf, K. K., and T. R. McCanne, "Relationship of Childhood Sexual, Physical, and Combined Sexual and Physical Abuse to Adult Victimization and Posttraumatic Stress Disorder," *Child Abuse and Neglect*, Vol. 22, 1998, pp. 1119–33.

van der Kolk, B. A., A. C. McFarlane, and L. Weisaeth, eds. *Traumatic Stress: The Effects of Overwhelming Experience on Mind, Body, and Society* (New York: Guilford Press, 1996), pp. 3–23.

Zeitlin, S. B., R. J. McNally, and K. L. Cassiday, "Alexithymia in Victims of Sexual Assault: An Effect of Repeated Traumatization?" *American Journal of Psychiatry*, Vol. 150, no. 4, 1993, pp. 661–66.

Chapter Four

Diagnostic and Statistical Manual of Mental Disorders—Fourth Edition, Text Revision (DSM-IV-TR) (Washington DC: American Psychiatric Association; 2000).

MacMillan, H. L., J. E. Fleming, D. L. Streiner, E. Lin, M. H. Boyle, E. Jamieson, E. K. Duku, C. A. Walsh, M. Y.-Y. Wong, and W. R. Beardslee, "Childhood Abuse and Lifetime Psychopathology in a Community Sample," *American Journal of Psychiatry*, Vol. 158, 2001, pp. 1878–83.

Pelcovitz, D., B. A. van der Kolk, S. Roth, F. Mandel, S. Kaplan, and P. Resick, "Development of a Criteria Set and a Structured Interview for Disorders of Extreme Stress (SIDES)," *Journal of Traumatic Stress*, Vol. 10, no. 1, 1996, pp. 3–16.

Widom, C. S., "Posttraumatic Stress Disorder in Abused and Neglected Children Grown Up," *American Journal Psychiatry*, Vol. 156, August 1999, pp. 1223–29.

Chapter Five

Gold, S. N., B. A. Lucenko, J. D. Elhai, J. M. Swingle, and A. H. Sellers, "A Comparison of Psychological/Psychiatric Symptomatology of Women and Men Sexually Abused as Children," *Child Abuse and Neglect*, Vol. 23, no. 7, 1999, pp. 683–92.

Goodman, M., A. New, and L. Siever, "Trauma, Genes, and the Neurobiology of Personality Disorders," *Annals of the New York Academy of Sciences*, Vol. 1032, 2004, pp. 104–16.

Holmes, T., and R. Rahe, "Social Readjustment Rating Scale," *Journal of Psychosomatic Research*, Vol. 11, 1967, p. 214.

Paris, J., H. Zweig-Frank, M. Bond, and J. Guzder, "Defense Styles, Hostility, and Psychological Risk Factors in Male Patients with Personality Disorders." *Journal of Nervous & Mental Disease*, Vol. 184, no. 3, 1996, pp 153–58.

Paris, J., H. Zweig-Frank, and J. Guzder, "Risk Factors for Borderline Personality in Male Outpatients," *Journal of Nervous & Mental Disease*, Vol. 182, no. 7, 1994, pp. 375–80.

Paivio, S., and C. Laurent, "Empathy and Emotion Regulation: Reprocessing Memories of Childhood Abuse," *Journal of Clinical Psychology*, Vol. 57, 2001, pp. 213–26.

Salzman, J. P., C. Salzman, A. N. Wolfson, M. Albanese, J. Looper, M. Ostacher, J. Schwartz, G. Chinman, W. Land, and E. Miyawaki, "Association between Borderline Personality Structure and History of Childhood Abuse in Adult Volunteers," *Comprehensive Psychiatry*, Vol. 34, no. 4, 1993, pp. 254–57.

Chapter Six

Fabry, J., *Guideposts to Meaning: Discovering What Really Matters* (Oakland, CA: New Harbinger, 1988).

Frankl, V. E., *Man's Search for Meaning: An Introduction to Logotherapy* (Boston, MA: Beacon Press, 1962, 1970).

Hoffman, E., *The Drive for Self: Alfred Adler and the Founding of Individual Psychology* (Reading, MA: Perseus Books, 1996).

Lear, J., *Open-Minded: Working Out the Logic of the Soul* (Cambridge, MA: Harvard University Press, 1998).

Pennebaker, J. W., *Opening Up: The Healing Power of Expressing Emotions* (New York: Guilford Press, 1997).

Pennebaker, James W. *Writing to Heal: A Guided Journal for Recovering from Trauma and Emotional Upheaval* (Oakland, CA: New Harbinger, 2004).

Pennebaker, J. W., J. K. Kiecolt-Glaser, and R. Glaser, "Disclosure of Traumas and Immune Function: Health Implications for Psychotherapy," *Journal of Consulting and Clinical Psychology*, Vol. 56, 1988, pp. 239–45.

Chapter Seven

Dube, S. R., R. F. Anda, C. L. Whitfield, D. W. Brown, V. J. Felitti, M. Dong, and W. H. Giles, "Long-Term Consequences of Childhood Sexual Abuse by Gender of Victim," *American Journal of Preventive Medicine*, Vol. 28, 2005, pp. 430–38.

Lyons, D., "Sex, God & Greed," *Forbes Magazine*, 9 June 2003, *www.forbes.com/forbes/2003/0609/066.html*.

Schaefer, J., P. Montemurri, and A. Capeloto, "Tom Paciorek Breaks Silence: Ex-Baseball Star: Priest Abused Me 'God, Is This Ever Going to End?' He Recalls Thinking at 16," *Detroit Free Press*, 22 March 2002, *www.freep.com/news/metro/priest22_20020322.htm*.

Chapter Eight

Beattie, M., *Codependent No More: How to Stop Controlling Others and Start Caring for Yourself* (San Francisco: Harper/Hazelden, 1987).

Briere, J., and J. Conte, "Self-Reported Amnesia for Abuse in Adults Molested as Children," *Journal of Traumatic Stress*, Vol. 6, no. 1, 1993, pp. 21–31.

Collins, B. G., "Reconstruing Codependency Using Self-in-Relation Theory: A Feminist Perspective," *Social Work*, Vol. 38, no. 4, 1993, pp. 470–76.

Cowan, G., M. Bommersbach, and S. Curtis, "Codependency, Loss of Self, and Power," *Psychology of Women Quarterly*, Vol. 19, no. 2, 1995, pp. 221–36.

Fischer, J., R. Wampler, K. Lyness, and E. Thomas, "Offspring Codependency: Blocking the Impact of the Family of Origin," *Family Dynamics of Addiction Quarterly*, Vol. 2, 1992, pp. 1–12.

Fortin, N., K. Agster, and H. Eichenbaum, "Critical Role of the Hippocampus in Memory for Sequences of Events," *Nature Neuroscience*, Vol. 5, no. 5, 2002, pp. 458–62.

Freyd, J. J., "Betrayal Trauma: Traumatic Amnesia as an Adaptive Response to Childhood Abuse," *Ethics & Behavior*, Vol. 4, no. 4, 1994, pp. 307–29, *www.dynamic.uoregon.edu/~jjf/articles/freyd94.pdf.*

Harkness, D., M. Swenson, K. Madsen-Hampton, and R. Hale, "The Development, Reliability, and Validity of a Clinical Rating Scale for Co-Dependency," *Journal of Psychoactive Drugs*, Vol. 33, no. 2, 2001, pp. 159–71.

Jordan, J. V., A. J. Kaplan, J. B. Miller, I. P. Stiver, and J. L. Surrey. *Women's Growth in Connecting: Writings from the Stone Center* (New York: Guilford Press, 1991).

Love, P., and S. Shulkin, "Imago Theory and the Psychology of Attraction," *The Family Journal*, Vol. 9, no. 3, 2001, pp. 246–49.

Whitfield, C. L., J. Silberg, and P. J. Fink, eds., *Misinformation Concerning Child Sexual Abuse and Adult Survivors* (Binghamton, NY: Haworth Press, 2002).

Chapter Nine

Black, C. A., and R. R. DeBlassie, "Sexual Abuse in Male Children and Adolescents: Indicators, Effects, and Treatments," *Adolescence*, Vol. 28, no. 109, spring 1993, pp. 123–33, *www.findarticles.com/p/articles/mi_m2248/is_n109_v28/ai_13885848.*

Briere, J. N., *Child Abuse Trauma: Theory and Treatment of the Lasting Effects.* (Newbury Park, CA: Sage, 1992).

Briere, J., D. Evans, M. Runtz, and T. Wall, "Symptomatology in Men Who Were Molested as Children: A Comparison Study," *American Journal of Orthopsychiatry.* Vol. 58, no. 3, July 1998, pp. 457–61.

Briere, J., and M. Runtz, "Symptomatology Associated with Childhood Sexual Victimization in a Nonclinical Adult Sample," *Child Abuse and Neglect*, Vol. 12, 1988, pp. 51–59.

Hendrix, H., *Getting the Love You Want* (New York: Owl Books, 2001).

Kreidler, W. J. *Creative Conflict Resolution: More Than 200 Activities for Keeping Peace in the Classroom* (Glenview, IL: Scott Foresman/Addison-Wesley, 1984).

Luterek, J. A., G. Harb, R. G. Heimberg, and B. P. Marx, "Interpersonal Rejection Sensitivity in Childhood Sexual Abuse Survivors," *Journal of Interpersonal Violence*, Vol. 19, no. 1, 2004, pp. 90–107. http://jiv .sagepub.com/cgi/reprint/19/1/90.

Mullen, P. E., and J. Fleming, "Long-Term Effects of Child Sexual Abuse." *Issues in Child Abuse Prevention*, 9, 1998.

Chapter Ten

Black, C. A., and R. R. DeBlassie, "Sexual Abuse in Male Children and Adolescents: Indicators, Effects, and Treatments," *Adolescence*, Vol. 28, no. 109, spring 1993, pp. 123–33, *www.findarticles.com/p/articles/mi_ m2248/is_n109_v28/ai_13885848.*

Browne, A., and D. Finkelhor, "Impact of Child Sexual Abuse: A Review of the Research," *Psychological Bulletin*, Vol. 99, no. 1, 1986, pp. 66–77.

Chapter Eleven

Battista, J., and R. Almond, "The Development of Meaning in Life," *Psychiatry*, Vol. 36, 1973, pp. 409–27.

Chamberlain, K., and S. Zika, "Measuring Meaning in Life: An Examination of Three Scales," *Personality and Individual Differences*, Vol. 9, 1988, pp. 589–96.

Crumbaugh, J. C., "Cross-Validation of Purpose in Life Test Based on Frankl's Concepts," *Journal of Individual Psychology*, Vol. 24, 1968, pp. 74–81.

Crumbaugh, J. C., and L. T. Maholick, "An Experimental Study in Existentialism: The Psychometric Approach to Frankl's Concept of Noogenic Neurosis," *Journal of Clinical Psychology*, Vol. 20, 1964, pp. 589–96.

Crumbaugh, J. C., and L. T. Maholick, *Manual of Instruction for the Purpose-in-Life-Test* (Munster, TN: Psychometric Affiliates, 1969).

Debats, D. L., P. M. van der Lubbe, and F. R. A. Wezeman, "On the Psychometric Properties of the Life Regard Index (LRI): A Measure of Meaningful Life. An Evaluation in Three Independent Samples Based on the Dutch

Version," *Personality and Individual Differences*, Vol. 14, 1993, pp. 337–45, *http://dissertations.ub.rug.nl/FILES/faculties/ppsw/1996/d.l.h.m.debats/c4.pdf.*

Frankl, V. E. *Man's Search for Meaning* (New York: Washington Square Press, 1963).

Hartman, D., and D. Zimberoff, "Existential Resistance to Life: Ambivalence, Avoidance & Control," *Journal of Heart-Centered Therapies*, spring 2004, *www.findarticles.com/p/articles/mi_m0FGV/is_1_7/ai_n6170890/pg_1.*

Lavee, Y., H. I. McCubbin, and D. H. Olson, "The Effect of Stressful Life Events and Transitions on Family Functioning and Well-Being," *Journal of Marriage and the Family*, Vol. 49, 1987, pp. 857–73.

Scheier, M. F., and C. S. Carver, "Optimism, Coping and Health: Assessment and Implications of Generalized Outcome Expectancies," *Health Psychology*, Vol. 4, 1985, pp. 219–47.

Spranger, E. *Types of Men: The Psychology and Ethics of Personality.* (New York: Johnson, 1966).

Zika, S., and K. Chamberlain, "On the Relationship Between Meaning in Life and Psychological Well-Being," *British Journal of Psychology*, Vol. 83, 1992, pp. 133–45.

Chapter Twelve

Alcohol Problems in Intimate Relationships. Identification and Intervention, A Guide for Marriage and Family Therapists. National Institute on Alcohol Abuse and Alcoholism (NIAAA), 5635 Fishers Lane, MSC 9304, Bethesda, MD 20892-9304, *http://pubs.niaaa.nih.gov/publications/niaaa-guide/NIAAA_AAMF_%20Final.pdf.*

Cosway, R., N. S. Endler, A. J. Sadler, and I. J. Deary, "The Coping Inventory for Stressful Situations: Factorial Structure and Associations with Personality Traits and Psychological Health," *Journal of Applied Biobehavioral Research*, Vol. 5, no. 2, 2000, pp. 121–143, *www.bellpub.com/jabr/2000/th000203.pdf.*

Endler, N. S., and J.D.A. Parker, *Coping Inventory for Stressful Situations (CISS) Manual* (Toronto, Canada: Multi-Health Systems, 1990).

Folkman, S., and R. S. Lazarus. *Manual for Ways of Coping Questionnaire* (Palo Alto, CA: Consulting Psychologists Press, 1988).

Holahan, C. J., and R. H. Moos, "Risk, Resistance, and Psychological Distress: A Longitudinal Analysis with Adults and Children," *Journal of Abnormal Psychology*, Vol. 96, 1987, pp. 3–13.

Krishnan, M., J. Orford, C. Bradbury, A. Copello, and R. Velleman, "Drug & Alcohol Problems: The Users' Perspective on Family Members' Coping," *Drug & Alcohol Review*, Vol. 20, 2001. pp. 385–93.

Lazarus, R. S. *Psychological Stress and the Coping Process* (New York: McGraw-Hill, 1966).

Lazarus, R. S., "Stress, Coping and Illness," in H. S. Friedman, ed., *Personality and Disease* (Chichester, UK: Wiley, 1990).

Lazarus, R. S., "Toward Better Research on Stress and Coping," *American Psychologist*, Vol. 55, 2000, pp. 665–73.

Lazarus, R. S., and S. Folkman. *Stress, Appraisal and Coping* (New York: Springer, 1984).

Moos, R. H., and B. S. Moos, *Family Environment Scale Manual: Development Applications, Research*, 3rd ed. (Palo Alto, CA: Consulting Psychologist Press, 1994).

Orford, J., G. Natera, J. Davies, A. Nava, J. Mora, K. Rigby, C. Bradbury, N. Bowie, A. Copello, and R. Velleman, "Tolerate, Engage, or Withdraw: A Study of the Structure of Families Coping with Alcohol and Drug Problems in Southwest England and Mexico," *Addiction*, Vol. 93, 1998, pp. 1799–1813.

Orford, J., L. Templeton, R. Velleman, and A. Copello, "Family Members of Relatives with Alcohol, Drug and Gambling Problems: A Set of Standardized Questionnaires for Assessing Stress, Coping and Strain," *Addiction*, Vol. 100, no. 11, 2005, pp. 1611–24.

Smith, J. E., "Time and Qualitative Time," *Review of Metaphysics*, Vol. 40, no. 1, 1986, pp. 3–16.

Chapter Thirteen

Ainsworth, M.D.S., M. C. Blehar, E. Waters, and S. Wall. *Patterns of Attachment: A Psychological Study of the Strange Situation* (Hillsdale, NJ: Erlbaum, 1978).

Becker, J., and W. Murphy, "What We Know and Don't Know About Assessing and Treating Sex Offenders," *Psychology, Public Policy and Law*, Vol. 4, 1998, pp. 116–37.

Bouvier, P., "Child Sexual Abuse: Vicious Circles of Fate or Paths to Resilience?" *The Lancet*, Vol. 361, no. 9356, 2003, pp. 446–47.

Bowlby, J. *Attachment and Loss:* Volume 1. *Attachment* (London, UK: Penguin, 1969).

Bowlby, J. *Attachment and Loss:* Volume 2. *Separation, Anxiety and Anger.* (New York: Basic Books, 1973).

Bowlby, J. *Attachment and Loss:* Volume 3. *Loss, Sadness and Depression.* (New York: Basic Books, 1980).

Campbell, S. B., "Behavior Problems in Preschool Children: Developmental and Family Issues," *Advances in Clinical Child Psychology*, Vol. 19, 1997, pp. 1–26.

Capaldi, D. M., and G. R. Patterson, "Relation of Parental Transitions to Boys' Adjustment Problems: I. A Linear Hypothesis. II. Mothers at Risk for Transitions and Unskilled Parenting," *Developmental Psychology*, Vol. 3, 1991, pp. 489–504.

Egeland, B., D. Jacobvitz, and L. A. Sroufe, "Breaking the Cycle of Abuse: Relationship Predictors," *Child Development*, Vol. 59, no. 4, 1988, pp. 1080–88.

Fonagy, P., M. Steele, H. Steele, T. Leigh, R. Kennedy, G. Mattoon, and M. Target, "The Predictive Validity of Mary Main's Adult Attachment Interview: A Psychoanalytic and Developmental Perspective on the Transgenerational Transmission of Attachment and Borderline States," in S. Goldberg, R. Muir, and J. Kerr, eds. *Attachment Theory: Social, Developmental and Clinical Perspectives* (Hillsdale, NJ: Analytic Press, 1995).

Gilgun, J. F. "Factors Mediating the Effects of Childhood Maltreatment," in M. Hunter, ed. *The Sexually Abused Male: Prevalence, Impact, and Treatment* (Lexington, MA: Lexington Books, 1990).

Hunter, J., and J. Becker, "Motivators of Adolescent Sex Offenders and Treatment Perspectives," in J. Shaw, ed. *Sexual Aggression* (Washington, DC: American Psychiatric Press, 1998).

Main, M., and E. Hesse, "Parents' Unresolved Traumatic Experiences Are Related to Infant Disorganized Attachment Status: Is Frightened/

Frightening Parental Behavior the Linking Mechanism?" in M. T. Greenberg, D. Cicchetti, and E. M. Cummings, eds., *Attachment in the Preschool Years: Theory, Research, and Intervention* (Chicago: University of Chicago Press, 1990).

Mcginty, S., "Paedophile Plans to Sue Church over Priest Abuse Allegations," *The Scotsman*, 20 August 2005, *http://thescotsman.scotsman.com/ index.cfm?id=1811602005.*

McHale, J., and J. Rasmussen, "Coparental and Family Group-Level Dynamics During Infancy: Early Family Precursors of Child and Family Functioning During Preschool," *Development & Psychopathology*, Vol. 10, 1998, pp. 39–58.

Salter, D., D. McMillan, M. Richards, T. Talbot, J. Hodges, A. Bentovim, R. Hastings, J. Stevenson, and D. Skuse, "Development of Sexually Abusive Behaviour in Sexually Victimised Males: A Longitudinal Study," *The Lancet*, Vol. 361, no. 9356, 2003, pp. 471–76, *http://www .psychology.soton.ac.uk/psyweb/staff/myprofile/myjournals/publications/ jsteven/salter%20et%20al%20Lanct%202003.pdf.*

Waters, T., "Learning to Love: From Your Mother's Arms to Your Lover's Arms," *The Medium (Voice of the University of Toronto)*, Vol. 30, no. 19, 2004, *www.psychology.sunysb.edu/attachment/online/twaters_ medium.pdf.*

Winnicott, D. W. *Mother and Child; A Primer of First Relationships* (New York: Basic Books, 1957).

Chapter Fourteen

Carlson, E. B., *Trauma Assessments: A Clinician's Guide* (New York: Guilford Press, 1997).

Corcoran, J., "In Defense of Mothers of Sexual Abuse Victims," *Families in Society*, Vol. 79, no. 4, 1998, pp. 358–69.

Emery, R. E., and L. Laumann-Billings, "An Overview of the Nature, Causes and Consequences of Abusive Family Relationships: Toward Differentiating Maltreatment and Violence," *American Psychologist*, Vol. 53, no. 2, 1998, pp. 121–35.

Massat, C. R., and M. Lundy, "'Reporting Costs' to Nonoffending Parents in Cases of Intrafamilial Child Sexual Abuse," *Child Welfare*, Vol. 78, no. 4, 1998, pp. 371–88.

Masten, A. S., and J. D. Coatsworth, "The Development of Competence in Favorable and Unfavorable Environments: Lessons from Research on Successful Children," *American Psychologist*, Vol. 53, 1998, pp. 205–20.

McFarlane, A. C., and G. De Girolamo, "The Nature of Traumatic Stressors and the Epidemiology of Posttraumatic Reactions," in B. A. van der Kolk, A. C. McFarlane, and L. Weisaeth, eds., *Traumatic Stress: The Effects of Overwhelming Experience on Mind, Body, and Society* (New York: Guilford Press, 1996).

Pfohl, W., S. R. Jimerson, and P. J. Lazarus, "Developmental Aspects of Psychological Trauma and Grief," in S. E. Brock, P. J. Lazarus, and S. R. Jimerson, eds., *Best Practices in School Crisis Prevention and Intervention.* (Bethesda, MD: National Association of School Psychologists, 2002).

Terr, L. C., "Childhood Traumas: An Outline and Overview," *American Journal of Psychiatry*, Vol. 148, 1991, pp. 10–20.

Wolfelt, A. D., "Children's Grief," in S. E. Brock, P. J. Lazarus, and S. R. Jimerson, eds., *Best Practices in School Crisis Prevention and Intervention.* (Bethesda, MD: National Association of School Psychologists, 2002).

Chapter Fifteen

Briggs, F., and R.M.F. Hawkins, "A Comparison of the Childhood Experiences of Male Child Molesters and Men Who Were Sexually Abused in Childhood and Claimed to Be Nonoffenders," *Child Abuse & Neglect*, Vol. 20, 1996, 221–33.

Bruckner, D. J., and P. E. Johnson, "Treatment for Adult Male Victims of Childhood Sexual Abuse," *Social Casework: The Journal of Contemporary Social Work*, Vol. 68, 1987, pp. 81–87.

Estes, L. S., and R. Tidwell, "Sexually Abused Children's Behaviours: Impact of Gender and Mother's Experience of Intra- and Extra-Familial Sexual Abuse," *Family Practice*, Vol. 19, no. 1, 2002, pp. 36–44, *http://fampra.oxfordjournals.org/cgi/content/full/19/1/36*.

Groth, A. N. "Sexual Trauma in the Life Histories of Rapists and Child Molesters," *Victimology: An International Journal*, Vol. 4, 1979, pp. 10–16.

Holmes, G. R., L. Offen, and G. Waller, G., "See No Evil, Hear No Evil, Speak No Evil: Why Do Relatively Few Male Victims of Childhood Sexual Abuse Receive Help for Abuse-Related Issues in Adulthood?" *Clinical Psychology Review*, Vol. 17, 1997, pp. 69–88.

Kaufman, J., and E. Zigler, "Do Abused Children Become Abusive Parents?" *American Journal of Orthopsychiatry*, Vol. 57, 1987, pp. 186–92.

Kwong, M. J., K. Bartholomew, A.J.Z. Henderson, and S. J. Trinke, "The Intergenerational Transmission of Relationship Violence," *Journal of Family Psychology*, Vol. 17, no. 3, 2003, pp. 288–301, *www.sfu.ca/psyc/faculty/bartholomew/research/publications/intgenviol.pdf*.

Loeb, T. B., J. K. Williams, J. V. Carmona, I. Rivkin, G. E. Wyatt, D. Chin, and A. Asuan-O'Brien, "Child Sexual Abuse: Associations with the Sexual Functioning of Adolescents and Adults," *Annual Review of Sex Research*, Vol. 13, 2002, pp. 307–45, *www.findarticles.com/p/articles/mi_qa3778/is_200201/ai_n9032344*.

Mathews, F., "The Invisible Boy: Revisioning the Victimization of Male Children and Teens," National Clearinghouse on Family Violence, Health Canada, 1996, *www.phac-aspc.gc.ca/ncfv-cnivf/familyviolence/pdfs/invisib.pdf*.

Mendel, M. P. *The Male Survivor: The Impact of Sexual Abuse.* (London, UK: SAGE, 1994).

Rabalais, A. E., "The Cycle of Abuse: Factors That Put Survivors at Risk for Perpetration of Child Physical and/or Sexual Abuse." Unpublished dissertation, the Eberly College of Arts and Sciences at West Virginia University, 2003, *http://kitkat.wvu.edu:8080/files/3080/Rabalais_Aline_dissertation.pdf*.

Schnitzer, P. G., and B. G. Ewigman, "Child Deaths Resulting from Inflicted Injuries: Household Risk Factors and Perpetrator Characteristics," *Pediatrics*, Vol. 116, no. 5, 2005, pp. 687–93, *http://pediatrics.aappublications.org/cgi/content/full/116/5/e687*.

Watkins, B., and A. Bentovim, "The Sexual Abuse of Male Children and Adolescents: A Review of Current Research," *Journal of Child Psychology & Psychiatry & Allied Disciplines*, Vol. 33, 1992, pp. 197–248.

Chapter Sixteen

Felitti, V. J., Kaiser Permanente Medical Care Program, 7060 Clairemont Mesa Blvd., San Diego, CA 92111. Personal Correspondence, 24 July 2005. See also "Adult Health Problems Linked to Traumatic Childhood Experiences," CDC, National Center for Chronic Disease Prevention & Health Promotion, Press Release, 14 May 1998, *www.cdc .gov/od/oc/media/pressrel/r980514.htm.*

Olson, D. H., D. H. Sprenkle, and C. S. Russell, "Circumplex Model of Marital and Family System: I. Cohesion and Adaptability Dimensions, Family Types, and Clinical Applications," *Family Process,* Vol. 18, 1979, pp. 3–28.

Schaefer, J., and A. Capeloto, "Stories of Broken Victims Lie Behind Catholic Summit," *Detroit Free Press,* 23 April 2002, *http://66.54.33.107/ news/religion/abused23_20020423.htm.*

"Sheldon Kennedy/Graham James Case: Sexual Abuse in Canadian Junior Hockey." Silent Edge (information about skating, sports, coaches, children, parents, and dangers of abuse) at: *www.silent-edge.org/ kennedy.html.*

Thomas, V., and T. J. Ozechowski, "A Test of the Circumplex Model of Marital and Family System Using the Clinical Rating Scale," *Journal of Marital Family Therapy,* Vol. 26, no. 4, 2000, pp. 523–34, *www.find articles.com/p/articles/mi_qa3658/is_200010/ai_n8913038.* Erratum in: *Journal of Marital Family Therapy,* 2001, Vol. 27. no. 1, p. 134.

Whitman, W. "A Noiseless Patient Spider," *Leaves of Grass.*

Resources

Chapter One

Adverse Childhood Experiences (ACE) Study, Department of Health and Human Services, Centers for Disease Control and Prevention: *www.cdc.gov/nccdphp/ace/index.htm*

Sexual Abuse of Males: Prevalence, Possible Lasting Effects, & Resources (Web site of Jim Hopper, Ph.D.): *www.jimhopper.com/male-ab*

Chapter Two

Boston Globe Clergy Abuse files: *www.boston.com/globe/spotlight/abuse/chronological.htm*

John Jay College of Criminal Justice Research Team, Terry, K. J., and J. Tallon, "Child Sexual Abuse: A Review of the Literature": *http://207.32.122.199/nrb/johnjaystudy/litreview.pdf*

Survivors Network of Those Abused by Priests: *www.snapnetwork.org*

Voice of the Faithful (Keep the Faith, Change the Church): *www.votf.org*

Chapter Three

John Briere, Ph.D., associate professor of psychiatry and psychology, Keck School of Medicine, University of Southern California, director of the Psychological Trauma Program of Los Angeles County and USC Medical Center: *www.johnbriere.com*

Oxnam, R. B. *A Fractured Mind: My Life with Multiple Personality Disorder*, (New York: Hyperion, 2005).

Sidran Organization: *www.sidran.org*

Chapter Four

American Psychiatric Association (APA): *www.psych.org*

Chapter Five

Mental Help Net: *http://mentalhelp.net*

Mitchell, S. A., and M. J. Black. *Freud and Beyond: A History of Modern Psychoanalytic Thought* (New York: HarperCollins, 1996).

Chapter Six

Abraham H. Maslow: Books, Articles, Audio/Visual, and Maslow's Personal Papers: *www.maslow.com*

Albert Ellis Institute (AEI): *www.rebt.org*

Allen,W. (Director), *Deconstructing Harry* [film], (1997)

American Art Therapy Association, Inc. (AATA): *www.arttherapy.org*

American Psychoanalytic Association: *www.apsa.org*

American Psychological Association (APA): *www.apa.org*

Cavalcade Productions, Inc. (1-800-345-5530): *Videos for Survivors*

The National Center for Complementary and Alternative Medicine at the National Institutes of Health: *http://nccam.nih.gov*

National Institute of Mental Health: *www.nimh.nih.gov*

National Mental Health Association: *www.nmha.org*

Substance Abuse and Mental Health Services Administration's (SAMHSA) National Mental Health Information Center: *www.mentalhealth.samhsa.gov*

Viktor Frankl Institute, Vienna: *logotherapy.univie.ac.at/e/indexe.htm*

Chapter Seven

Adult Survivors of Child Abuse (ASCA): *www.ascasupport.org*

Adverse Childhood Experiences (ACE) Study: *www.acestudy.org*

Berendzen, R., and L. Palmer. *Come Here: A Man Overcomes the Tragic Aftermath of Childhood Sexual Abuse* (New York: Villard Books, 1993).

Bishop Accountability Organization: *www.bishop-accountability.org*

Curtis, D., *Our Fathers* [TV film], (2005).

Deposition transcript of Bernard Cardinal Law on 8 May 2002, Boston, as part of sexual abuse civil suit filed by alleged victims of clergy, *www.thebostonchannel.com/News/1444317/detail.html*

Dave Pelzer (physical abuse survivor, bestselling author, inspirational speaker): *www.davepelzer.com*

Echo Bridge Productions. [USA video] *Trying to Get Some Dignity,* (1997)

France, D. *Our Fathers: The Secret Life of the Catholic Church in an Age of Scandal* (New York: Broadway Books, 2004).

Healthy Place (consumer mental health site): *www.healthyplace.com*

Jarecki, A., *Capturing the Friedmans* [film], (2003).

National Child Protection Act (NCPA, or the "Oprah Winfrey Act"): *www4. law.cornell.edu/uscode/html/uscode42/usc_sec_42_00005119----000-.html*

National Foundation to Prevent Child Sexual Abuse (NFPCSA): *www .fbifingerprintchecks.com*

National Organization on Male Sexual Victimization: *www.male survivor.org*

Oxnam, R. B. *A Fractured Mind: My Life with Multiple Personality Disorder,* (New York: Hyperion, 2005).

Philadelphia District Attorney Index Page: *www.philadelphiadistrict attorney.com*

Philadelphia Grand Jury Report, 21 September 2005, Philadelphia Archdiocese Sexual Abuse: *www.philadelphiadistrictattorney.com/images/ Grand_Jury_Report.pdf*

Ray, D. *The Endless Search: A Memoir.* (New York: Soft Skull Press, 2003).

Rhodes, G., and R. Rhodes, *Trying to Get Some Dignity: Stories of Triumph over Childhood Abuse,* (New York: Harper Perennial, 1998).

Rhodes, R. *A Hole in the World: An American Boyhood.* (New York: Simon & Schuster, 1990).

Rhodes, R. "In Depth," BookTV, 3 March 2000: *www.booktv.org/ InDepth/archive_2000.asp*

Richard Gartner, Ph.D. (past president of MaleSurvivor: National Organization against Sexual Victimization): *www.richardgartner.com*

Smith, J. N., *The Boys of St. Vincent* [TV film], (1992).

Survivors Network of Those Abused by Priests (SNAP): *www.snapnet work.org*

Voice of the Faithful (VOTF): *www.votf.org*

Volunteers for Children Act (42 U.S.C. Sec. 5119a): *www4.law.cornell .edu/uscode/html/uscode42/usc_sec_42_00005119---a000-.html*

The Zero (site of child advocate, attorney, consultant, Andrew Vachss): *www.vachss.com*

Chapter Eight

Alpert, J. L., L. S. Brown, and C. A. Courtois, "Symptomatic Clients and Memories of Childhood Abuse: What the Trauma and Child Sexual Abuse Literature Tells Us," APA Working Group Paper on the Investigation of Memories of Childhood Abuse, 1996. *www.apa.org/pi/memories_ report/section1.pdf.*

Alpert, J. L., L. S. Brown, and C. A. Courtois, "The Politics of Memory: A Response to Ornstein, Ceci and Loftus," APA Working Group Paper on the Investigation of Memories of Childhood Abuse, 1996, *www.apa .org/pi/memories_report/section3.pdf.*

Alpert, J. L., L. S. Brown, and C. A. Courtois, "Response to 'Adult Rec- ollections of Childhood Abuse: Cognitive and Developmental Perspec- tives,'" APA Working Group Paper on the Investigation of Memories of Childhood Abuse, 1996, *www.apa.org/pi/memories_report/section5.pdf.*

Co-Dependents Anonymous (CoDA): *www.codependents.org*

False Memory Syndrome Foundation: *www.fmsfonline.org*

"Final Conclusions of *APA Working Group Paper on the Investigation of Memories of Childhood Abuse, 1996,*" *www.apa.org/pi/memories_report/ section7.pdf.*

Freyd, J. J., *Betrayal Trauma: The Logic of Forgetting Childhood Abuse.* (Cambridge, MA: Harvard University Press, 1996).

Freyd, J. J., "What Is a Betrayal Trauma? What is Betrayal Trauma Theory?" 2005, *dynamic.uoregon.edu/~jjf/defineBT.html.*

Hendrix, H., *Getting the Love You Want,* (New York: Owl Books, 2001).

Imago Relationships International (Harville Hendrix, Ph.D., and Helen LaKelly Hunt, Ph.D.): *www.imagorelationships.org*

Miller, J. B. *Toward a New Psychology of Women* (Boston: Beacon Press, 1976).

Miller, J. B., and I. P. Stiver. *The Healing Connection: How Women Form Relationships in Therapy and in Life* (Boston: Beacon Press, 1997).

Ornstein, P. A., S. J. Ceci, and E. F. Loftus, "Reply to the Alpert, Brown and Courtois Document: The Science of Memory and the Practice of Psychotherapy," APA Working Group paper on the Investigation of Memories of Childhood Abuse, 1996, *www.apa.org/pi/memories_report/ section2.pdf.*

Ornstein, P. A., S. J. Ceci, and E. F. Loftus, "Adult Recollections of Childhood Abuse: Cognitive and Developmental Perspectives," *APA Working Group paper on the Investigation of Memories of Childhood Abuse, 1996, www.apa.org/pi/memories_report/section4.pdf*

Ornstein, Peter A., Stephen J. Ceci, and Elizabeth F. Loftus, "More on the Repressed Memory Debate: A Rejoinder to Alpert, Brown and Courtois," *APA Working Group paper on the Investigation of Memories of Childhood Abuse, 1996. www.apa.org/pi/memories_report/section6.pdf*

Chapter Nine

Preventive Medicine Research Institute, 900 Bridgeway, Sausalito, CA 94965, Phone: (415) 332-2525; Fax: (415) 332-5730; Web site: *www.PMRI .org*

Vincent J. Felitti, M.D., Kaiser Permanente Medical Care Program, 7060 Clairemont Mesa Blvd., San Diego, CA 92111: *www.ACEStudy .org*

Chapter Ten

American Association for Marriage and Family Therapy (AAMFT), 112 South Alfred Street, Alexandria, VA 22314-3061, Phone: (703) 838-9808; Fax: (703) 838-9805; Web site: *www.aamft.org*

American Association of Sex Educators, Counselors and Therapists (AASECT): *www.aasect.org*

Forever Families, from the School of Family Life at Brigham Young University: *www.foreverfamilies.net*

Maltz, W., *The Sexual Healing Journey: A Guide for Survivors of Sexual Abuse* (New York: Harper, 2001).

Recovering Couples Anonymous: *www.recovering-couples.org*

S-Anon (for family members of those attending SA): *www.sanon.org*

Sexaholics Anonymous (SA): *www.sa.org*

Sexual Recovery Anonymous (SRA): *sexualrecovery.org*

Sexual Recovery Institute: *www.sexualrecovery.com/resources/12step.php*

Chapter Eleven

Al-Anon Family Groups: *www.al-anon.alateen.org*

Antonovsky, A., *Unraveling the Mystery of Health: How People Manage Stress and Stay Well,* (San Francisco, CA: Jossey-Bass, 1987).

Berne, E. *Games People Play: The Basic Handbook of Transactional Analysis* (New York: Ballantine Books, 1996).

Steiner, Claude, M. *Emotional Literacy: Intelligence with a Heart*, (Fawnskin, CA: Personhood Press, 2003).

Steiner, C. M., *Games Alcoholics Play.* (New York: Ballantine Books, 1984).

Steiner, C. M., *Healing Alcoholism.* (New York: Grove/Atlantic, 1981).

Steiner, C. M., Web site for Emotional Literacy, Transactional Analysis (TA), and other matters: *www.emotional-literacy.com*

Steiner, C. M., *Scripts People Live: Transactional Analysis of Life Scripts.* (New York: Grove/Atlantic, 1990).

Chapter Twelve

Benson, H., and M. Z. Klipper., *The Relaxation Response.* (New York: Avon Books, 2000).

Burns, D. D., *Feeling Good: The New Mood Therapy* (New York: Quill, 2000).

Mind-Body Medical Institute: *www.mbmi.org*

Weil Lifestyle, LLC, Dr. Andrew Weil's Web site: *www.drweil.com*

Chapter Thirteen

Attachment Resources: *www.psychology.sunysb.edu/attachment*

Families Through Time Study, understanding how couples with infants and young children coparent: *http://ftt.clarku.edu*

Jane F. Gilgun, Web site: *http://ssw.che.umn.edu/Faculty_Profiles/Gilgun_Jane/Gilgun_pubs.html*

James McHale, Web site: *www.clarku.edu/faculty/jmchale*

Chapter Fourteen

Dick, K., (Director), *Twist of Faith* [Motion picture], (2005).

FBI Investigative Programs Crimes Against Children Web site: *www.fbi.gov/hq/cid/cac/states.htm*

National Association of School Psychologists Web site: *www.nasponline.org*

NYU Child Study Center Web site: *www.aboutourkids.org*

Prevent Child Abuse America, 200 S. Michigan Avenue, 17th Floor, Chicago, IL 60604-2404, Phone: (312) 663-3520; Fax: (312) 939-8962; Web site: *www.preventchildabuse.org*

Chapter Fifteen

Child Abuse Prevention and Treatment Act (CAPTA): *www4.law.cornell.edu/uscode/html/uscode42/usc_sec_42_00005106---g000-.html*

Children's Bureau, Administration on Children, Youth and Families, 370 L'Enfant Promenade SW, Washington, DC 20447, Phone: (800) 394-3366 or (703) 385-7565; Fax: (703) 385-3206; E-mail: *nccanch@caliber.com*; Web site: *http://nccanch.acf.hhs.gov/pubs/factsheets/signs.cfm*

J.S. v. R.T.H., 155 N.J. 330 (1998), *lawlibrary.rutgers.edu/courts/supreme/a-98-97.opn.html*

National Clearinghouse on Child Abuse and Neglect Information (NCCANCH)

The National Domestic Violence Hotline: *www.ndvh.org*

Stop It Now! 351 Pleasant Street, Suite B319, Northampton, MA 01060, Help line: 1-888-PREVENT (1-888-773-8368); Phone: (413) 587-3500; Fax: (413) 587-3505; E-mail: *info@stopitnow.org*; Web site: *www.stopitnow.com*

Chapter Sixteen

Greenberg, L. S., and S. M. Johnson, *Emotionally Focused Therapy for Couples* (New York: Guilford Press, 1988).

Relationship Institute, Co-Directors: Joe Bavonese, Ph.D., & Shirley Bavonese, 27172 Woodward Avenue, Suite 200, Royal Oak, Michigan 48067, Phone: (248) 546-0407, M.S.W. Web site: *www.relationship-institute.com*

Index